Remembering Anthony Vidler (1941–2023)

As a teenager, Tony Vidler already showed a talent for architectural perspectives in this 1956 drawing, which he titled "Our Drawing Room" and initialed A.V. Just a few years later, he would leave this home to study architecture at Cambridge University, from 1960 to 1966. He then headed to the US, where he would become a teacher and a dean, an architecture historian, and a writer one wanted to read. Drawing courtesy Emily Apter.

Editor
Cynthia Davidson

Managing Editor
Patrick Templeton

Editorial Intern
Motuma Tulu

Protagonists
Thomas Daniell
Todd Gannon
Catherine Ingraham
Sanford Kwinter
Manuel Orazi
Bryony Roberts
Julie Rose
Sarah Whiting

As we prepared to go to press with this issue of *Log*, I learned that architecture historian Kurt Forster had died. Kurt's passing was the fourth recent death of towering figures in architecture theory, history, and criticism, all of whom wrote for *Log*: Jean-Louis Cohen, 74, in August; George Baird, 84, and Anthony Vidler, 82, in October; and now Kurt, 88, on January 6, 2024. It feels like the sudden felling of giant oaks.

I have had the honor of knowing and working with each of them through the Anyone project. Jean-Louis and I together planned the Anymore conference in Paris, which he hosted in the old Cinémathèque française in the Palais de Chaillot, in 1999. Among the hundreds of articles he wrote, four appeared in *ANY* magazine and six in *Log*. Recently I reread Jean-Louis's texts in *Le Corbusier: An Atlas for Modern Landscapes*, the catalog of the dazzling exhibition he guest curated, with Barry Bergdoll, at the Museum of Modern Art, in 2013. Coincidentally, the postcard for *Log* 59 is related to Jean-Louis's involvement in the restoration of Eileen Gray's E-1027 house, in Roquebrune-Cap-Martin.

George was a practicing architect, an academic dean, and a prolific writer. The disciplinary debates in *Meaning in Architecture*, the book George coedited with Charles Jencks, in 1969, still resonate today, particularly the applicability of semiology in architecture. The book still sits on the shelf above my desk, along with George's collected essays, *Writings on Architecture and the City*, published in 2015.

Tony became a friend the day I met him, and he and his wife, Emily Apter, often prepared a great New Year's Eve dinner. He participated in several Any conferences and guest edited *ANY* 18: Public Fear, which we conceived in 1997, after the terror bombings of buildings in Oklahoma City and in Buenos Aires. He also guest edited *Log* 28: Stocktaking, with Peter Eisenman, taking the temperature, so to speak, of the state of architecture in 2013. I edited Tony's book *Histories of the Immediate Present*, published in the Writing Architecture Series, with MIT Press, and he was completing a new book for the series, which will be published posthumously.

And then there is Kurt. In early 1991, I flew to Los Angeles with Jeffrey Kipnis to meet Kurt, whom I did not know, and to discuss how we might launch the Any conferences at the Getty. I was overwhelmed by Kurt's loquacity; Kipnis chided me for not getting a word in, but everything Kurt said was spot on and exciting. With Kurt and the Getty as hosts, the first Any conference, Anyone, went ahead that May. Over the years, Kurt and his wife, Elisabetta Terragni, became dear friends. I have fond memories of times together in Milan, Zurich, Berlin, and New York. Equally memorable are Kurt's "Hey, Sailor. . . ," a tribute to Paul Rudolph in *ANY* 21, and in *Log* 32, "Sebald's Burning Train Stations and Monstrous Courthouses."

Jean-Louis Cohen, George Baird, Anthony Vidler, and Kurt Forster – all of them extraordinary teachers and generous mentors, all of them important writers, all of them key players in developing a critical discourse on the culture of architecture and architecture history. Their absence has created a perceptible void, but the intelligence and ideas they sparked in their students and colleagues, and through their books and articles, are still with us. We can still listen and learn. – CD

www.anycorp.com

Log 59 Copyright © 2023 Anyone Corporation. All Rights Reserved. ISSN: 1547-4690. ISBN: 978-1-7365007-7-4. Printed in USA. *Log* is published three times a year by Anyone Corporation, a nonprofit corporation in the State of New York with editorial and business offices at 1133 Broadway, Suite 330, New York, NY 10010. Subscription for 3 issues: $45 US; $49 CAN/MEX; $69 International. Single issues are available in print or as PDFs for $18, plus shipping if applicable. The opinions expressed herein are not necessarily those of the protagonists or of the board of the Anyone Corporation. Send inquiries, letters, and submissions to log@anycorp.com.

Log 59

Fall 2023 — Observations on architecture and the contemporary city

Author	Page	Title
Savinien Caracostea & Anders Frederik Steen	175	Eat the World We Want to Live In
Thomas Daniell & Maki Onishi	33	The Positive Power of Architecture
Cynthia Davidson	11	A Seat at the Table
Cynthia Davidson with K. Michael Hays, Andrew Holder & Anna Neimark	185	Toward a Theory of Inscription
Peter Eisenman & Valerio Olgiati	115	Making Sense of the Non-Referential
Dora Epstein Jones & Katharine Hayhoe	169	Hope Begins in a Dark Place
Darell Wayne Fields & Milton S.F. Curry	87	This Is a Time for Manifestos
Mark Foster Gage & David Chalmers	215	Architecture, AI & the Hard Problem of Consciousness
Todd Gannon & Caroline Levine	99	Everybody Needs to Breathe Oxygen
Elisa Iturbe & Maria Shéhérazade Giudici	69	Carbon Modernity's Domestic Typologies
Jaffer Kolb & Lucas LaRochelle	160	Something Lost, Something Found
Sanford Kwinter & Ursula Biemann	224	*Sentipensar*; or, How to Become Earth
Phyllis Lambert	181	Remembering Jean-Louis Cohen
Sylvia Lavin	144	Birdcalls; or, Criticism in the Environment
Ann Lui & Juliet Sorensen	79	Building Justice
Michael Meredith & Alex Da Corte	108	A Conversation Pit
Ana Miljački & Cristina Gamboa	47	Housing Makes a Community
Anna Neimark & Andrew Atwood	41	Stone on Stone
Manuel Orazi & Emanuele Coccia	13	Architecture; or, The Science of the Planet

Florencia Pita	120	Ephemerality Will Kill Us All
& Carla Fernández		
Mónica Ponce de León	21	Architecture Is the Intersection of Material and Ideas
with Amale Andraos,		
Sean Canty,		
Preston Scott Cohen,		
Mira Henry		
& Meejin Yoon		
Bryony Roberts	151	Expanding Embodiment
& S.E. Eisterer		
François Roche / S/he	237	An Archaeological Retro-future
with Emanuele Coccia		
Anthony Vidler	1	Our Drawing Room
Anthony Vidler	248	Palladio's Rialto Bridge
Sarah M. Whiting	59	From Abstraction to the Longhouse
& Pier Vittorio Aureli		
Cameron Wu	203	Form, Words, and Artificial Intelligence
& Patrik Schumacher		

General Observations:	Jada Cannon on Avian Cohabitants 202 ...
	Taylor Dover on an Average Home 58 ...
	Pia Ednie-Brown on the Year of Barbie 129 ...
	Arseny Pekurovsky on the Supermarket 98 ...
Cover Story:	Roquebrune-Cap-Martin, France
	Postcard: Le Corbusier, Cabanon de vacances, 1951.
	Photo: Iwan Baan, 2022.

Lars Müller Publishers wish the team
at Log many congratulations for reaching
twenty. Two decades is no mean feat
in the world of printed matter.
Over this time, we have thoroughly enjoyed
your critical exploration of architecture
and the built environment.
We share your passion for interrogating
the constructed world in which
we live and support your implicit invitation
to dream up progressive solutions to
contemporary problems.
We look forward to many more of
your contributors' rigorous observations
and philosophical provocations.

Lars Müller Publishers
Est. 1983

Books on architecture, design,
photography, art and society

www.lars-mueller-publishers.com

DELACAVE Architectes | Architectural Think Tank

info@delacave.net
delacave.net

Courtesy DELACAVE Association For Art | Stuart Alexander Schibli
Special thanks to Ernest Schilliger

Architecture and Architects

From Park Books

Montessori Architecture
A Design Instrument for Schools
Steve Lawrence and Benjamin Stæhli

Montessori Architecture is the first book to comprehensively address the architectural design, construction, and use of materials in and the furnishing of educational spaces according to Maria Montessori's visionary ideas.
Paper $50.00

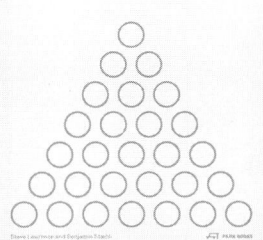

The Advanced School of Collective Feeling
Inhabiting Modern Physical Culture 1926–38
Edited by Nile Greenberg and Matthew Kennedy

The authors explore the impact of physical culture during the 1920s and '30s on the thinking of some of modern architecture's most influential figures. Using archival photographs, diagrams, and redrawn plans, they reconstruct a fascinating constellation of domestic projects by Marcel Breuer, Charlotte Perriand, Richard Neutra, and others.
Paper $40.00

Neighbours
A Manifesto, a Play for Two Pavilions, and Ten Conversations
Edited by Karin Sander and Philip Ursprung

An exploration of the relationship between the Swiss and Venezuelan pavilions at the Giardini della Biennale in Venice.
Paper $35.00

From Scheidegger & Spiess

In the Summer of 2009
Photographs by Walter Pfeiffer, Design by Matteo Thun
Walter Pfeiffer and Matteo Thun

Swiss artist Walter Pfeiffer's photographic homage to Italian architect and designer Matteo Thun.
Cloth $50.00

Distributed by the University of Chicago Press www.press.uchicago.edu

Experience art and architecture in harmony with nature

Visit the Architectural Archive + Research Library, galleries, art installation trail, and experimental architecture on the 'T' Space Reserve. Guided tours and appointments offered year-round.

tspacerhinebeck.org

SYNTHESIS OF THE ARTS
'T' Space inspires cross-pollination of art, architecture, music, and poetry to foster creativity and to amplify interdisciplinary thinking.

EDUCATION
The resources of the Archive, Residency program, lecture series, and academic tours encourage critical thinking about the connections between architecture, the arts, and ecology.

ECOLOGY
Though ecological architecture and programs, 'T' Space seeks to revitalize the unity of humanity and nature.

Operated by the Steven Myron Holl Foundation, 'T' Space stimulates critical and theoretical exchange of ideas in the context of today's cultural, economic and technological conditions.

'T' Space
RHINEBECK

Revu par / Selected by

**Studio Muoto
Claudia Shmidt
Pezo Von Ellrichshausen**

**Sortis du cadre
Out of the Box**

AMANCIO WILLIAMS

Sala para el espectáculo plástico y el sonido en el espacio, Córdoba, Argentine, par Amancio Williams, 1943–1945. Amancio Williams Fonds, CCA. Gift of Amancio Williams's children. Photo: Matthieu Brouillard (c) CCA

CCA

June 2023 to May 2024

AP205

cca.qc.ca

Urban Living

From Chicago
The Lost Subways of North America
A Cartographic Guide to the Past, Present, and What Might Have Been
Jake Berman

"Berman's many exceptional maps are provocations worth thousands of words each, conveying a history of relative transportation abundance in the U.S. There is no other book on public transportation like it."—Steven Higashide, author of *Better Buses, Better Cities*
Cloth $35.00

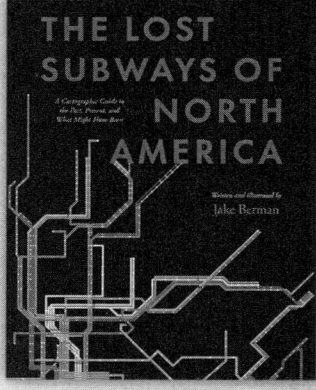

Chicago Reflected
A Skyline Drawing from the Chicago River
Ryan Chester
With an Essay by Thomas Dyja

"Chester's precise, inventive, remarkable drawing slices through the city, through infrastructure, and through time itself to capture America's greatest architectural ensemble in a way that viewers cannot have experienced. It is a delightful tour de force."—Reed Kroloff, Illinois Institute of Technology School of Architecture
Cloth $29.95

The Stray Shopping Carts of Eastern North America
A Guide to Field Identification
Julian Montague

"Montague's sly masterpiece is back, a Baedeker equal parts Ballard, Borges, and Buffalo, New York. Don't leave home without it."—Ed Park, author of *Same Bed Different Dreams*
Paper $22.00

From Park Books
Institutions and the City
The Role of Architecture
Edited by Gérald Ledent and Cécile Vandernoot
With Contributions by Delphine Dulong, Dietmar Eberle, Christian Gilot, Gérald Ledent, Sophia Psarra, and Cécile Vandernoot

This volume offers a groundbreaking study of architecture's role in the establishment, identification, and perpetuation of public institutions that shape both societies and individual lives.
Paper $45.00

The University of Chicago Press www.press.uchicago.edu

Cynthia Davidson

A Seat at the Table

To mark the 20th anniversary of *Log*, the 26 individuals who guest edited a thematic number or a special section of an issue were asked to interview someone whose work resonated with their current thinking or concerns – even with what keeps them up at night. In addition, *Log*'s protagonists – the informal sounding board that helps keep this magazine on a course of investigation and discovery – were asked to interview someone. The idea was that their conversations would expand beyond what one could stage in a live event, such as what *Log* presented for its 10th anniversary, in 2013. For example, the 16 participants in the 2013 event spoke to an audience of 400, and here, in the pages that follow, there are 55 participants with a potential audience of several thousand readers.[1] In effect, there is a seat at the table for anyone who's interested.

When *Log* began, in 2003, New York was in the wake of the terrorist attack on the World Trade Center. The entries to the design competition for rebuilding the site were stylistically different but largely aggressive proposals, as if recognizing architecture's potential to assert the wounded city's prominence in the world. Overall, however, architecture seemed to be drifting, having shed terms like *deconstructivism* and *postmodernism* and refusing parametricism while grappling with rapidly changing technologies and growing environmental concerns. This magazine set out to record, through critical observations and writing, the various movements, watching to see where they would lead. Since then, nearly 600 people have contributed some 1,200 observations, essays, and arguments that, seen in hindsight, track not only developments in architecture but also in the social, economic, political, and natural environments.

So, 20 years on, where is architecture? Or better, where is the world that architecture in many ways shapes? *Log* 1 included protagonist Julie Rose's report from Hong Kong on the SARS "panic pandemic," as she called it. *Log* 49 was a "work-from-home" production during the height of the global Covid pandemic – as was the production of the next four issues. Covid changed how people, and architecture, began to think about domestic space and commuting to

1. The event, "In Pursuit of Architecture," was held September 21, 2013, at the Museum of Modern Art in New York. Pia Ednie-Brown and Peggy Deamer each wrote unsolicited critical analyses of the event, which were published in *Log* 30. For video recordings, see https://vimeo.com/showcase/10928188.

work – all design problems. *Log* 8 was a critique of the concept of sustainability, in 2006; *Log* 47, guest edited by Elisa Iturbe, in 2019, named the environmental problem of "carbon form." While both issues sold out, the ongoing sale of PDF copies has made the latter the best-selling issue in *Log*'s history. Then there is technology. In *Log* 2, Chantal Thomas, in "From Proust to the Mobile Phone," observed "the mania for communication . . . in the public arena; the constant concern to reach and be reachable" that the mobile phone had ushered in – four years before the introduction of the game-changing iPhone. In this issue, *Log* 59, Emanuele Coccia suggests that the iPhone is now our new mobile home – home in our hands or our pockets, not in a place.

    The "public arena" that today challenges not only how we share and receive information, but also the idea of public space, began to expand rapidly in 2004 with the introduction of Facebook; then Twitter, in 2006; Instagram, in 2010; Tiktok, in 2016. Online architecture feeds began to appear, including *ArchDaily*, in 2006, and *eflux Architecture*, in 2016. The effects of apps on social interaction – and hence, public space – were the subject of Andrés Jaque's "Grindr Archiurbanism" in *Log* 41. Even conversation has changed. The interviews that guest editors Anthony Vidler and Peter Eisenman conducted for *Log* 28: Stocktaking, in 2013, were largely recorded in person (two interviewees submitted written responses). Only two of the interviews for *Log* 59 were conducted in person; the rest were email exchanges or recorded via Zoom, regardless of the participants' locations.

    At the close of his introduction to *Log* 28, Vidler wrote that, even with recognizing the impact of the digital on architecture, the interviewees "still remain quite adamant as to the various authorities on which the discipline should be based: formal, typological, technological, programmatic, or simply 'post-theoretical' and pragmatic." The multidisciplinary conversations in *Log* 59 also tend toward the pragmatic, but they take different tacks. Material and construction; cooperative housing and business models; social and racial justice law; climate change and the human-nature relationship. And behind it all, the coming AI revolution.

    Given the state of the world today, what all of this will look like in the next 10 years is difficult to imagine. What is certain, however, is that architecture, as the multidimensional manifestation of cultural aspirations, will persist. Must persist.

Cynthia Davidson founded *Log* in 2003.

Manuel Orazi
& Emanuele Coccia

Architecture; or, The Science of the Planet

Philosophy of the Home: Domestic Space and Happiness by Emanuele Coccia, 2024. 208 pages. Penguin.

Emanuele Coccia is an associate professor of philosophy at the École des Hautes Études en Sciences Sociales in Paris. Coccia collaborated for many years with Giorgio Agamben before starting his teaching career in Freiburg, Germany. He has taught in Buenos Aires and Tokyo, was an Invited Research Fellow of the Italian Academy at Columbia University in 2015–16, and in 2022, taught a philosophy class at Harvard called The Ego in Things: Fashion as a Moral Library. Among his many books, the most widely translated is The Life of Plants: A Metaphysics of Mixture *(2018).* The Life of Forms: Philosophy of The Re-Enchantment, *written with fashion designer Alessandro Michele, is forthcoming. We talked via Zoom in October 2023; he is in Paris, I in Macerata.* – MO

MANUEL ORAZI: Emanuele, nice to see you again. I can't think of anyone better to talk to about the future of architecture.

EMANUELE COCCIA: I can think a lot of people, actually.

MO: Your most recent book, *Philosophy of the Home*, which will be published in English, in April 2024, is your first book to actually address architecture. Ten years ago, your book *Il Bene nelle cose* [The Good in Things] touched on architecture and the city, because there were some metropolitan issues, but they were not the core of the book. This time you touch on architecture, so we might think that, after a consistent philosophical career, you have decided to approach architecture and the city directly. Why?

EC: First of all, thank you. *Log* is one of the most important magazines I read, and I am so happy to have a conversation with you because we haven't had a dialog in a while. You are right, architecture was always more than just an interest for me. It was – it is – a constant field of research and reading. My book on advertising, *Goods: Advertising, Urban Space, and the Moral Law of the Image*, was, in a way, a footnote to Venturi's book about Las Vegas.[1] Architectural theory played a huge role in my education, and books by Venturi, Scott Brown, Rem Koolhaas, and Kevin Lynch have had a lasting influence on the

1. See Robert Venturi, Denise Scott Brown, and Steven Izenour, *Learning From Las Vegas* (Cambridge: MIT Press, 1972).

way I relate to the world. They still represent patterns of thinking and writing.

In *Philosophy of the Home* the emphasis is not on the city but on domestic space because I think the home has been a kind of black hole, or blind spot, in architectural theory and practice over the past decades. Apart from the remarkable work of Dogma, no architect has thought about what it means to build a home that corresponds to the new forms of love and what will follow patriarchy.

Now I am returning to urban space for a residency in Laren, the birthplace of the De Stijl movement, where I would like to organize a workshop with architects, urban planners, botanists, zoologists, and lawyers on how the coexistence of species can be thought of as an urban reality. Essentially, the urban landscape emerged as a result of humanity transitioning from a hunter-gatherer lifestyle to establishing enduring connections with specific trees and shrubs for sustenance. This marked the inception of the first gardens, where a unique commitment to plant life gave rise to urban spaces. The relationship between species is not merely a peripheral aspect of architecture; rather, it constitutes the fundamental urban reality. Cities, at their core, sustain themselves through interactions with cultivated plants and domesticated animals. The interplay between different species is not only a prerequisite but also the very essence shaping all cities. From its origins, urbanism embodies a multispecies reality.

Never before have Koolhaas's words, in his preface to the Italian translation of *Singapore Songlines*, seemed more true to me – namely, that urban thinking in Western society stopped around the 1980s. It moved on to Asia, particularly China.

I am also working a lot on the relationship between architecture and digital space. Since the birth of cybernetics, the development of digital technologies has opened up a new space, which has different rules, forms, and metabolisms from the geographical space we were used to inhabiting. For example, digital space is a space of absolutely unlimited physical and temporal contiguity. Thanks to my phone, I live next to any other human being, within voice range, and we are all always in the same time zone. Architecture seems to have neglected, even removed, this space as an object of design and architecture. This is also, and especially, why social media is so ugly and poorly done, because no architect or urban planner has worked on it. We don't consider it as a space, as an object of planning, of actual design. We are still considering the main object of architecture as stone and not this space made only of information, or of pure semiosis, as Venturi and Scott Brown suggested.

So, the question is perhaps not why architecture now, but why I don't write on architecture all the time. I think architecture is the main science, the main way of thinking about making the world livable. And since today, the city coincides with the planet – after all, one definition of the Anthropocene could be the idea that the planet is now a huge city – the science of the planet is necessarily architecture and not ecology.

I say this in opposition to the trend seen at the last few Venice biennales and the contemporary debate. You cannot stop building. Instead, you need to build the planet for all species and not just for us. It is also something different from what Charles Waldheim and others have called "landscape urbanism." We should finally admit that thinking about a new cohabitation of all species means thinking about the city, though obviously on a different basis. Ecology must disappear because there is nothing natural, even in the non-human world, in the way species decide to cohabit and modify the world to do so. They, too, are architects. And to deal with ecology is therefore to deal with architecture without knowing it.

MO: I have known you for about 20 years. I have the impression that there was a turning point in your career more or less around the publication of *Il bene nelle cose*. It's as if you did more theoretical work in the first part of your career and refused certain work because you were thinking about metaphysical issues, and then you decided to approach the problems of the real world like advertising, fashion, and plants. Like, at first, Wittgenstein focused on logical empiricism and then focused on language, there seems to be a first Coccia and a second Coccia. It makes sense that you would approach architecture in considering the problems of the world, because architecture itself is a problem of the world.

Nevertheless, for me, *Philosophy of the Home* is a utopian book because you try to offer the reader the possibility of an emerging, totally different house, of a nonexisting architecture. I would define it as a virtual dimension of the house, which is something more concrete. So even if the book touches on the problematic aspects of private domestic life, it has a utopian drive. This is rare in architecture today because for the most radical thinkers in architecture, or the young generation in architecture, utopia is a refusal of concrete architecture. It's an escape from architecture. *Philosophy of the Home* tries to open up new possibilities for domestic living that are concrete but also optimistic, if not utopian. I say this because, listening to you, I am reminded of when Koolhaas said the lack of any utopian drive in recent times is as problematic as when there was an overwhelming utopian drive in the 1960s and '70s.

EC: First of all, yes, I have huge hope. I don't know if there is a first and second part of my work, but let's say that the book about advertising was a turning point in the sense that it brought the city into my thinking, and I started to work much more directly on modernity. Maybe that's why architectural theory has become so important. I absolutely agree that there is a huge problem, not in general, but in the European and US world. On the one hand, there is a huge sense of guilt on the part of architects who feel that architecture is the main culprit of climate change and not the key to its solution. On the other hand, since the 1980s, a bitter reflection on the failure of modern urban rationality has been emerging from European urbanism, expressed, in its most radical form, in Manfredo Tafuri's *Architecture and Utopia*. Modernity is described as a Piranesian dialectic with reason folding in on itself to produce sublime prisons. The urban form becomes a trap. And it is this dual sense of failure that has crippled cities in Europe. I live in Paris, which is the perfect example of a city that has refused to consider itself modern. They have frozen the civic center into a museum of 19th-century modernization. Paris is the city that has turned Haussmannian modernity into irretrievable archaeology, which is why it is gravely responsible for the decadence of contemporary European urban thinking. Evidence of this is its absolute immobility for the 2024 Olympic Games.

European cities refuse to recognize that architecture is an operation of constant transformation of urban reality and that it must radically rethink the city at every moment. We prefer to live in medieval huts instead of taking note that we must respond to contemporary demographics with contemporary housing. They peddle this laziness as a respect for heritage, but it is an elitist attitude because, of course, the civic center is within the reach of only a small number of people. Today, more than ever, we need new thinking, urban invention, not anti-urban spirit. Cities are and will remain our horizon. We have exploded demographically and will continue to do so. We need more architecture, not moratoriums on construction. And we need more architecture, not less, because all other species are now inhabitants of the one city that is as big as our planet, that is the Anthropocene. Therefore, the lack of vision, political sense, and realism on the part of architects is extremely dangerous. This also applies to landscape architects, urban planners, and so on.

Moreover, during the pandemic, we discovered that we not only live in mineral space, not only in spaces made of stone, we also live in digital space produced and accessed through our smartphones, which are actually an extremely important habitat. The smartphone today is a kind of mobile home, like a domestic space that moves with us, that has no connection to geographic space. It has no connection with land or territory, but it is still a form of space in which everyone is connected and everyone occupies the same space without differences in time. Today, the home is probably this space. We should, and I often repeat this, consider WhatsApp as the new form of modularity. We should consider our smartphone as the module of our time. And perhaps we should rethink cities and homes from this space, or rebuild cities as a kind of hybrid space produced by mineral infrastructure and digital infrastructure. In summary, we need a new architectural renaissance today, because without architects we are doomed.

Climate change has introduced a kind of romantic misunderstanding that we can, in a sense, overcome architecture or design to have an immediate relationship with other species. Nothing could be more naive. As Jeanne Gang reminds us, we cannot have a nonarchitectural connection with nature. We need houses, we need roads, we need designed spaces. And not only for our species. After all, the forest itself is a built object, thus an architectural object. Cesare Leonardi and Franca Stagi suggested this 40 years ago. If we lose our relationship with architecture and design, we lose our relationship with the planet, with nature, and with other species. We need architecture to start to entertain a relationship with the world. After all, architecture is a mobile and active relationship with the whole planet.

MO: You are utopian in this sense, because architects basically have such a negative, dystopian attitude. But there is something in what you say about the smartphone and what digital life has taken to a radical point – the process of data deterritorialization prophesized by Deleuze, or, simply, globalization. I think that architects, who are a great part of your readership, don't know that you don't teach architecture. Many people think, because of your recent interest, that you must teach architecture every day. But actually, you teach on many different issues. You even studied angels. What is your usual focus as a teacher, or as a researcher?

EC: I got a teaching position in Paris almost 15 years ago. I was supposed to teach something called History of Christian Normativity, which is a sort of mix of the history of theology, history of canon law, and history of ideas in the Middle Ages and late antiquity. But I switched after two or three years to something else because it was too complex to teach such topics in France. Religions, in France, are considered forms of ideology and not forms of cosmic imagination. I actually started to teach about aesthetics. So for at least 10 years, I've been in an art theory and art history department, where I teach art theory, landscape, fashion, and ecology. It's all very free. Now, for instance, I'm also teaching a class about cybernetics. I have the privilege to be teaching in a school that was the birthplace of French theory. Barthes, Levi-Strauss, Bourdieu, and Derrida used to teach here. It's a school where you have the freedom to teach whatever you want, even the subject you are writing on. For instance, last year I taught about love because I'm writing a book about love. But teaching is more and more just a part of my work. Now I'm working a lot with museums and art centers, such as Fondation Cartier, the Milan Triennale, and the Pinault Collection, organizing public programs or cocurating exhibitions. I'm now cocurating an exhibition on art and ecology in Kanazawa, Japan, and another on fashion in Trieste. I'm also teaching a lot about fashion history. I just wrote a book with the former creative director of Gucci, Alessandro Michele.

MO: Surely you don't have the problem of alienation in your daily work because it's so various. From what I understand, it's in line with your definition of philosophy. You have said several times that you can do philosophy with almost every branch of human life and human thinking.

EC: Yes. I don't think there is a definition of philosophy. The name *philosophy* itself is strange, because it was a provocation. In the face of those who claimed to be experts (the so-called sophists), figures emerge who claim to be what, in French, is called an *amateur* – that is, someone whose relation to knowledge is not defined by a method (thus by the certainty of truth), nor by a master (thus by the evidence of authority), but by an inordinate and perhaps even somewhat toxic passion, by a desire that burns your soul and does not let you free for a second and often forces you to ruin your days. Philosophy is not a discipline, it is the mode of being of any form of knowledge that has been produced or generated by desire, by love, by a form of passion. So from this point of view, you cannot decide in advance what is philosophical or not. You can only recognize that something, some subject, has become philosophical because someone has invested an inordinate passion and desire in it. And love and desire are things that you cannot completely master. There is no method for love, and there is also no clear prediction of what will happen when you love. That is why it is so difficult to say that something will be philosophical or not. It depends on the intensity of the desire that leads you toward an idea.

MO: I'd like to ask you about contemporary architecture. When you hear many architects talk about an issue in architecture today, nearly everybody starts to talk about universal problems that go beyond architecture. It's extremely rare that someone gives you an example from architecture, or even a small part of a city, a street, a museum, a park, or a space along a river. For example, in the Venice Architecture Biennale this year, I couldn't find concrete examples of cities or of architecture that we could emulate, whether from Africa or from Australia. Contemporary architecture seems to have vanished in this sense. Are there examples of good architecture or parts of cities that you find successful or that should be imitated?

EC: A tremendous amount. There are many extremely beautiful examples of good architecture in the world today. Jeanne Gang is a genius. What she did at the Museum of Natural History in New York is incredible. Junya Ishigami is incredible. Everything he does is extremely interesting. Freddy Mamani is also a genius. Every building he has done is incredible. Wang Shu and Lu Wenyu are just stunning. All of their work is incredible. Last week [September 28, 2023] they were all in Milan for The World Around, organized by Beatrice Galilee and Béatrice Grenier of Fondation Cartier. But I think there is a huge number of successful buildings of different kinds – museums, houses, installations. And a lot of interesting people are building. Another genius is Bernard Khoury, the Lebanese architect who works mostly in Beirut. And Andrés Jacque is doing something extremely original and innovative in Europe.

What is probably missing is a more coherent and contemporary way of thinking about urban planning. It is missing because we have stopped thinking about it. We have many new challenges that require a new form of imagination. That's why it is perhaps more difficult to find good examples of urban planning in Europe and the United States. But you are right when you say that biennales and the public discourse on architecture emphasize the negative aspects. Maybe the problem is the biennale formula. There are two problems. The first is that there are not many museums dedicated to architecture. Or the museums that do architecture exhibitions do bad exhibitions. MAXXI in Rome is doing a very good program, and there is the Canadian Centre for Architecture, but there are not many spaces dedicated to architectural theory and reflection. Second, biennales are often given to people who are not curators, which is a problem.

MO: So you are against Gregotti's idea that only architects should be the curator of the Venice Architecture Biennale?

EC: That's bullshit. You need curators to do a good job.

MO: You mentioned that the exhibition of contemporary art is another area you are working in. What do you think about Yona Friedman's idea of the role of the museum? He said that museums were mostly powerful means of communication. Not just places where we can expect to find memorable works of art but places where we can send messages – in other words, an alternative place of communication.

When I go to exhibitions, sometimes I think of this idea because I expect too much from museums. The word *museum* makes you expect a lot in general, when it is actually a place that should be familiar to the majority of people. I think Friedman's statement also has to do with democratization of art activity in general. What do you think?

EC: What happens in museums is a much deeper and bigger process, not just something to do with democratization. And I'm not just talking about museums as institutions related to a nation's heritage, but the power of exhibitions.

Exhibitions came into existence before the establishment of museums. They played a huge role in the production of modern cities – that's what people, from Walter Benjamin to Koolhaas, from Venturi and Scott Brown to Giuliana Bruno, have understood by working on the city. And it is what Baudelaire already sensed. A city becomes modern when it is structured as an open-air exhibition. Only when urban space becomes an exhibition of the world and exposes the inhabitants to themselves is the metropolis born. From this point of view, exhibition is at the heart of urban modernity. That is why museums are so important today.

Exhibitions are also the heart of modern commerce in the form of storefronts. They're like the opposite of the panopticon. The people are not controlled, rather an object is presented for all to see. Unlike with storefronts, where your relationship to the object on display is defined by your economic status, in museums, the display device puts everyone on an equal footing. From that point of view, the exhibition is a huge tool for democratizing the experience of the world.

I would say there are two or three other elements that make exhibitions a key figure in the contemporary world. First of all, the exhibition is the ultimate cognitive device in the way we produce knowledge in a much more interesting way than we produce it in college. Producing knowledge normally means producing a discussion about knowledge, saying something that is only semantically related to known reality. In the move to produce knowledge you take on the object itself. You don't produce a discourse about reality. It is material reality itself that, thanks to the exhibition, begins to speak.

Second, precisely because knowledge is produced through things themselves, it is possible to use all the senses. Knowledge produced by exhibitions is the explosion of sensible life and media because all the senses are activated. At the university, it is still believed that knowledge exists only in the exclusive medium of writing an essay with footnotes.

There is also the fact that in the last, let's say, 50 years, there was the birth of exhibition language, starting with Harald Szeemann and his "documenta 5." That exhibition taught that it is possible to produce a discourse that does not coincide with the artist's discourse. This is what Daniel Buren opposed in "documenta 5." He said, *You are using me to make my artwork say something that is not what I am saying*. But thanks to Szeemann, and later, to Lyotard's "Les Immatériaux," the exhibition became a medium for producing thought. It is no coincidence that since the 1970s and '80s, many artists have reappropriated the exhibition as a medium for producing art. Think, for example, of Philippe Parreno in France. From this point of view, the exhibition became something through which art produced its own history.

My last point is that exhibitions are important, or museums in general, because they have become the paradigm of digital space. If you think about it, our smartphone is a portable museum. And in a way, what we do through Instagram or Facebook is like producing an exhibition. We exhibit our friends, the faces of our friends, and pictures of the experiences we love. Through this device, we all become curators. From this point of view, curating has become our main relationship with the world. That is why museums today are the most important cultural device.

MO: It's the democratization of the curator. After everybody became a photographer, now we're all curators.

EC: Yeah, everybody's a photographer and everybody's a curator. But that doesn't mean everybody is good at it.

MO: Like Antonio Gramsci said, that everybody's a philosopher doesn't mean that everybody's a good philosopher. Traditionally, the Italian intellectual is a nihilist thinker, but you find many possibilities that seem to open up opportunities to reshape not only the museum but any kind of space with events. Events like Friedman's street museum, showing objects selected by inhabitants of a simple street. Do you think that events in general – and not only artistic events – more and more characterize the city, and that the city, in relation to the countryside, is also radicalized in a way because of this? It seems that the suburb, or the countryside, feels left out of this. And that they react by voting to turn back the clock to a golden era when the world seemed simpler to them.

EC: This is a huge question. First of all, I would say that the opposition between the city and the countryside is nonexistent. The countryside is such an urbanized space. It is even more urbanized than a city. A real metropolis is much wilder than the countryside, which, especially in Europe, is the exact opposite of nature. After all, in the cultivated countryside everything is defined by design. Agriculture is the absolute design space – not only space but also plant life is the object of design. That is why in the countryside there is much more control over everything. If you live in the countryside in Italy, France, or Germany, it means that everything, even the growth of the most insignificant of species, is planned and controlled. From this point of view, the problem with the countryside is that nothing can really be free. Whereas the metropolis is an uncontrollable jungle. There is so much density that it is impossible to control everything. This is the real opposition.

The development of social media, smartphones, and digital space has also produced a general metropolitan space that is no longer based on being in one place, no matter whether it is city or country. But the big problem – and this is Koolhaas again – is that since the 1980s there has been no real urban thinking in the West. I go back to the example of Paris. Benoit Jallon and Umberto Napolitano, with their exhibition "Paris Haussmann," tried to show that if we love Paris, it is because of the density formula invented by Haussmann. Paris should renew its density projects, radicalizing what Haussmann did. Instead there is talk about de-densifying, and that is a huge mistake. Ecology must not think about de-densification, it must transform the culture of metropolitan congestion into congestion that is no longer monospecific. Instead of cultivating dreams of a return to premodern wilderness, metropolises should become more metropolises, more modern, and welcome into modernity all the species on the planet. Stefano Boeri is right. The forest should become the name of the skyscraper, not of what exists outside the city. We have to think of the forest as something that structures the city and urban modernity. We need to think of nature as something that produces a future, not as a past that we have abandoned.

MO: In France, some intellectuals whom you know very well – I'm thinking of Francis Hallé and Gilles Clément – are working on this problem. Clément said that the best honey is produced in the city of Paris because of the biodiversity of flora compared to the countryside. This is only one example of how a city means diversity more than the countryside. If we look to these thinkers in the area of cultivation, maybe they can teach us things.

EC: Yes and no. You mentioned two geniuses, but they belong to another generation, not to the current generation. The problem is that there was an extraordinary generation – Clément, Hallé, Bruno Latour – that was extremely intelligent and lucid. Now there is a younger generation, which is extremely romantic, extremely antimodern, extremely anti-technological, and extremely anti-progress. That's why the situation in France is complicated. It's an exaggeration, but when you go into an architecture bookstore, you'll find books about cheese making in the mountains or living in cabins or food architecture as a solution to everything, or ways to produce buildings from the earth. It's not that these books are not interesting, but they are clearly forms of consolatory thinking, a very romantic and nostalgic way of thinking. Moreover, they are not political, because they focus on extremely local and small spaces, whereas today we need planetary solutions. It is not possible to think of solutions for our situation by thinking about a local space. The local no longer exists after the invention of digital space. We have to think from a planetary point of view, because ecological, financial, and health problems can only be solved from the point of view of the planet itself, not from the view of a single country or village. That is why this way of thinking is clearly a reactionary form of consolation.

Manuel Orazi, a *Log* protagonist, was guest editor, with Alicia Imperiale, of *Log* 53: Why Italy Now? (2021). He works for the Italian publishing house Quodlibet and is a visiting professor at the Accademia di architettura in Mendrisio, Switzerland. In 2021, he curated "Carlo Aymonino: Loyalty to Betrayal," for the Milan Triennale.

Mónica Ponce de León with Amale Andraos, Sean Canty, Preston Scott Cohen, Mira Henry & Meejin Yoon

Architecture Is The Intersection of Material and Ideas

When Log *approached me with the invitation to participate in this issue, I decided to structure a conversation among practitioners with robust academic careers and who see building as an intellectual practice: Amale Andraos, Sean Canty, Preston Scott Cohen, Mira Henry, and Meejin Yoon. Specifically, we explored the relationship between form, space, and design process as it pertains to architecture's cultural significance. Andraos is a cofounder of WORKac, a professor, and dean emeritus of Columbia GSAAP. Canty is codirector of Office III, the founder of Studio Sean Canty, as well as an associate professor at Harvard's Graduate School of Design. Cohen is a professor at the GSD and the founding principal of Preston Scott Cohen, Inc. Henry is coprincipal of Current Interests and design faculty at SCI-Arc. And Yoon, principal of Höweler + Yoon, is the dean of Cornell's College of Architecture, Art, and Planning. The six of us got together on November 2, 2023, via Zoom. – MPDL*

MÓNICA PONCE DE LEÓN: The five of you are all academics who have pursued your academic project through the making of buildings, as opposed to, let's say, other pedagogues who have focused on writing or teaching alone. I'm interested in the point of view of those who are embedded in these two worlds simultaneously, as I think it can offer greater insight into architecture's impact on society.

Many of you have heard me say that I believe architecture is a creative practice very similar to musical composition or creative writing, but we deal with buildings – a material world of a large scale. As such, the discipline of architecture occupies a very special place in the academy. Architecture's cultural relevance emerges from our ability to imagine and materialize alternatives to the status quo. This is what I consider the power of architecture. Meejin, I want to kick us off by asking you to talk about the University of Virginia Memorial to Enslaved Laborers and about the memorial in the context of the university itself. But also in the larger context of the history of Confederate monuments in Virginia and in the South.

MEEJIN YOON: Thanks, Monica. What is interesting and maybe not well-known about the Memorial to Enslaved Laborers is that its name comes from a student group that organized to propose a student design competition, under that title, to imagine a memorial in recognition of the history of slavery at the institution. The prompt for the student proposal came out of an assignment in a course taught by Dr. Frank Dukes at UVA, in 2007, in which he asked his students to find recognition of the history of slavery at the university. When the students found the only recognition was in the form of a small plaque underfoot near the rotunda, they were shocked by the form and scale of the recognition. UVA was founded by Thomas Jefferson, the third president, a signer of the Declaration of Independence, and owner of over 600 enslaved men, women, and children in his lifetime. On the University of Virginia Historical Markers on the Grounds, there is no mention of slavery. What we heard consistently from the UVA alumni community was how this history was not discussed. I think the story behind the memorial demonstrates the power of the classroom, the role of teachers, the optimism and agency of students to organize this competition, and also the process and time it takes for an institution to tell hard truths about its own history and to move forward. Even though the student design competition was held in 2011, it would be several years before the president of the university created a commission on slavery and engaged the faculty in doing research and making recommendations, of which the memorial was just one part. In terms of the process of the memorial, the most important thing was recognizing that while architecture was a part of the memorial, so much more was needed to create a memorial that could acknowledge the history of slavery.

It started with, of course, the creation of a team with broad expertise: Dr. Dukes, distinguished fellow at the Institute for Engagement and Negotiation; Dr. Mabel O. Wilson, an alum of UVA, designer, historian of American history, and professor of architecture and African American and African diasporic studies; Gregg Bleam, landscape architect; and artist Eto Otitigbe. Throughout the project I learned the power of our discipline, but also maybe its inadequacies. Through additional and expanded expertise and perspectives, and working with the university, we were able to iterate and discover together. At the outset, the university did not have a designated site or a designated budget.

The memorial was being designed in parallel with the local debates taking place to remove the Robert E. Lee statue in Charlottesville. The Lee statue was the flashpoint for the Unite the Right rally [in August 2017]. As Confederate monuments were being debated, we learned the history of when these monuments were placed in our public spaces – not immediately following the Civil War but later, during Jim Crow, as a form of intimidation. And I think that made it very clear that the Memorial to Enslaved Laborers could not be an object or a "thing" that you assign meaning to, but a space and place to gather to do the work of racial justice.

MIRA HENRY: Meejin, as you talk about this project, I am reminded how practice and pedagogy operate at such different time scales. Can you tell us more about the time and process of that work?

MY: I feel like we, the design team, came in at the very tail end of a process a decade in the making, and our work was built on the scholarship that was produced by members of that president's commission, who are architectural historians and historians of American history. I feel like we are just a small part of this longer time line. What was important

Höweler + Yoon Architecture in collaboration with Dr. Mabel O. Wilson, Gregg Bleam, Dr. Frank Dukes, and Eto Otitigbe, Memorial to Enslaved Laborers, University of Virginia, Charlottesville, 2020. Photo courtesy the architects.

about the project was we had six months to actively listen and engage the community, testing various possibilities, scales, and sites.

This is what I meant about realizing how powerful our discipline is in expanding and furthering conversations. I remember at some of the first meetings that sometimes, as the architect, you're between the institution and the community. But what that enables is a possibility for the community to have conversations with the leadership of an institution, which otherwise might not be available. In the early community conversations, no one wanted to talk about the memorial per se, but wanted to engage in dialog on the need for repair and the history of injustice.

Without those multiple months, or if there had been a rush in terms of the design project and process, I feel like the memorial would have fallen short on many fronts. The space and time for those conversations to happen was as important as the final memorial itself. During those six months, and the following year, during design and development, the nation was grappling with racialized violence. The Unite the Right rally, in which Heather Heyer was killed; the murder of Ahmaud Arbery; police shootings of unarmed Black men and women; and then, right as the memorial was completed, in 2020, the murder of George Floyd.

SEAN CANTY: In that process, given the inadequacy of the initial acknowledgment of that history, how did you all arrive at the appropriate formal solution?

MY: Through the design process, every initial design option felt wrong. We knew it, or we heard it from UVA or from members of the community. The powerful thing was that we were able to build trust with the descendant community through the design process – they had a very strong voice in the design review and were instrumental in the process up to the end. And now they are an independent nonprofit called the Descendants of Enslaved Communities and are official co-stewards of the Memorial to Enslaved Laborers with the university.

Initially, we were very interested in pursuing a distributed and ephemeral memorial. One proposal was the planting of a dense field of crocuses on the Lawn, the most central and historic space. We thought the community would want the memorial to be in the most prominent place, but then we heard from the descendant community and the Charlottesville community that the Lawn was a very intimidating space for non-UVA community members, and that it should be more accessible and closer to the Corner, the abutting commercial street of the city.

The other thing we learned is that if we sat around a room and all talked about aspirations and ideas, 90 percent of the descriptive words would align. But then, if you developed a scheme and presented it, it became clear that there were gaps between words and the interpretation of the words into form. It was a highly iterative process. Having the tools of representation and ability to do quick design tests and options deepened and enabled that conversation. And because we didn't start with a design with the goal of trying to convince others of the qualities of that design, but the design emerged through the feedback process, we were successful in creating a memorial that the community, and particularly the descendant community, embraced.

MPDL: It's interesting that you focused on the idea of space – architecture creating a framework for space – but when you gave examples where there was less architecture, those you engaged with in the process wanted more architecture.

MY: That's right.

MPDL: I am curious to hear from everybody if you have had similar experiences in which you went into a project thinking architecture is going to be with a lowercase *a*. Believing that the design was going to be more about creating interactions between different components of the program, and then your client pushed you in a direction where there was more architecture rather than less.

MY: What we heard was that they wanted something durable, multigenerational, something that would last as long as traditional monuments and memorials. Even though we thought ephemerality can be very powerful, the question of architecture, not only for this time, but for future generations, came up more than we anticipated. And that has led me to think more and more about architecture as holding values that are transmitted to future generations.

AMALE ANDRAOS: A conversation about architecture that begins with a monument is very helpful because a monument is the ultimate architectural gesture, right? It has everything we dream architecture can be. It brings people together, it lasts across time, it is imbued with meaning. It's a really interesting entry point. And I will say that what's great, Meejin, in terms of hearing the story, is that we are in a moment when everything is simultaneously an instantaneous statement and no one is listening to anyone. In the creation of a memorial, we all have to come together, and it is possible to recognize that the design process is going to take a long time. In your process, Meejin, working so closely with clients, various stakeholders, and the community, you sent the message that you weren't going to make a statement. You were just figuring this out.

Monica, to your question, we've never had a client who wanted less architecture. I feel this is something that, as architects, we are very self-conscious of. They want an architecture that works. They don't want everything to be…

MPDL: No, my question was the opposite. That you came in thinking you're going to do something minimal, and then the client wanted more, more, more.

AA: Clients still believe there is value in architecture. Otherwise, they wouldn't be there. For us in our work, we try to not overdesign everything. We try to be strategic. There's big *A* here, and then there's whatever else is needed over there. There's space for both the super-designed and the more straightforward.

I remember when [architecture critic] Alexandra Lange first visited the Adams Street Library in Dumbo. She said it felt like we put everything in the center and then the rest around it was not so designed. And we were like, yep. She read it as a budget thing. It could have been budget, but it was more a design strategy.

Sometimes I feel like we are more self-conscious than the clients might be. The thing is, you want to do the right thing. You do want to engage. This is not one-way. And that's why, Meejin, I like your story about so many people coming together, the community, different constituents, and the fact that it was a collaboration. All these strategies, I think, are helping us make things that can maybe find relevance somehow.

PRESTON SCOTT COHEN: I want to bring up something else about the memorial that I think is compelling as a takeoff from Monica's initial point, and speak more about the particulars of its form, the specific way this circular form, which has to do with enclosure, tilts, allowing access to the interior that would have been otherwise closed. What I find compelling here is that the strategy by which that opening occurs conveys what Meejin said about how so much of this story had never been told. There is a reference to the closure and then opening in the very form of the project. I don't know if that's intended, but I think the tilting and the opening of something closed is unique to this particular project. It's not Richard Serra's *Tilted Arc*. I'm trying to think of other paradigms. If I were to think, in contrast, about the Memorial to the Murdered Jews of Europe by Peter Eisenman in Berlin, there, one is completely immersed in the memorial. I think you're trying to address paradigmatically this very particular question of an untold narrative and its opening. I love the fact that the project relies on these very clear, almost irreducible devices, represented in cross sections that disclose the interior as you move by, and that also conceal it at a certain point, which I remember you spoke about in another context. To my mind, this is the strategy that makes it happen and makes it mean what it means. It's a really phenomenal project for these reasons.

It's very rare to see a project that has such a clear and irreducible strategy to express a point and to make meaning that way. I'm responding to what Monica said about the work, which is something artistic, because it's not just about the research. There had to be a lot of research done to make the memorial, but its expression in form is not the moment of research. Where do you leave research and begin the project that you're describing, Monica?

MPDL: I would say that research becomes background at the moment that the architectural imagination takes over the creative process. The moment that you begin to imagine ways in which form can make present alternatives to the status quo.

PSC: I think this project is both. I think the memorial is a perfect example of the two

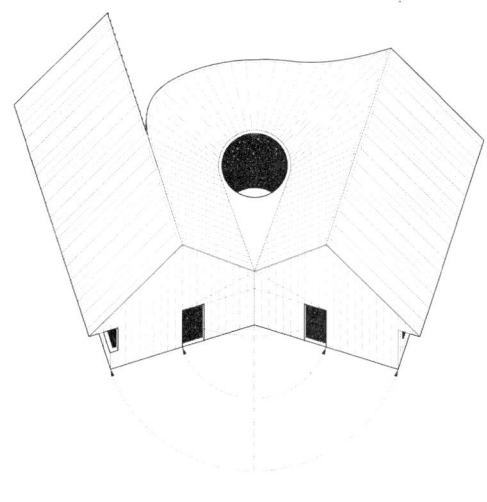

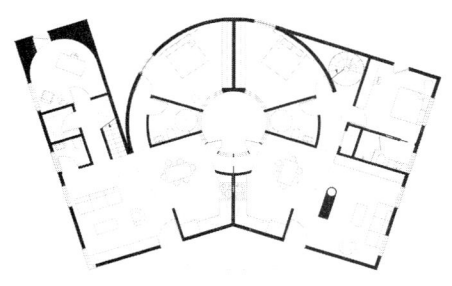

Studio Sean Canty, Janus House, unbuilt, Concord, Massachusetts, 2018. Drawing courtesy the architect.

sides of this question. The preamble is all of the research. Ultimately, both the research and form bring forth the whole idea that knowledge had been suppressed and that Jefferson had been celebrated for so long without the story ever having been told.

MPDL: I would argue that this is what architecture does very well. At the end of the day, isn't the power of architecture that we can imagine ways to embody ideas, to materialize cultural forces? Students at UVA were surprised to find out how repressed the history was, but the truth is that everyone knew the history, and the memorial now makes it powerfully visible.

MY: There are other ways to make a circle, right, Monica?

MPDL: No, no, the opposite. I can imagine a different architect who is not as good as Höweler + Yoon, who does the same research, goes through the same participatory process, and ends up with a completely different intervention that would not have been half as successful or half as powerful. I do think that our contribution to the world, what makes up our contribution to society, is our imagination and our ability to think through all of these different forces and to come up with the form that embodies them.

MY: I was thinking back on what you said in terms of cultural relevance and the discipline of architecture. I spent my early years as an architect trying to not make architecture, focusing on very ephemeral things, but what architecture does, as Scott was able to articulate, is make space. Coming to terms with the precision of how to make space through material, but using a level of precision that intersects between the horizon line and the landscape, how a curb can gradually become a wall, how there's resonance with context and the like – those are all the tools we have as architects.

MPDL: That intersection of material and ideas – giving form and shape to ideas through materials – is what we do. In that sense, I'm interested in the way that all of you take on certain typological standards and then massage, adjust, and transform them. I know that the word *typology* has fallen out of favor, and I see academics making strenuous efforts to not use it. They use *morphology*, etc., but just indulge me in using *typology* as a shortcut. That's also something I think is interesting about all of your work, that you look at preexisting models, manipulate them, transform them, appropriate them, and shift them.

I think, Sean, what you do with the single-family home is extraordinary. I want to build all of them and move right in. They're just absolutely exquisite. Sean, could you talk about your manipulation of given types as a way of engaging culturally with the world?

SC: Part of the inspiration of working typologically is reflecting on the ways in which types, particularly within the African American community, are received as something to be inhabited and not of one's own creation or authorship. But the ways in which those things become embodied or inhabited by individuals and transformed through day-to-day lived experiences has always been profound to me. Meaning, in Philadelphia, I could go next door to my neighbor's house, which had the same row house framework but was completely, radically different on the interior.

MPDL: But in the end, I don't look at your work and think of it as only received from a particular history. I see your work as manipulating and using form as a way of creating other kinds of experiences, interpretations, and futures.

SC: In some ways, they are meditations on how those received types have been altered in my own experiences. I am trying to reproject them into the work to think about them. It's hard to explain, but in the ways in which I transform the types, they're kind of undone as if they were not meant to be inhabited. Often it's about being a little bit more collective, a little bit more shared, a different take or attitude toward privacy or roominess. So I am trying to find the "offness" in each of them – just picking up on my own experience going into people's homes as a kid and seeing how they actually used the spaces, particularly Black homes. How there's always something slightly different to them from what was intended with the original type, and trying to reproject that.

It's taken me some time to reflect on this obsession with homemaking as a form of agency. I think each house, or each study, is a different meditation on this theme through different means, usually through geometry, in my case, but also geometry in parallel with working from a typological framework.

MPDL: Scott, this reminds me quite a bit of the kinds of transformations that I have seen you do in synagogues, taking preestablished cultural norms that are embedded in a building and then shifting them. Can you talk about your work on synagogues in the context of typological manipulation?

PSC: I think it would be fun, instead, to talk about Taubman College, the addition to the Art and Architecture building at the University of Michigan, since you were the dean then. That makes it interesting, because who the client is is always an important part of the project. It wasn't only a matter of working with the university and the architecture and planning departments as a client. There was also an idea about a longer tradition, following from Mies's interpretation of industrial architecture, which was so much part of the original building and pervasive in that part of the country. This brought about the studio space as a kind of factory, which came out of students influenced by IIT and other pedagogies. And, as I have told Monica before, the project was influenced by her own practice involving material interpretations that are also related to this architectural culture. The inspiration for some of the ways we treated the facade came out of our conversations. Monica found the silver brick, for example. It is an unusual occasion when the client is so educated and dedicated in a very particular way.

AA: It's very interesting. If I can bring up another word that has gone out of fashion – *precedent*. It's interesting to me, Sean, that you're working through your personal memories and experience. Scott, you're referencing Mies and the history of the design of campuses. If we're trying to undo the discipline and its references, what is it that we have to not repeat? In this conversation, I feel like a lot has been said about references in the archive that we dig out, but not enough about the references that are negated. This ties to what Meejin was saying about the untold stories.

PSC: That's an interesting way to think about it. In many of these cases, there's a kind of intervention in the way we think about something that exists and that we're going to modify, whether it's the story of the enslaved or it's a story about the origins of these houses that otherwise isn't understood. I'm not sure I had the same task to reveal something that was not recognized, but I would say that the initial idea I had for the addition is very odd for this building. It was kind of a Matta-Clark intervention, which was to clip the corner of the existing Miesian building because it is a very closed building. Maybe this connects back to the Memorial for Enslaved Laborers, about the closed form and how to open it. Here we were adding onto the corner by means of subtraction, by cutting open the structure of that building. This is a very different attitude for an addition than those that contrast with an old building by means of mere abutment, as well as those that seek to establish seamless continuity. The diagonality of that negated corner developed into the unexpected geometry of the atrium we added. The task was to create a center, despite being located along an edge. How do you make the edge the center of life? A paradox, which was perfect for me. I love this kind of problem. As much as I felt that it should not be a highly expressive and differentiated building, there was never any doubt that it would have to contain a powerful and centered antidote within. Ultimately, this became the pair of stacked oblique hexagonal ramps bound together by a spiraling stair as if tied in a knot. As a result, the interior sequence is quite wrought, nothing like the directionless Miesian open plan of the existing building.

MY: I have a question for Sean related to typology. There's an exquisiteness to your work because it's both familiar and unfamiliar and executed through very precise control of form and geometry. I am curious about this question of "just enough." They are meditations, but I'm looking for a different word than *meditation* because I feel like there's a moment when there is just enough tension with the familiar, the unfamiliar, the form, and the intrinsic qualities, the balance of which is the beauty of the work. I am curious how you reach that process of just enough. I feel like, Scott, you do that too.

SC: I've been thinking about this and Monica's question since my lecture at Princeton [March 27, 2023] because I think I adhere to a looser framework of typology. For me, Charles Moore's *The Place of Houses* is maybe the realm of typology that I'm more interested in because he deals with more elemental aspects of the room, the machine, the ritual. I try to hold on to those things diagrammatically or paradigmatically, but I'm always trying to open up typologies to something that's slightly more collective than the single-family home. Even if it's for a single-family program, there's a way in which singularity and multiplicity might be embedded in one proposition. The "just enough" is trying to find the right confluence of form, material, and spatial experience to satisfy the problem.

MY: I guess, back to how Monica started with the affinity of our creative practice to things like music, there is this control of the medium that happens through creative

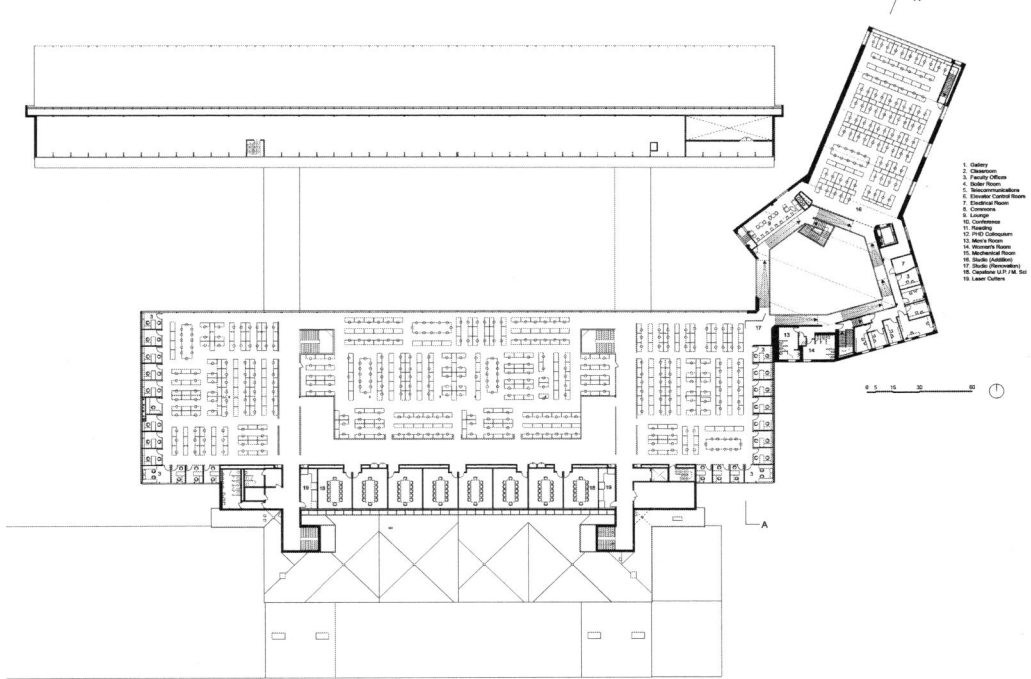

Preston Scott Cohen, Inc., Taubman College of Architecture and Urban Planning, University of Michigan, Ann Arbor, Michigan, 2017. Third-floor plan. Drawing courtesy the architect.

practice and iteration. And I think you have control of the medium.

SC: Part of it is just knowing your assets and your skill sets but also profoundly leaning into one's intuition to know what feels right for the problem, what feels right for the brief, what feels right for the form. It's taken me some time to be okay with that.

MH: I am enjoying hearing you speak about your work in terms of Black domesticity. As a graduate student, I studied architecture in LA, and I never knew that thousands of buildings in the city were designed by a Paul R. Williams. Now that his archive has been acquired by USC and the Getty, important new scholarship is emerging on the impact of his work. I recently heard LeRonn Brooks, a historian at the Getty, speak about Williams's churches. Being one of the only Black-owned communal spaces in the early part of the 20th century, churches had to take on a lot of distinct programs. The church was also a library, a kindergarten, a community center. And while from the exterior the building reads like a typical church, the section reveals some pretty incredible spatial sandwich conditions with all these things happening inside. So I'm just thinking about Amale's point about precedent and also about space making and placemaking and the interior, especially in the Black tradition. Sean, your work does have that tension. Spaces are being shifted and programs are encountering each other in a powerful way.

MPDL: Mira, can you speak about your own work vis-à-vis material choices, material selection, material accumulation? You talk a lot about gathering. I wonder if you can frame your question to Sean vis-à-vis your own work.

Current Interests, Terracotta House, Los Angeles, 2023. Photo courtesy the architects.

MH: Reflecting on Meejin's project and how, ultimately, they developed a complex project with a simple form, I would say that is very much how we work. We could say, let's just work on a box, but when you cut the section of that box, it is going to look pretty intense because of the layered systems in how that box would get built.

We started building work over the last five years, which allowed us to engage with material detail. That's really where the pleasure has been. Currently we are working on using existing components like structural terra-cotta block that we have split to expose it in new ways. We have also been working on different kinds of sound insulation systems to develop padding layers. It's very much a love for the process of building. We are working in a zone between craft practice and typical construction, which requires an understanding of what subcontractors can do. We are beginning to interface with an economy of making that's bigger than ourselves – one that's related to the people who are making it on site.

SC: There's an interesting component of enclosure that is always contested in your work. There's a softness that I think resists the boundaries of delineations between rooms and between inside and outside. The forms may look like types we recognize, but the way they're operating is radically different because of that material and tectonic expression you're talking about. I find the layered enclosure fascinating, from the facade to the roomness of your and Matthew [Au]'s work, which is undoing some other aspect of typology or undoing some other paradigmatic aspect of interior and exterior. That's unique and also quite refreshing.

AA: It's such a refreshing resistance to the mode of shopping in the US. We collaborated on two community centers in Mexico City with Ignacio Urquiza Arquitectos. And it was like, Let's color concrete! Oh, yum, yum, yum. Versus working here, it's…

MH: It's brutal.

AA: It's unbelievable where the profession has been taken, and I find this conversation so refreshing to remind ourselves of the fun and the pleasure of making form using materials, resisting through craft, using your imagination. This gets eroded on a daily basis.

MH: Last year, when we were teaching an option studio at Princeton, we took our students to Brazil. We got a chance to just spend a lot of time with Lina Bo Bardi's work. It wasn't the first time I had been, but something about this time in my life, having multiple buildings in construction right now, made the trip so meaningful. There is a certain exhilaration and a kind of pain in

WORKac with Ignacio Urquiza Arquitectos, Pilares Lomas de Becerra, Mexico City, 2022. The concrete is bright blue. Photo courtesy the architects.

trying to do something new. I loved going to Bo Bardi's house and thinking about how many years it took to build. It is a bit leaky and moldy, and utterly fantastic. The rawness of her work brought up a lot of emotion for me around the risks of construction. Architecture's success also contains failure. In these types of encounters with buildings, I feel it is iterative, quite literally, not just through drawing, but iterative through building. It's a long game.

MPDL: This brings to mind another topic that I want to introduce: taking risks in the design process. I don't mean risk from a liability point of view, but rather the risk of using unusual materials, of putting vegetation on a facade, of working outside your comfort zone, the risk of going all out on a geometry that may or may not get built. I think that risk is as much a part of the architectural imagination as anything else that we do as architects. If we are not willing to take risks, then we're not producing architecture. Do you agree or disagree?

AA: I'll just say I agree. But there's not just me, there's Dan [Wood], there's the office, and there's the client, and I feel like we take turns taking risks, and this is where the process is important. First of all, long ago we agreed never to disagree. Meaning, if there's a disagreement, that means we need to find another way to do it. Scott, you mentioned excitement. The thing is, when everyone is excited, then everyone at some point is like, let's just take the risk. You need a group to take the risk, because you can't do it alone.

MPDL: With risk you are putting new ideas on the table. Amale, I love the facade of Anthropologie Dos Lagos, with green growing on it and circles cut out of it. I've never seen anything like it. I can imagine, when drawing, modeling, etc., getting excited about it as a personal exploration and then thinking, Wait, does this look good? How is this going to be received by my peers? Am I sure I want to do this? That's the risk I mean. I think that taking leaps of faith is essential to the practice of the architect. Perhaps we don't talk about that enough.

MY: Earlier you mentioned finding alternatives to the status quo, which means you're taking a risk. I think everyone here does that through their creative practice. To me, maybe on the education side, I've been wondering how we support sustained creative risk taking. Because at some point, there's a kind of wearing down into the status quo. How do we support risk in the discipline and with our students? How do we support it for ourselves and for each other?

The creative risk part is exposing yourself – not in terms of legal liability but in terms of exposing yourself to failure. I think we should find ways to embrace creative risk more. I feel like you can't take on risk if you're not okay with failure. But our discipline doesn't support or reward failure. I don't mean to imply that our discipline should be like the tech industry, which has a "fail fast" model. I think we put things out there, through creative practice, tied to what Mira was saying earlier, that take time. If it's buildings that are the risk, that risk might be in the creative expression, or be in the use of materials that might not be warranted because you're using them in a different way or creating a new system and/or approach to building something more sustainably that hasn't been tested before. So I think Amale is right. You can take on more risk when everybody is supporting it, when everyone agrees that risk is worth taking – not only by the team, but by the client, community, and the discipline.

Mónica Ponce de León cocurated, with Cynthia Davidson, "The Architectural Imagination," the US Pavilion at the 2016 Venice Architecture Biennale, the catalog for which was *Log* 37. She is the principal of MPdL Studio and the dean of the School of Architecture at Princeton University.

Thomas Daniell
& Maki Onishi

The Positive Power Of Architecture

Maki Onishi is cofounder of onishimaki+hyakudayuki architects / o+h, a partnership with her husband Yuki Hyakuda. A monograph on the office's work, titled onishimaki + hyakudayuki / o+h: 8 stories, *was published in 2014. Currently a professor at Yokohama National University and a visiting professor at Kyoto University, Onishi was curator of the Japanese Pavilion at the 18th Venice Architecture Biennale. The installation was largely a celebration of the accumulated memories of artists, architects, and visitors who have been in the Japanese Pavilion since its completion, in 1956, to the design of Le Corbusier disciple Takamasa Yoshizaka. Onishi was inspired by Yoshizaka's view that "building things means transmitting life to them," and reinvigorated the architecture with the addition of a canopy made of recycled polyester and an outdoor space for social interactions, composed of waste wood and glass vessels that produced fragrances distilled from locally collected leaves. Our conversation took place on October 2, 2023, in her Tokyo office. I translated the transcript from the Japanese to present it here.* – TD

THOMAS DANIELL: What distinguishes your generation of Japanese architects from the preceding generations?

MAKI ONISHI: I became an architect in 2011, the year of the Tohoku earthquake. So I would say that we are the generation that started making architecture after the earthquake. To experience the Tohoku earthquake right at the moment we entered the workforce had a great impact on our thinking about architecture. Of course, even prior to that, rather than architects just designing whatever they want, particularly among young people, there had been a shift toward emphasizing the importance of discussions with the local community during the design process, leading to an interest in renovation and community development rather than just large-scale, new construction projects. But I feel that the Tohoku earthquake gave a decisive impetus for such values.

TD: Clearly the earthquake triggered a change in priorities and relationships for the design process, but what does that imply for the architecture itself?

Toyo Ito & Associates, Architects + Maki Onishi / o+h, Home for All for Children in Higashimatsushima, Miyagi, Japan, 2013. All images courtesy onishimaki + hyakudayuki architects / o+h. Photo: Iwan Baan. For color photos and drawings, see pages 130–131.

MO: I believe that architectural thinking entails the construction of society starting from place. For that reason, it's important that architecture is not an isolated box, but relates to the activities of the people who visit that place. And of course it's important to link architecture with the surrounding landscape and with regional ways of life. That is why we emphasize the importance of discussions and of spending time in the local community during the process of making architecture. To take a stance valorizing people's activities and the community itself may seem to imply a rejection of design, as it suggests that human activities are more important than anything else and so there is no need for special architecture, but I don't think that's true. Louis Kahn said, "In a small room with just another person, what you say may never have been said before." The ways people encounter each other and spend time together change dramatically depending on the kind of place created. Thinking about architecture through discussions with local people may lead to an expansion of the possibilities of architecture, to the creation of unprecedented architecture, and even to a new society.

TD: In fact, I think you began working as an architect before 2011. You graduated from Kyoto University in 2006, receiving a national award for your undergraduate thesis project, and then your first real project, Double Helix House, was published soon after that. But indeed, you came to prominence in 2011 with the children's center designed in collaboration with Toyo Ito and built as part of the reconstruction efforts after the Tohoku earthquake. How did that come about?

MO: Well, I went on to do my master's degree at the University of Tokyo, which I completed in 2008, and then started some small projects while I was doing the doctoral program, but I and my husband Yuki Hyakuda officially founded our office in 2011. I was invited by Ito to collaborate on the design of Home for All for Children in Higashimatsushima as part of Home for All, an organization founded after the Tohoku earthquake by Ito and Kazuyo

Sejima, among others. Many architects have built Home for All projects in the affected areas. My proposal was to create a place for children among the disaster-relief housing in Higashimatsushima, where six or seven hundred families were then living. What shocked me was that the abstract language I had been using to discuss architecture while I was at university was completely useless in communicating with the local people. At that time, I had a very small office – just me and one staff member – so for six months we rented a room in a disaster-relief housing complex and observed the construction. While drinking and singing karaoke with the other residents, I felt how wonderful it was to see architecture gradually emerging within the scenery of their daily lives. At the same time, I began to think that this should not be limited to the Tohoku region. I wanted to return to Tokyo and to think about architecture while connecting with the local community in the same way. So I moved my office, which had been on the fifth floor of a building in the Meguro district, to the ground floor of a building in a downtown neighborhood called Nihonbashihamacho. It used to be a parking garage, so when the shutters are lifted, the office is fully open to the street. Local children will stop by to look at the models on their way home from school.

TD: For Home for All, Ito gathered Japan's most radical, experimental architects and then asked them to design projects that were relatively humble, unspectacular, and inexpensive. At that time, you were almost completely unknown and certainly the youngest architect involved, invited by Ito due to his belief in your potential. How did you negotiate the demands of Home for All and your need to create a significant debut work?

MO: Our first design proposal was, like many of the other Home for All projects, an extremely simple shed. Then one day, Ito summoned us to his office and said, *This design seems utterly unlike you!* But at the same time, he insisted that Home for All is not about creating "works of architecture," so we had somehow thought that we should be making an anonymous building. I then realized that it is not necessarily a contradiction to build with the users' feelings in mind while creating a special architecture that expresses the designer's personality. So I created Home for All for Children in Higashimatsushima to be like a town of many small huts on wheels. Looking around the disaster-relief housing, I saw children playing everywhere – in ditches, on fences, and all kinds of other places – so I proposed that, rather than making a fixed facility, it would be fun to make architecture that can move along with the children's play.

TD: Aesthetically, it looks like something from a children's picture book, very cute and friendly.

MO: That's right. Ever since I was young, I have loved children's stories and picture books. As I said, I was shocked that the language I had been using was incomprehensible to the people in Higashimatsushima. I wondered how to communicate with them, and started to make drawings like what might be found in a children's picture book to show them, instead of speaking. But when construction was completed, the people turned out to be much more adaptable than I imagined. They were able to use the architecture very freely. After witnessing that, I came to realize that it is not necessary to make the process easy to understand. It is more important to trust the adaptability, generosity, and creativity of human beings.

TD: The work also has a tactile quality that seems very different from the abstract,

onishimaki + hyakudayuki architects / o+h, Double Helix House, Yanaka, Tokyo, 2011. Photo: Kai Nakamura.

diagrammatic architecture produced by many of your peers.

MO: That's right. From my earliest projects, such as my thesis project and Double Helix House, as well as Weekend House in Sengataki – which was our office's first real project, though it was never built – I was interested in the inherent presence of architecture, in how architecture might be captured by different senses such as sight, touch, smell, and so on. For example, Double Helix House has stairs of different widths ascending in a spiral, and though we cannot see into the spaces ahead, we can feel their presence. The roof of Weekend House in Sengataki is clad in shingles so as to resemble animal fur, whereas the interior has smooth white surfaces, two opposed textures that trigger very different tactile images. Rather than a form that is simply an artifact, I want to create something that somehow feels as if it were alive, that triggers all five human senses.

TD: Some years after the project in Higashi-matsushima, you did another community center in Fukushima called Alberobello. Was that also part of Home for All?

MO: No. Prior to that, we designed Good Job! Center KASHIBA, in Nara, a workplace for people with disabilities. The client for Alberobello commissioned us after seeing that project. Alberobello is a home for elderly people with disabilities, and we designed it as something like a village that gives rise to places where you can be on your own or spend time with others while enjoying the surrounding greenery.

TD: Your Shelter Inclusive Place Copal is also for disabled people. Is this emphasis due to your own interests or is it in response to requests from the client?

MO: We designed Good Job! Center KASHIBA after winning an open competition for young architects. The client was Tanpopo-No-Ye, an organization based in Nara that, for nearly 50 years, has been involved in supporting handicraft and other creative activities of people with disabilities. It was an experience that changed my viewpoint on society 180 degrees. Before the project began, we visited Tanpopo-No-Ye, and I asked a staff member if there were any special considerations in designing buildings for people with disabilities. He said no, that the spaces where we feel comfortable are spaces where people with disabilities will also feel comfortable, and spaces where we feel uncomfortable will also feel uncomfortable to people with disabilities. Hearing something so obvious, I felt ashamed for having unconsciously made a distinction between myself and people with disabilities. I realized that what we designers should do is interrogate our own bodies and think about the kinds of spaces that are truly comfortable, the kinds of spaces that are truly inviting. Through designing in collaboration with everyone at Tanpopo-No-Ye, I was compelled to pause and fundamentally rethink all those elements of architecture that I usually design without giving them any deep consideration. For example, imagine blind people visiting a place. Some of them will walk around while touching the walls with their hands, so one aspect of the design is where and how the rough or smooth wall textures will alternate in the space. Or, if you imagine a person who has difficulty balancing while sitting on the floor, you might prefer to make the floor soft and comfortable to lie on rather than hard and cold. In this way, if we imagine the diversity of people who might visit a building, we can redesign every architectural element that we normally take for granted, and I believe that this opens up new architectural possibilities. Architecture itself comprises dominant elements that have accumulated over a long history, whether you take a single window or a single stair, and there is a tendency to copy and paste. I want to reexamine and redesign each one of these areas.

TD: But doesn't designing for the disabled entail following Japan's very precise accessibility regulations?

MO: It is true that there are many regulations concerning barrier-free access and so on, but what I learned through designing Good Job! Center KASHIBA is that making a building barrier-free and making it inclusive follow fundamentally different vectors of thinking. In barrier-free design, when, for example, installing a ramp at a train station, the width and incline are determined to be easy to use for as many people as possible, right? Inevitably, the design becomes impersonal, and you can no longer see who the design is for or the faces of the individuals at the heart of the design. Inclusive design thinking is a little different. For example, if you design a handbag that is easy to use for a person who is paralyzed in half of his or her body, it will

onishimaki + hyakudayuki architects / o+h, study models for Weekend House in Sengataki, 2012.

also be easy to use for a mother who is breastfeeding and has difficulty moving the arm that is holding the baby. This suggests that a design conceived through deep consideration of the needs of a specific "individual" may also be appropriate for other people. So inclusive design is not about individuals, but about building a circle of empathy that is tolerant and accepting of others.

I believe that such inclusive thinking is not limited to making buildings for people with disabilities, such as Good Job! Center KASHIBA. It can also be applied to designing through discussion with local people when creating public buildings. Recently we have had many opportunities to hold workshops and briefings with locals, but as public buildings have lifespans of many decades, I started feeling a little uncomfortable talking with only the very limited number of people joining our workshops and briefings. But while I was working on a project on Shodoshima Island, I attended a local festival. A crowd of men carried portable shrines toward the sea, while a crowd of island dwellers sat on the piers with their drinks and lunch boxes,

Above and opposite page: onishimaki + hyakudayuki architects / o+h, Good Job! Center KASHIBA, 2016. Photos: Yoshiro Masuda.

cheering. I realized that such scenes have been occurring here for a long time and will continue for a long time to come. Even though the people with whom we were able to meet and talk were only those currently living there, I felt that by engaging with them deeply we might be able to connect with the past and the future, beyond those particular people.

TD: Whereas most young Japanese architects tend to become famous for a series of small experimental houses, your office quickly became known for community-related projects. Was that a strategy? Or just the type of commission you happened to receive?

MO: I would say both. We are interested in community-related projects and actively participate in competitions for them, but sometimes a client will commission us after seeing our previous projects. What is interesting about Home for All is that, unlike public places maintained by the national government or local municipalities, these are examples of places that local people establish and maintain on their own. I feel that the production of places by one's own hands is becoming increasingly important in Japanese society. A public place that is created by one's own hands could be a part of a house or it could be a welfare facility. In that sense, I am interested in thinking about architecture that functions like a community center, even if it is not necessarily called a community center.

TD: Why do you say that the production of places by hand is becoming increasingly important in Japanese society?

MO: Because it is increasingly important to view the creation and use of architecture as a continuous process. Rather than aiming for superlatively beautiful architecture at the moment of its completion, we want to emphasize continuous relationships between humans and architecture so that architecture can continue to grow and develop as it is used and modified over a long period of time.

TD: Your cohousing/coworking project Residential Incubator Toberu is also a kind of community center, or an attempt to implement new forms of social organization and interaction.

MO: That's right. When it comes to creating a place for a community, there are many ways to open up the place. I spent my student years in Kyoto, and not everywhere in Kyoto is fully open to the public. There are alleyways that contain bookstores and coffee shops where people can quietly gather, but only those willing to venture into their depths. Such places are not necessarily very open but tucked away and only open to those who make the effort. Such places give a city its charm. At Residential Incubator Toberu, we wanted to create a communal space that is both closed and open, with a sense of depth.

TD: Despite all this talk about community and people and inclusiveness, I think you are also interested in architecture for its own sake, in beautiful compositions of structure, form, and material, such as the use of timber in Taga Community Center or the roof forms of Shelter Inclusive Place Copal and Kumamoto Earthquake Museum KIOKU.

MO: Yes, I believe that the beauty of architectural form is very important, but it should be evaluated first and foremost in terms of its suitability for the site, particularly in terms of its scale. For example, in Kumamoto Earthquake Museum KIOKU, which we completed this year, we wanted to create an architecture that responds to the magnificent surrounding landscape, so we intensively studied the size of roof that would be appropriate for the site. Even with a single building, I believe it is possible to create a relationship in which the architecture responds to the wider landscape. As I mentioned earlier, I have been thinking about how the beauty and interest of architectural form itself can be an enhancement rather than a refusal of engagement with social movements and communities.

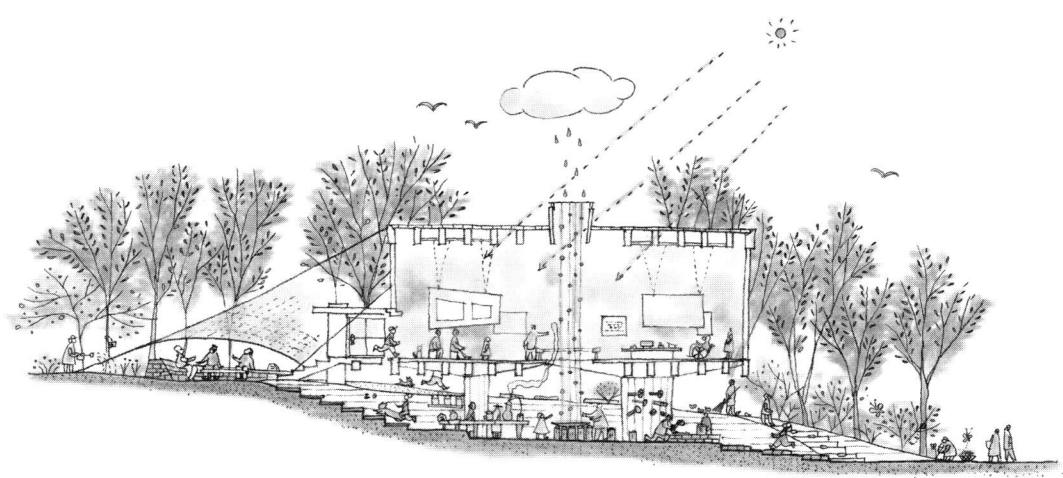

onishimaki + hyakudayuki architects / o+h, "Architecture, a place to be loved," Japanese Pavilion, 18th Venice Architecture Biennale, 2023.

TD: You were curator of the Japanese Pavilion at the Venice Architecture Biennale this year. How did you respond to the overall theme set by curator Lesley Lokko? Does Japanese architecture still have lessons to offer the rest of the world?

MO: I titled the exhibition "Architecture, a place to be loved" with the subtitle "when architecture is seen as a living creature." I wanted to suggest that architecture should not be seen as an artificial object but as an organism imbued with life. Viewing architecture as a living creature will engender the desire to nurture a place from the viewpoint that even its flaws are part of its individuality. By loving the irreplaceable presence of architecture itself, I believe that the relationship between architecture and human beings will become more interactive and reciprocal, transcending the "used-user" relationship. The notion of finding life in artifacts is connected to the animistic thinking that has existed in Japan since ancient times. Being able to love and cherish the various things that coexist in this world – humans, animals, and plants, as well as rocks and mountains and even architecture – as much as oneself is a sensibility that we have cultivated in the Japanese climate, and I believe it may be an important viewpoint for the wider world.

TD: What are your hopes or expectations for the future of architecture?

MO: I would like to broaden the meaning of the word *architecture* to include not only the completed building but also the process of its making, the activities it enables after its completion, and its relationship with the surrounding environment. I myself wanted to become an architect because of my experience of the exuberance and splendor of architecture rising up in the city. So I want to think about ways of creating architecture that will share its inherent positive power and festive nature with local communities.

Thomas Daniell is a *Log* protagonist and a professor of architecture at Kyoto University. His review of the 18th Venice Architecture Biennale is in *Log* 58.

*Anna Neimark
& Andrew Atwood*

Stone on Stone

It takes time to adjust your eyes to the darkness, especially in Los Angeles. The Los Angeles County Museum of Art (LACMA) campus feels particularly exposed, with large expanses of grass and sky encompassing the grounds. Outside, brightness and contrast attack our senses. Michael Heizer's granite rock hovers over a concrete ditch. Renzo Piano's travertine grid reflects the harsh sun. Peter Zumthor's construction site rings with a high pitch. The air smells of the tar that permeates the fossil-rich ground. Everyone arrives wearing sunglasses.

But inside one of the Resnick Pavilion galleries, the architects of The Los Angeles Design Group (The LADG), Andrew Holder and Benjamin Freyinger, blacked out the skylights and dimmed the lights. They packed the room with veneered plywood panels that effectively dampen the sound. And they reduced the atmosphere to a kind of off-black that recedes into the background, extending the compact gallery with deep pockets of seemingly infinite space. The muted ambience of the "Eternal Medium" exhibition relaxes our senses and gives us a break from LA's harsh atmosphere. The reset is necessary to appreciate the delicate pattern, tone, and texture on display. Only in this dark air can our pupils dilate and color correct to see both the stones and deep into the stones at once.

The subtitle of the exhibition, "Seeing the World in Stone," brings awareness to the process of seeing the ephemeral worlds that surround and inhabit this seemingly hard material. In a famous story that now resembles a myth, Ludwig Mies van der Rohe envisaged an entire pavilion trapped inside the symmetry of an onyx slab. But for a few contemporary exceptions, like Young & Ayata's "hot stone objects," architects have forgotten how to see the things of this world – modern pavilions, mystical landscapes, inkblot clouds, spotted animals – petrified in rock. For our generation – a generation that has traded medium specificity for immaterial platitude – this exhibition is a lesson in remembering. We recalled that stone is hard and heavy, that it contains veins and grain, that it is quarried and traded with great difficulty, that it emits images and mediates phantoms, that it is really beautiful and beautifully real.

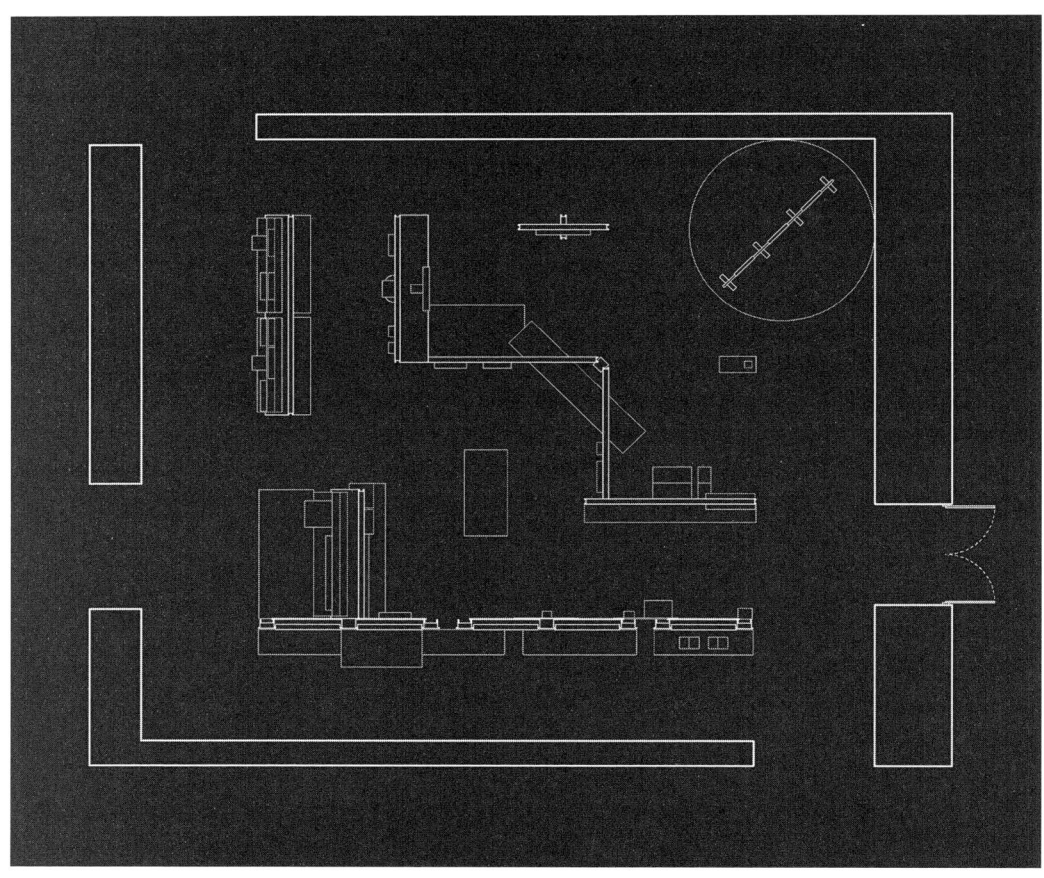

The Los Angeles Design Group, plan for "Eternal Medium: Seeing the World in Stone," Resnick Pavilion, Los Angeles County Museum of Art, August 20, 2023 – February 11, 2024. Drawing courtesy the architects.

As part of an international collaboration, the exhibition's polymath curator, Rosie Mills, The Rosalinde and Arthur Gilbert Associate Curator of Decorative Arts and Design at LACMA, developed this transhistorical exhibition across departments and time periods, with knowledge and specimens gathered from LACMA, the Rosalinde and Arthur Gilbert Collection, and the Victoria and Albert Museum in London. She organized 125 objects into nine categories of display, across which, at different scales and in diverse forms, stone is everywhere present, and it also represents. And despite the singular word *medium* in the title of the exhibition, there are many media grouped to communicate with one another to develop the idea of stone's capacity to mediate. There are animals formed of rock, paints made of minerals, stones marked with pigment, pictures clad in stone, landscapes pictured in gems, stones depicted with paint. The artifacts range in measure from a cubic centimeter to feet in length; in weight, from paper to marble slab; in format, from flat to volumetric; in value, from minimal to maximum security glass.

The LADG's partitions, pedestals, and tables for "Eternal Medium." Photo © Marten Elder. Courtesy the architects. See a color photo of the installation on page 134.

Mills directed The LADG to pull it all together without "bleaching" the objects. Thus they faced the old-school problem of the *nine-square*: how to squeeze nine thematic groupings into a single rectangular space with a high degree of scalar looseness and local differentiation. But the result is not the formal nine-square of John Hejduk. Its corners are blunt, its edges lean, it has gaps. The substructure of the nine-square grid is set up only to be unpacked and undermined. There are normal panels that support leaning platforms that support cantilevering pedestals that support extruded plinths that support the glass panes that support the wedged plates that support the vinyl text. This pile of supporting material is painted black, Dunn-Edwards Black Bay, to be specific. And, of course, it is the opposite of the white box gallery. But as eyes adjust to the dark, it becomes apparent that this black is also not quite the black of a black box theater. It's softer and grayer than its more dramatic black box counterpart. Just as the nine-square grid establishes an organizational foil to slowly be eroded, Black Bay establishes an obvious binary to also be adjusted, blurred, transgressed, and ultimately destroyed.

Dresden Snuffbox in the Shape of a Dog, circa 1740–1750. Photo © Museum Associates/LACMA.

Many things here feel intentional. There is almost no neutrality, not in the box, not in the paint, and definitely not in walking into the nine-square grid. And there are many corner problems, too. For the most part, corners, like the nine-square, are either butted or eroded. To assist the visitor in comparative viewing, the architects cut window boxes out of the walls. They stretched tables diagonally across the corners and loaded them with delicacies of rock. Two seemingly distinct sections, "Hard" Stones and Fooling the Eye, become entwined by one such projecting surface that holds up glass boxes that hold the artifacts that hold our gaze from multiple perspectives at once. The museum staff will even offer a loupe to zoom in on the revealing details. A 17th-century Indian Dagger of Emperor Aurangzeb flaunts a white horse head handle whose tinged nephrite veins follow the wavy nature of the mare's mane. An 18th-century Dresden Snuffbox in the Shape of a Dog emerges from a moss agate whose dark inclusions uncannily capture the hound's spots. A Yunnan 19th-century Marble Slab disk suggests an ink-like landscape whose crystalline bands weave a mountain range along a horizon. These miniature objects mediate microcosmic details. Imaging shapes in stone expands the term *medium* to encompass its mystical meaning. Medium means middle – *in medias res* – it is the site of transmission. With some imagination, stone can fluctuate between its materiality as an obdurate fact and its textuality as a prolix oracle.

Analia Saban, *Draped Marble (Carrara, St. Laurent, Brown Onyx)*, 2016. © Analia Saban. Photo © Museum Associates/LACMA.

The section titled Seeing Images in Stone focuses on what Mills calls "the stone's pictorial potential," developing the public's visual imaginary through the concept of pareidolia. The *Oxford English Dictionary* explains that the term stems from the prefix that is "analogous to but separate from" the root that is defined as "an insubstantial manifestation or an apparition." Several other sections, Manipulating Multicolored Stones, Flora and Fauna, Heaven and Earth, and Fooling the Eye, build on the curator's idea to train our imaginary capacity for "pareidolic vision" by focusing on natural phenomena, treelike textures, and trompe l'oeil effects of stone's mineral variations. Other sections are more down to earth. Sourcing Specimens traces stone from around the globe extracted from quarries or spoliated from ancient monuments. One gridded game table features polychromatic stones gathered from disparate origins. The section "Hard" Stones plays with our expectations of stone's solidity, mass, and weight by showcasing bloodstone, nephrite jade, porphyry, and marble that have been carved, cracked, and lathed to appear effervescent, light, and sinuous.

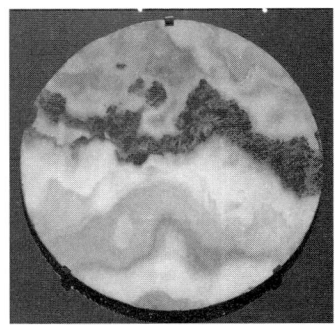

Marble Slab from Yunnan, China, circa 1800–1872. Victoria and Albert Museum, London. Photo © Museum Associates/LACMA.

In a theatrical staging, artist Analia Saban hangs three slabs of stone like laundry over a sawhorse in her *Draped Marble* installation. The stone cracks into a calcified aggregate of loose rock, seemingly made plastic by gravity. The section Transcending Stone depicts materials such as porcelain posing for the hard stones that they are not, while Stone for Stone explores ways in which stone can reflexively represent itself. In one pictorial urban mosaic, a building's shadow falling onto the stone-clad plaza is depicted with a slightly darker shade of the sourced mineral. This reminded us of Viollet-le-Duc's Alpine house called La Vedette, where the painted mural of the craggy rock-scape spills out of its frame as wainscoting of a cabinet clad in thin slabs of broken stone.

On our mission to review the exhibition design, we intended to look past the objects, to focus on the background. But we couldn't take our eyes off the astonishing array of artifacts. Small and precious amethysts converse with large oil paintings. Peter and Jesus – literally the rocks of the Christian faith – mix with secular snuffboxes and petrified landscapes. Ancient craftsmen are brought into dialog with contemporary artists. Thematic and visual affinities curate the madness of genres, sizes, and materials. To use Holder and Freyinger's term, it is an irreverent "gathering" of things. The curator and the architects clearly took pleasure in the absurd amount of labor that went into making these objects as they thoughtfully staged stone on stone in physical and referential proximity. There is no one order or proper sequence for viewing the work. Instead, piles, lists, labels, groupings, relations, sightlines, proximities, and multiple points of entry produce something of a peep show, a proffer of stone against a series of props, seducing in the quiet dark.

Anna Neimark and Andrew Atwood are cofounding principals of First Office. Anna teaches at SCI-Arc; Andrew teaches at UC Berkeley.

Ana Miljački & Cristina Gamboa

Housing Makes A Community

Cristina Gamboa is one of 14 cofounders of Lacol, a cooperative of architects in Barcelona. Their cooperative housing project La Borda, of which she is a member, received the 2022 EU Mies van der Rohe Prize for Emerging Architecture. At Lacol, Gamboa has been researching participatory approaches to design and developing cooperative housing and housing policies, which are constantly tested in Lacol's ongoing projects and initiatives. Gamboa also teaches at the Architectural Association in London and the Escola Tècnica Superior d'Arquitectura de Barcelona. I sat down with her at a Zoom table on September 10, 2023, to record this conversation, with the idea that it would complement the conversations and topics in Log 54: Coauthoring. *– AM*

ANA MILJAČKI: I went to Barcelona this summer. One of my purposes was to see La Borda. I also saw La Balma. The area near La Borda, as you know, is a big construction site at the moment. That industrial scape seemed to be getting turned into various types of social infrastructure. My family and I were sneaking around it, in the sweltering infamous European heat wave, to get a peek into the building.

Lacol and its architectural work, which have been on my radar, are lighting up architectural social media with ever greater frequency, including the presentation of last year's Mies Award – congratulations on that. I just taught the third installment of the Collective Architecture Studio at MIT [see *Log* 48], which grapples with collective authorship, collective ownership, and collective living simultaneously, and all that in the context of an ex-socialist country where there's still a memory of socialism and of self-management. I take MIT students to Belgrade because I feel there's still a memory of an older dream of collectivity there, and therefore of an alternative to the neoliberal, capitalist business as usual. In working through some of these topics with students, historians, and activists in Belgrade, Lacol became very important to the studio, both as an architectural solution and as a proof, of sorts, of concept. We are fans.

Let's start by talking about how Lacol is organized. How have some of these co-op housing and working buildings come about? What might they suggest for our future? Can you imagine the model repeating?

CRISTINA GAMBOA: Thank you for this introduction. It is always interesting to understand the context and motivations for a conversation. While you were talking, I was reminded of my exchanges with colleagues in Eastern European countries, who recognize that cooperative ideas in Spain register as a radical alternative, and thus have an audience, whereas in their contexts, it seems that cooperatives are a reminder of an unwelcome past, which hinders the view of this model.

AM: I'm a historian of some of the socialist architecture in the Czech Republic, but I am from Belgrade, Yugoslavia – a place in time and geography – and my research and experience confirm your sense that there are different memories of socialism across Eastern Europe. You might know Ana Džokić, a founder and member of a number of different cooperative groups in Belgrade and the ex-Yugoslavian region. She is a veteran of the fight for cooperative thinking and acting, as well as for cooperative housing, and is currently attempting to mount a platform that enables interested parties to organize co-ops around different needs, something like your Coopolis. We learned from her that there are many legal and financial barriers to realizing, and especially to financing, cooperatives in the Serbian and ex-Yugoslavian context. Foreign banks, mostly Western European, that operate in that context simply don't offer the financial instruments that would enable collective ownership.

So there are barriers, but there are also activists and the general population who do not remember socialism as all bad. In fact, in the ex-Yugoslavian context, memories of socialism fair well when measured against the contemporary situation.

You launched Lacol in 2009. All descriptions of it suggest that you were friends and colleagues at school. How many were you? Has the group grown, has it evolved and how?

CG: Yeah, Lacol combined two groups of students. We are 14 cofounders, two groups of friends (seven and seven) that started university together. One of the two groups rented a space to work together. When half of each group went on their Erasmus exchanges with other universities, the remaining people joined together in the same space. Upon returning from these exchanges, there were 21 of us sharing the space. Our school of architecture in Barcelona is large, students are expected to work quite autonomously. The school provides some space, but this model does not include studios and shops. One works alone, at home. So having a studio together meant we had a space where we could share ideas with one another, as well as the resources we needed to do our work. In this shared space, we also had the opportunity to start discussing what was working and what was not working in the profession. As we entered the final stages of our diploma work, half, or even more, of Lacol decided to try to understand and undertake an alternative form of the final project. At our school final projects tended to be typological exercises, big facilities, large stadia, etc. But we were in 2008, 2009.

AM: In the middle of the financial crisis?

CG: Exactly. The crisis was palpable, yet the university was offering an obsolete model. We discussed how we might be able to collectively offer something different. We proposed to the university to work with a committee of three female architects and engage deeply with a specific neighborhood for our work. Our experience of sharing ideas in our workspace helped us transform the curriculum.

For our final project we proposed and implemented different initiatives in a neighborhood with which we have since established a lasting relationship.

It all developed organically, including a way of understanding our responsibility as architects in the midst of a financial crisis. There were no jobs to be had, everyone was living in pain, and yet there was so much to be done. So, 21 of us were sharing the studio space. We all finished our studies within a year of one another, around 2011, when Lacol started to operate. We realized that our mode of work, and Lacol, could become a professional reality.

During those nearly five years, from 2009 to 2014, Lacol became more consistent and more clearly formalized as a professional project. Fourteen members of the original group officially founded the co-op in 2014, while some of the others dispersed to follow different paths. Many things already linked us together: our age, our politics, shared experiences at the university and in the studio we rented together, as well as our choice to follow this particular collective path.

Lacol has been a space for growing, in the sense that we were figuring out what interests we could share. We are architects, but we are also sociologists, carpenters, and urban planners. As we were working, we understood who could do what, and this kind of interdisciplinary umbrella was of interest to us. From the 14 founding members, we are now 11 cofounders, working full-time, and two collaborators. It has been quite an intense evolution. We have been working together for more than 10 years. The group has been really consistent. Right now, we also have six people working with us, and we can start imagining how we might grow and evolve.

AM: In a recent interview, you said that Lacol developed in parallel with the development of La Borda as a cooperative. There is a title of a piece on your work that I like very much, something like, making housing makes a community. Sometimes you need a community to precede a project, other times the making of a project produces the community. Can you talk about that relationship between the community and the architecture that houses it, or about the relationship between La Borda and Lacol?

CG: I think that relates to your first question. Three members of Lacol chose Can Batllo as a site to develop their diploma project. In a way, Can Batllo and La Borda have been our school. It was through the initial engagement with Can Batllo that we began to understand the role of the user and of citizenship in the production of urban space and in the process of producing architecture. With this paradigmatic experience in the self-managed construction of the city, the housing initiative emerged. So in the middle of a financial crisis, and within the framework of a self-managed and activist project, a group of neighbors started discussing alternative forms of tenancy and ownership. Housing is one of Barcelona's main challenges. People are being displaced and evicted. In this context, we became part of a group of neighbors that was trying to understand cooperative housing models around the world, from Denmark to Uruguay. We were looking for references and trying to understand how we might bring about a similar proposal to fit our legal and cultural frameworks. In the midst of these overlapping crises, we understood how political our own activity could be. It felt good. It was fulfilling to understand our role and the agency that we can have.

La Borda is, first of all, about policy. It's about understanding a model of ownership, a relationship with the municipal government in which it leases the land for 75 years to a co-op as a nonprofit entity. La Borda is both an architectural outcome and a system.

At Lacol we sometimes call this combination "community infrastructure." Community infrastructure involves devices that are set in a specific space and led by a community, but are part of a system that can be replicated. This is the main idea.

AM: You said that you need to know the context in order to do the kind of work you do. I am wondering about the political importance of being in the vicinity of and participating in the strengthening of the cooperative model across different fields, which was happening at that point in Spain, and in Barcelona specifically. What has been the importance of the historical moment, the locality itself, and about the transferability of the project?

CG: You mentioned this idea of building housing to build a community. This was critical. We understood the process as being led and controlled by a community, but in the process of facing many conflicts together, the group's capacity to solve problems and discuss architectural and economic issues was increasing. They/we were getting to know one another through the process. So, regarding your question, we always want to acknowledge that we were operating in a working-class neighborhood with a long tradition of cooperativism. That is a big part of the reason why we, too, are a cooperative. We know the model and the values of cooperativism and its characteristics through local genealogies, and there was an extensive network of people from different projects and initiatives. It was possible to do what we did because we didn't do it alone.

For example, downstairs from our studio, there is a co-op that researches cooperativism in the neighborhood, and we've learned a lot from them. Sometimes we are materializing, spatializing, and giving shape to ideas that are shared across many collectives in the area. Without that network of ideas and people, our work would not be possible. At the same time, it came out of a specific political moment after the financial crisis, following the 2011 anti-austerity "movement of the squares," and then, of course, with a progressive government, Barcelona en Comú, voted into power in 2015.

Over the last eight years, we have operated outside of the formal political space. The idea of working that way was crucial not only for the independence it provided but also because it allowed us to be involved in the coproduction of policies. We had an opportunity to take advantage of our collaborations within the policy frameworks put forth by the new Catalan government, both regarding housing co-ops and social economy incubators. When we talk with colleagues and collectives in other countries, it has been important to acknowledge the local specificity of our situation. It is difficult for us to imagine working in another place.

Between 2015 and 2023, we experienced a period of political support in Barcelona. But processes of opposition and construction follow cycles. We have to see how things will unfold in the future.

AM: There are two ways in which I am wondering about replicating or not replicating the cooperative model, but I am resisting using words that are part of the business vocabulary. What are the ingredients we might need in order to replicate your model of practice? Can you imagine the academy transforming to foster that model? I love the idea that the pre-Lacol group began producing its academic work outside of the academy in order to respond to a lack, of sorts, and I love imagining the school transforming accordingly. Could the academic context enable young architects to think differently and outside of the engrained status quo?

CG: During these processes of creating our

co-op and La Borda, we discovered architects and practices that offered useful management strategies, tools, and methodologies. We had to look for our own references – knowledge that the school had not supplied us. For us, La Borda provided the opportunity to understand what kind of architecture we were interested in and why. And sometimes the key idea revolved around popular architecture – what might we need for the production of popular architecture and to whom do we look to learn about participation? Besides the richness of the context we inhabit, we lacked appropriate references. From this point of view, it would be amazing if schools were to offer other histories of architecture. The contemporary feminist academics are writing these now, involving the agency of the architect as well as certain kinds of informal, bottom-up work.

For us it was really important to understand the tools, language, vocabulary, etc. If architecture schools were to present the plurality of possible modes of practicing and provide the tools necessary to support those, all of this would be different. As Lacol, we have been sharing tools with many other colleagues in co-ops. As you mentioned, we formed Coopolis, a foundation for sharing and promoting knowledge about cooperatives. We are continuously looking for spaces for knowledge transfer. Academia is one, but professional and human networks are also important. We used to understand architectural practice through the framework of competition, but I think this makes little sense today. When we worked on our second housing co-op, La Balma, we did it with another co-op of architects. In fact, since La Borda, we have done two projects with two different co-ops. These co-ops are now doing similar projects by themselves.

AM: You talked about La Borda being a school for members of Lacol. What would you

Lacol, La Balma, Barcelona, 2021. Top-floor circulation space as a communal balcony. Photo: Milena Villalba. All photos courtesy the architects. For color photographs of Lacol's work, see pages 136–137.

say were the main lessons from La Borda, and what was different in La Balma?

CG: Well, sometimes we say that our spatial research and all the discussions we had during the making of La Borda defined a framework of operations – certain ideas that are not exactly rules but guides for understanding participation as a process in which the community has control over the development, and the user won't be the owner of the flat. Understanding how the community participated in decisions about development but not about the specific units was important. In the collages of decisions made in our participatory workshops, there was clear recognition of the items that were defined by individuals and the areas that recorded collective thinking and were imbued with a developing

Lacol, La Borda, Barcelona, 2018. A food co-op storefront on the ground floor of the north facade. Photo: Baku Akazawa.

sense of belonging. It was important for us to understand that collective ownership involved collective decisions on items that impacted the life span of the building. The second set of important issues had to do with collective living, how the community spaces would operate in the building, and how they might accommodate change. We did not produce a dichotomy between common areas and the rest of the building. We designed the connections between the private and common spaces, as well as transitions to the public. All of this involved challenging cultural norms about individual spaces and the space of the family. Our responsibility as architects was to help people understand the instrumentality of spatial organization and architecture. For example, why we might not want to have a corridor with many doors closing off everything. We presented on topics like these, as well as on gender roles in the domestic sphere. The key lesson for all was the ideal model of sustainability in which the user is an active participant, not just a passive recipient of a "high-performance" building. It was important to understand the potential of daily practices in order to get at more sustainable collective living. The last issue involves the way sustainability and economy are linked. When you save energy, you are saving people's money. We kept discussing ways to reduce the cost of the construction, while also ensuring that the energy performance of the building would be really high. In the end, La Borda fused together ideas of participation, community living, and economic issues. We are implementing this combination of concerns in other projects. The specific mechanisms we implemented in La Borda may need to be adjusted for different contexts, but the same concerns and ideas run through them.

AM: Are there design tools that you brought to the table and included in your conversations with the various stakeholders, including future inhabitants and members of the co-op? Or, conversely, are there architectural tools that you might not have had before you engaged in these projects that you now think we should all have?

CG: Conversations with different stakeholders involve navigating different power differentials. Beyond the clear role that architects have in the assembly of a building, we also have to make architectural ideas accessible. I think that architects' drawings and vocabulary are sometimes very exclusive. In that sense, a beautiful drawing, the drawing by and for architects, is not helpful. We try to make accessible drawings, which, to architects, may seem like a reduction in the quality of the drawing, but every once in a while, it is useful to break our own habits and to unlearn, so to speak. Even on the construction site, are we drawing something for the worker to understand or because it is beautiful?

The most important tool for us has been dialog. Our idea of authorship has been collective, in the sense that many members of Lacol are working on a project. In La Borda, we also engaged various other collaborators – the environmental consultancy, the acoustic experts – and everyone felt that it was a project that could demonstrate an alternative way of doing things. Since we did not have all this knowledge internally, and because we were very young, we ended up collaborating with teams that had much more experience than we did. They recognized our enthusiasm and energy, and may have thought that we were naive, too, which made them protective. The architecture of La Borda took form through discussions and learning all around, including the representatives of the municipality.

With La Borda, we challenged regulations. We pushed for changes in the metropolitan parking regulations. We were installing certain environmental devices that were new, which involved discussions with our collaborators and users and also with the housing and permitting agencies. It was important to make people in these regulating bodies understand that we were seeking partners, that we were not fighting with anyone. We wanted to propose housing in which units could get bigger or smaller. The technicians were incredulous. We had to have the housing agency lawyer come in to discuss introducing a new type of contract that described the apartment growing and changing. Many of the things we accomplished at La Borda were products of these types of conversations.

AM: You mentioned having to change minds. It's interesting that you are at the table with agencies and with people who are involved in drafting the procedures that regulate the space you are working in and changing. Did you encounter any barriers that remain? Or is this precisely what is amazing about your context in Barcelona, that it enables this kind of work?

CG: Well, collective ownership was possible at La Borda because of local cooperative networks. La Borda was funded by a financial services union, Coop57. Coop57 collectivized all the money, operated as a bank outside of the banking system, and generated this project. It had its own regulations, with a maximum of 200,000 euros to give to a project. But when they realized the potential of this housing project in the context of Barcelona, they changed their own regulations, took a risk, and offered 1.6 million euros.

The idea of taking a risk together is crucial here. It is applicable at the level of the local municipality as well, and it always depends on finding the right people for it. Because we were trying to push through changes, we had to establish a certain kind of space for dialog. We were constantly inviting the housing agency or the energy agency to be part of the conversation to understand the conflicts produced by the regulations and attempt to think of different frameworks together. At La Borda, for example, the idea of clustered living was not possible because the housing regulation is based on a dated, heteronormative idea of couples.

Our massive efforts on this front have finally resulted in a new housing regulation that allows for clustered living, and we have been relying on it for our newer projects. Sometimes antiquated regulations limit a project, but through facing them head-on, and with the right people, and especially by being propositional, we can produce change. We are always trying to be propositional and projective.

AM: Let's zoom out a little. What would you say is your own definition of the role of the architect and the role of architecture?

CG: Well, after 10 years of working together – just after Covid – we sat down together because it seemed like we needed to articulate our collective vision. We formulated the idea of "community infrastructure" to describe our desire to be engaged in generating a sustainable life through architecture, cooperativism, and participation. The community is at the center, and it manages and controls this infrastructure. As a response to a systemic environmental, economic, and social crisis, our housing co-ops offer collective attempts at sustaining life.

But now we are also proposing energy co-ops, because we need to share energy resources as well as housing. All the devices are controlled by the community in order to produce a collective response to a shared problem. Architecture is a tool produced and managed through participation and cooperativism as a set of values, but architecture is not at the center of all the solutions we need as a society. The energy community is not an architectural proposal but, first, a legal entity. The idea that management of the urban realm is at stake is more and more present in our work. I live in La Borda, so I experience closely the needs and ways of that collective.

AM: I want to talk about the fact that members of Lacol are also often part of the collective they are working for, the community that you're describing "at the center." And also, the sustainability question now pertains to how you sustain the housing collective and how you sustain yourselves as a community and a collective of architects. I imagine that your definition of architecture now encompasses management, cooperativism, and the ability to produce platforms for co-ops to be made.

CG: Exactly. But caring about ourselves as workers is also crucial. When we say that a detail is economical, we refer to the cost of construction, but at the same time, a detail is economical because we understand that we have limits as workers. We know that we cannot produce 2,000 models and 200 plans. We cannot afford that. We need to be self-aware about our work, otherwise we may end up exploiting ourselves. This is really important. And in that sense, even the diversity of the lines of work at Lacol – which are based on our specific interests but also give us a certain kind of stability – are important. This diversity has enabled a multifaceted approach and a certain economic equilibrium.

AM: You were talking about architecture not being the central concern in all of this work. I prefer to think that architecture is everywhere in your work and in a different way than we've been used to imagining it. But where would you say aesthetic concerns fit in this model, and how? When I look at La Borda and La Balma, as well as your project for the workspace La Comunal, I see aesthetic consistency across them. There are certain details and certain ways of treating architecture spatially, materially, etc. that are extremely coherent. They don't strike me as sidesteps or as marginal.

CG: Aesthetics are so subjective. Recently, an architect told us that La Borda is really beautiful. And I responded, Well, people living in La Borda sometimes think it's not. As a resident, I experience a kind of comfort that I never have before. This is what the inhabitants of La Borda appreciate, though they might not all love the mesh on the balconies or the metal sheets on the facade. For us, the final look was the outcome of trying to make the most out of little and of trying to establish a strategy of prioritizing our efforts. So, if you want to reduce the environmental impact of the building and have a low budget to work with, you have to be really strategic about each construction decision. If a layer of plasterboard solves two requirements, you do that. La Borda is the outcome of a series

Lacol, La Borda, Barcelona, 2018. Co-op meeting in the double-height community space off the seven-story atrium. Photo: Institut Municipal de l'Habitatge i Rehabilitació de Barcelona.

of such decisions. Even so, we are sometimes critical. I'm thinking, should La Borda be so different from the rest of the collective housing projects around it? When we worked on it, we were interested in visualizing the collective as a big house. The idea of unity is present in the form and in the facade. As we work, sometimes aesthetic ideas and preferences change, but the material details, which we are pretty sure about, remain.

AM: Well, as an architect and critic who went to see it, I found that simple materials were ennobled by the ways they were deployed. Even that balcony mesh, or the roller blinds, right? Something that is fairly cheap and ubiquitous was deployed in a way that produces a considered aesthetic effect.

You have described the work of Lacol as "taking architecture out of the traditional client-user commissioning relationship and politicizing it." What does that mean?

CG: We understood that an alternative housing model was needed to respond to the lack of housing, to a need to diversify this sector of building. Our recognition of a general need and our being active about it was also a way for us to produce work for ourselves. We understood from the beginning that La Borda provided us a space for research. It provided a direct connection with our activism and with the networks that we want to reinforce and cultivate. At Lacol, around 70 percent of our time is dedicated to earning projects that are paid. The other 30 percent is spent on activism, interactions, and discussions. We are careful to recognize both productive and reproductive work. They have the same value. In an architectural project that we are getting paid for, someone is working on the building, someone is cultivating the networks, often in the afternoons or evenings. All of this work has value and allows us to invest in the world.

Lacol, La Borda, Barcelona, 2018. Kitchen and living space. Photo: Lluc Miralles.

AM: You just painted a pie chart of your time with words, right? There is a certain amount of time and we divide it like this. I have been doing interviews with architects about things they would prefer not to do, and about the ways they discuss these types of decisions in their firms. Are there things you would prefer not to do as a collective? Do you have that conversation at Lacol? How do you make decisions and stick to them as a collective?

CG: Well, Lacol has been evolving continuously. I don't think we have ever spent more than a year organizing ourselves in the same way. We are very clear about what we don't want to do in terms of work. We have a set of values and a set of lines we don't want to cross. For example, we would not collaborate with private real-estate initiatives whose only goals are speculation and profit. Sometimes it's more difficult to say yes to projects than it is to say no, and in the process of thinking through these things we have learned a lot about all the members of Lacol. Perhaps I have an interest in a project and see it as an opportunity, while someone else might be totally against it. Over time we understood that we need to provide space for these kinds of discussions. I would say that the most important organizational question pertains to the kinds of discussions we need to have. We have set aside time and space, a couple of times a year, for a conversation about the evolution of Lacol in terms of economic issues and the direction we are taking. We need this dedicated space because this topic requires focus. Right now we are organized in different areas of work. After a decade of working together we trust each other and we delegate. This idea of delegation and trust is the core of Lacol. We cannot take all decisions collectively.

AM: So you're allowing decisions to be made locally?

CG: It's not a hierarchical structure but more of a fractal situation. I am working especially on architectural projects linked to housing. But some Lacol members are dedicated to working on energy communities, and we make decisions within our domains. But we discuss things together weekly, and this allows for a cross-sectional conversation among different groups.

AM: You certainly gave us a sense of how the decision-making unfolds at Lacol. Have you had to say no to something?

CG: We received a proposal to collaborate from another office. It turned out to be a really speculative development, huge, and in wood, but really challenging the housing price in a certain area of the city. We said no to that. That project was opposed to our values, despite it being about housing, and we made this decision together.

AM: In one interview, you talked about the way cooperatives often form from groups of people who already trust each other, know each other, are often homogeneous in some way because life has brought them together and they are bonded over those shared experiences. You suggested that there are ways to open that up and think about diversity within the logics of the cooperatives.

CG: Yeah, I think this would be applicable even to Lacol itself because, in the end, there is a certain homogeneity in our approach. We have been having conversations about the ways that Lacol can grow and open up, but perhaps more important, we have been having conversations about this in the case of La Borda and the larger cooperative housing project. La Borda was a Trojan horse, and those who worked on it were activists. But once the project is built and people live together, you realize that we are all alike. We have diversity in terms of inhabitants' economic situations, but we are discussing how we could make La Borda more inclusive. When a flat opens up right now, we have a series of criteria and interviews in place, with the hope of opening up the co-op to different people. These processes take a long time. It is clearer to us now that there are many different issues that contribute to the way a co-op is formed. Who can participate in these conversations? Who has access to the relevant networks? Who understands the language in which the conversations are conducted? Who has the need and the stability that motivate and enable them to participate? And then, how can we produce more flexible and inclusive frameworks and protocols? How do we establish mechanisms of economic solidarity, and how will it all be replicated?

We are learning by doing. We are evolving Lacol's structure because we are learning from our mistakes and about things that are missing. The same is true of the housing co-op.

AM: You now have a few people who support the work but are not partners or owners of the firm. I read that you have a mechanism in place that enables them to opt in to the co-op eventually. But do you think you have to grow in terms of numbers?

CG: Well, we have been growing. But instead of Lacol becoming a monster with many heads, we generate projects and collaborations that we can continue to contribute to but are not internal to Lacol. Lacol has helped initiate a housing co-op platform and, more recently, an energy hub with an engineering co-op. These were needs that we helped address, and now these are friendly initiatives. Internally, we have grown a little, we are fewer than 20 people. But here the discussion is about creating a space in which those who join us can feel they can challenge habits and frameworks produced over all these years of working. We would like Lacol to be about all of its members.

Ana Miljački guest edited *Log* 54: Coauthoring (2022) with Ann Lui. She is a critic, curator, and professor of architecture at MIT, where she teaches history, theory, and design and directs the Critical Broadcasting Lab. Since 2021, she has been collaborating with the Architectural League of New York on a podcast series titled *I Would Prefer Not To*.

Observations on an Average Home

307a, Greenville, South Carolina, 2023. Photo: Taylor Dover.

This is an average affordable house in Greenville, South Carolina. Standing two stories tall, with its covered porch and surrounding lawn, number 307a is a moderate walk from the small but growing downtown. A drive around the immediate neighborhood reveals that the average charm of 307a is not unique. A handful of other houses follow an identical design, recognizable despite their distinctly colored front doors.

Greenville's 2018 Affordable Housing Action Plan defines the budget for an affordable house by calculating 30 percent or less of the monthly income of a household earning 80 percent or less of the city's median income of $60,000. Following this equation, in 2023, an affordable house costs $250,000 or less. Nationwide, the average price of a single-family home is $430,000. While the interior of 307a isn't visible from this sidewalk view, and the latest sale price isn't publicly listed, Zillow's "zestimated" price is $223,400. The $206,600 gap between the zestimate and the median selling price in America shows just how uncommon it is to be both affordable and "average."

Ninety percent of the buildings in the US are single-family houses. These roughly 102 million structures constitute 60 percent of the country's habitable dwellings. The "starter home," which accounted for more than 70 percent of housing construction in 1950, now represents less than eight percent nationwide. Who is designing and building these increasingly rare homes? While the local Greenville government's substantial incentives for affordable housing have resulted in more than 600 affordable units currently in planning around the downtown, the majority of these are apartments in large-scale multiunit buildings. An investigation of Greenville's building record does not identify an architect for 307a, rather, like most average affordable homes in this community, it was built by a nonprofit corporation, Allen Temple Community Economic Development Corporation, who have built or renovated 86 homes in upstate South Carolina since 2006. – Taylor Dover

Sarah M. Whiting
& Pier Vittorio Aureli

From Abstraction To the Longhouse

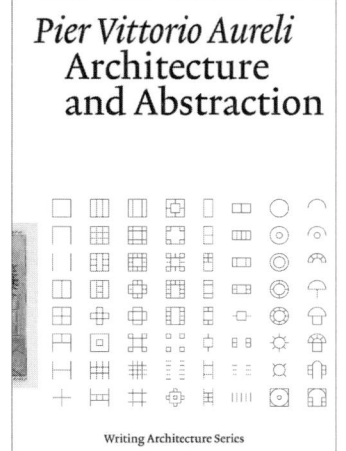

Architecture and Abstraction by Pier Vittorio Aureli, 2023. 320 pages. MIT Press, Writing Architecture Series.

On the evening of November 9, 2023, Pier Vittorio Aureli lectured on "The Longhouse" at Harvard's Graduate School of Design. Aureli is a partner in the Brussels-based architecture office Dogma and teaches at the École Polytechnique Féderale de Lausanne (EPFL), where he directs the Theory and Project of Domestic Space laboratory. He is also the author of numerous articles and books, most recently Architecture and Abstraction *(2023). We talked together at the GSD the morning after his lecture.* – SMW

SARAH M. WHITING: Thank you for your fascinating talk on "The Longhouse" yesterday. There are a couple of reasons I want to interview you, Pier Vittorio. In addition to talking about your longhouse research, I'd like to discuss your new book, *Architecture and Abstraction*, and I'm curious about what it's like for you to now be teaching at the EPFL after years of teaching at the AA and at Yale – all of them significant institutions.

But first, let's talk about your book. For me, *Architecture and Abstraction* is a reminder of the importance of what Bob Somol and I termed the "projective" so many years ago in *Log* 5, which we guest edited. I'll note for the umpteenth time that I have never used the term *postcritical* (despite many people's assumptions). The point of the projective was precisely to push the critical *beyond* criticism, which we argued had become formulaic. We were impatient to cast some forward directions for architecture: "The critical project opened productive horizons in our discipline," we noted in our introduction, "but we now need to explore what those horizons *look like* and *how they work.*"

That forward casting has proven to be incredibly hard. Most architectural production that surrounds us right now is referential and image based. Gabled roofs, arches, pastel colors, muted forms all evoke postmodern examples from the '70s and '80s, and even the attention to "materiality" (whatever happened to the word *materials*?) hearkens back to the tectonic resurgence of the mid-'80s. Rather than moving ahead, we are doubling back and flattening architecture to an image of its recent past. What I have always appreciated in talking with you and reading your work is that you always foreground form and space and the specifics of architecture. And indeed, *Architecture and Abstraction* delights me with its specificities. It lays out a history of what architecture has looked like and how it has worked, but I miss finding in its pages where architecture might be headed. I fear it reads more as a tale of the architectural possibility of abstraction being eclipsed by the economic abstraction of capital.

PIER VITTORIO AURELI: The book, as basically all of my books, grew out of my teaching. The books are often like the written extensions of my classes. When teaching, I refrain from immediately drawing conclusions. I try instead to lay things on the table, navigating, with the students, how something historically happened, what the most interesting evidence is, or some interesting authors who have addressed this problem. So I don't feel an urgency to deliver some sort of message or conclusion. The class becomes a sort of laboratory where we deconstruct the problem.

SMW: Have you ever been surprised by a conclusion that you didn't anticipate?

PVA: All the time. I believe that teaching and research should be a moment of discovery, a moment when you change yourself, rather than just supporting your own hypothesis. Of course, my teaching always starts with a proposition. But I think it's a problem when you use the material of your teaching to support that conjecture unconditionally. There should always be a moment of discovery. There is always a moment when you have to revise your initial assumptions. This was very much the case with my book on abstraction, because my point of entry into the issue of abstraction was simply a complete fascination with it. I've always been interested in abstraction.

One of the biggest influences on my work is abstract painting. I know it sounds very obvious, but a painter who had a great impact on me was Mondrian, and especially his writings. Another painter who had a strong influence on my work – and especially on my writing – is Peter Halley, who belongs to a generation that started to problematize abstraction. For Halley, abstraction was no longer an idealization of the world but rather the way the world actually operates.

SMW: In your book, abstraction concerns practice and the role of the architect. It also concerns the abstraction of capital. Dogma's housing proposals – A Simple Heart, for example – present issues of capitalism and labor in terms of the worker being housed, but in the book, you bring architecture and capitalism together more directly.

PVA: Yes. In a way, architecture has always been driven by abstractions because its production has always implied the division of labor. The rise of geometry and calculus were fundamental preconditions for conceiving and building architecture. But then, of course, this subsumption of architecture through abstraction escalates with the rise of capitalism, especially because capitalism relies on monetary value and on unprecedented levels of the production of material things.

The first impact of this condition was the split between manual and intellectual labor, which became even more pronounced with the rise of capitalism. And then the fragmentation of the building process into a plethora of roles, where the act of building becomes completely driven by exchange value and no longer by use value. My intention was to explain how that happened historically and what kind of consequences this transformation had on the ways we think about architecture.

So, although the main topic is abstraction, it's really a history of the architectural *project*. A project is essentially an act of anticipation of something that doesn't exist yet. The word itself emerged in the 15th century, when there was an increasing need to predesign or anticipate the design of buildings, especially within the field of military architecture, where there was much more pressure in terms of timing and budget. This more symbiotic relationship between thinking and doing, which was very common in medieval architecture, was no longer sustainable, because with the building of fortresses, especially with the rise of firearms, which escalated armed conflicts, the timing was dramatically reduced. And it's at that point that the idea of project – the idea of designing architecture through a very detailed plan that is conceived before construction – became stringent. Later on, this mentality affected the whole production of architecture.

SMW: How do you see the transformation of the project today versus that 15th-century definition?

PVA: There are two tendencies. One, especially in the last century, is when the project becomes essentially the architect's claim to authorship. Today, when we talk about a project in architecture, we immediately think about an architect who has an idea about something and expresses that idea through her or his work. The other tendency is the rise of the project as the precondition for the production of architecture – the series of mediations through drawing, through technology, through budget, through the organization of the workforce, through the constant challenge of programs that have to be addressed. We usually assume that the rise of the project happened in the 15th century. This is true in theory, and architects also existed before the Renaissance, but in practice the project as an all-encompassing plan consolidated only in the 19th century, with the process of industrialization. Take the factory, for example, which was a major trigger for almost reinventing the idea of construction and the idea of how architects or engineers were professionally related to architecture. Paradoxically, it is when the project becomes the absolute precondition for the production of architecture that architects are no longer the protagonist and their role is fragmented into a multitude of competences and specific professional roles.

In writing *Architecture and Abstraction*, this second understanding of the project was more interesting because I also wanted to criticize the romantic, authorial idea of the architect that excludes this larger picture of the production of architecture.

SMW: Today, in schools at least, that larger picture of practice is definitely acknowledged. Can you situate how you sit within the group of people who acknowledge the issue of labor in architecture today?

PVA: A focus on how architecture is produced rather than just on how it looks has always been part of my teaching history and theories of architecture. I think we should try to make it something that we teach from the very first year of our students' education: that architecture involves capital, involves labor, and that we cannot exclude these things from the way we study architecture.

SMW: To return to the book, how would you characterize its broad arc?

PVA: I was attempting to write a genealogy of the architectural project, particularly where abstraction plays a very important role, because projects inevitably, constantly abstract everything that pertains to experience. I'm trying to show how architecture has been transformed under these conditions. The last chapter is more of a personal interpretation of this topic, focusing on a group of architects who have been very influential in my understanding of architecture. It's a book that ultimately problematizes my strong commitment to architecture. It's almost like trying to understand architecture's deepest problems in order to find a way that retains a space for something emancipatory.

SMW: I appreciate you saying there's an emancipatory potential because, at a certain point in the reading, I was overwhelmed by capitalism's reach – its dictatorial definition of what we can do, of the idea that everything is controlled. While I love Hannes Meyer, I don't think he offers us a way forward today. And the data centers you bring up at the end are totally overwhelming – Meyer on steroids, you could say.

PVA: But the way data centers are designed and built is the opposite of what Meyer was trying to do. Data centers represent – among other things – the complete dissolution of any "project." Meyer's work was an attempt to recompose the possibility for an architectural project as an act of cooperation rather than as an individual pursuit.

SMW: Reading the book, I felt, for the first time, that you had succumbed to a Tafurian narrative. You lay out a very clear history and end up with an argument that seems to say that it's simply impossible for architects to have any agency – to use the *mot du jour* – within our global capitalist system.

PVA: Indeed.

SMW: So where is the emancipation?

PVA: Well, that's a very good question. To be honest with you, I don't believe that a pessimism of intelligence blocks an optimism of will. Sometimes it is more productive to open up all the problems than to rush toward some solution.

Sometimes, forcing ourselves to say okay, let's be optimistic, can be more counterproductive than just admitting all the issues we're presented with. This book is really about that. And about coming to terms with something that is very dear to me, which is the idea of the project, which I still believe in. But, in order to remain supportive of the idea that architecture has some capacity, I really have to come to terms with all of its shortcomings. And I think that this, for me, was extremely important, and this book is a step in that trajectory.

As for Tafuri, you might be interested to know that, together with a group of doctoral students from the EPFL, I am compiling an anthology of Tafuri's articles, essays, and interviews. The anthology is inevitably a very succinct collection, given that he wrote more than 400 essays and 22 books. Yet, the goal is to give an overall presentation of Tafuri's work by showing how his interests in modern and Renaissance architecture were deeply intertwined, rather than being just the products of different "stages" of his career.

As far as my own work is concerned, I am, on the contrary, committed to searching for ways for architecture to evolve into a more emancipatory practice. That is the goal of *Architecture and Abstraction* – to develop critical tools to understand what we are doing and why. It is my firm belief that it is only by clearly addressing the very roots of our problems that we can then think how to move forward.

With Tafuri, it is important to emphasize that his critique of architecture and the role of the architect is not a critique tout court but a "critique of ideology," which was addressed to the more "progressive," "avant-garde" trends in modern architecture. This critique was formulated in the late 1960s and 1970s when, particularly in Italy, the workers movement was at the peak of its political power and many intellectuals, including architects, were leaning to the Left. These architects were often taking positions that were similar to their predecessors facing similar problems and dilemmas. To put it simply, Tafuri was not critical of architects in general. He was not even critical of capitalism per se. He was critical of how, historically, politically committed architects, especially leftist architects, responded to or worked through capitalist development by becoming, at best, the ideological harbingers of such development. In fact, when he was dealing with architects outside of the leftist or avant-garde milieu, he was sometimes surprisingly sympathetic. For example, he had a great appreciation for architects such as Carlo Scarpa, on whom he wrote one of his most beautiful essays, "Il Frammento, la 'figura,' il gioco. Carlo Scarpa e la cultura architettonica italiana," published on the occasion of the first posthumous retrospective of the Venetian architect, in 1985. Another architect he liked a lot was Jacopo Sansovino. He wrote a monographic study, *Jacopo Sansovino e l'architettura del' 500 a Venezia*, one of his best books, in my opinion, and devoted beautiful pages in both *Venice and the Renaissance* and *Interpreting the Renaissance* to Sansovino's work. Tafuri noted that Sansovino was a brilliant virtuoso architect practicing in early 16th-century Rome, but when he worked in Venice, he gradually moved from prestigious commissions to very humble works like housing. In doing so, he immersed himself in very practical problems, de facto becoming more of an architect-as-technician than architect-as-artist.

On a more personal note, I would add that however skeptical toward the "agency" of architects Tafuri was, as a pedagogue he was the finest reader of architectural projects I've ever witnessed at work. His classes were based on very rigorous close readings of buildings and drawings, and he took the architect's work very seriously, patiently describing how design decisions take form vis-à-vis the plethora of constraints that surround the making of architecture. I must say that while his student, I learned much more about design from Tafuri than from my studio professors, whose teaching was often based on vague concepts, metaphors, or discourses borrowed from other disciplines. So, to go back to your question, in spite of his negativity – and the "negative" was certainly the main ethos of his critique – Tafuri was a great teacher of architecture, the one who really instilled in me and my classmates a passion for architecture. He had the rare ability to talk about formal issues, always giving them their proper historical context. For me, teaching is also independent of my wishes. I want to be as honest as possible with students and allow them to really understand the problems, while never making the problems too overwhelming for them.

SW: Do you see any impact of your history teaching on the students' studio work? If I'm understanding you correctly, at the EPFL you are not teaching studio, only history, whereas at Yale and the AA you taught both, no?

PVA: I can't really assess the impact of my teaching on students, but I've always recommended to them the importance of history as a way to understand critically the present condition. Before focusing on teaching history and theory at the EPFL, for more than 20 years I taught studio as well. I've always insisted that my history and theory classes are not meant to "support" my design studio or to give it a "theoretical foundation." At Yale, I even discouraged my studio students from taking my history and theory class. However, in my studios I would always ask the students to start by researching the issues at stake in their project from a historical perspective, so that their design decisions would be influenced by an awareness of what had happened on their site or with their program. This means that I see my history classes more as "cautionary tales" about architecture rather than as offering them "inspiration" for their design projects. I believe that even if the history of architecture is not immediately helpful in the practice of design, it is a fundamental resource in terms of critical awareness of what architecture is about and how it can be done differently.

SMW: Maybe you can explain how your reading of the longhouse plays into such an understanding of history. While listening to your lecture about it, I was thinking that it could be an analysis that offers a way forward because it helped situate the earlier housing projects by Dogma. It seems that long communal typologies have long been part of your work.

PVA: In a way, yes.

SMW: I've always loved Dogma's extraordinarily meticulous drawings of those super-scaled housing projects, but they have always seemed impossibly utopian because of their scale. Your deep dive into a smaller scale but still long typology offers up a kind of promise that could be folded back onto that larger scale. Have you found that the longhouse, as a basic typology, could actually be a starting point for architectural practice and for communal living once again?

PVA: Large-scale housing projects are only a part of our work. In other projects that focus on communal living we have explored different scales for housing such as the urban villa, or even transforming suburban housing, as in Opposite Shore, a design research commissioned by the Department of Spatial Planning in Flanders. Our research on the longhouse comes from a larger investigation on domestic space, which we have developed in several books and essays. This investigation, to a certain extent, responds to a series of housing movements that in the last decades have tried to find ways to decommodify domestic space. These movements proposed a radical way of conceiving domestic space at the moment when housing went through a process of hyper-commodification thanks to the rise of real estate as the dominant industry of our time. In a way, these researches and projects give these movements a sort of historical perspective, highlighting the fact that before the rise of capitalism these ways of living were not an exception, but were the norm.

For me, this is very important, because otherwise, the risk is that we consider these contemporary forms of communal living, or decommodified housing, as exceptions, or as something that people would not appreciate or support on a large scale. It's important for us to show that, on the contrary, in the past, this way of living was not exceptional. It was not only common, there was also an active process by the state and, later, by capitalism to destroy them.

SMW: Can you point to contemporary examples where we might still have some emancipatory hope?

PVA: Community land trusts, tenant syndicates – groups and initiatives that try to withdraw housing from the market. To put it simply, with these examples you cannot use your house as an asset. You can't buy the property and then expect to sell it at a major gain. Such organizations prevent that from happening. They essentially force residents to use their house as a house, not as a future asset.

Of course, the problem at the moment is that these are very small initiatives compared to the great need for affordable housing. I hope in the future there will be some legislative mechanisms advanced by municipalities to scale them up, to make them much bigger than what they are right now.

Dogma, The Opposite Shore, model for communal housing, 17th Venice Architecture Biennale, 2021.

SMW: But such a system also only works in a context where there is some assurance of assets once you stop working – like adequate social security or some form of adequate pension. That's why the house is used as an asset in the US. It has traditionally been a way to ensure future income.

PVA: It is true that home ownership is a form of security against the power of landlords. However, unconditional state support for home ownership has resulted in limiting access to housing to those who cannot afford to own a house. This is exactly what housing movements such as syndicates and community land trusts address by trying to find an alternative to ownership and the landlord system. In some cases – like the model of the tenant syndicates, which is achieving interesting results in Germany – the tenants not only co-own their house, they're also renting, not from a landlord, but from the community of which they are a part. This way there is no external actor who can extract profit from this transaction. For me, the problem is that these initiatives are not yet at scale. But this should be the goal.

SMW: So let's tie this back to your lecture on the longhouse last night. You put this type into a very broad context, saying it's a global type. You looked at the specifics in each example and how they affected how people lived together. I think you got a little pushback for having relied on secondary sources for that social context. How do we, as architects, expand beyond reading form, proportion, and material and also engage the specifics of context when not always having the time or money to do extensive fieldwork? And how do you propose we deal with the broader challenge of studying the noncanonical without falling into Western tropes?

PVA: Our research on the longhouse is primarily a gathering of scholarship that has already been produced on the many versions of this type. There is already plenty of fieldwork done by archaeologists and anthropologists, but their scholarship is always focused on single cases.

Our original contribution on the topic of the longhouse is that we have redrawn a selection of these case studies, not to find some universalizing principle, but to emphasize the specificity of each example. Being ourselves Western architects, it is impossible for us to abandon our Western lens, especially the idea of representing everything through a set of drawing techniques, which has certainly evolved out of a specific Western/European tradition – although one should say that plan and axonometric views were also used by non-Western cultures. And yet, as I said in my lecture, our study of the longhouse tries to bring awareness to the fact that, in different places, at different times, these types of buildings were destroyed together with the people who lived in them. Our intention is to show how our modern domesticity, based on the private apartment or the single-family house, was conceived not in order to provide a more comfortable or cheaper home for everyone but to eliminate the variety of ways of dwelling and building houses that already existed in many parts of the world. Let's not forget that the spread of colonialism and capitalism aimed at the imposition and universalization of property relationships on everything and everyone. This forced the elimination of any form of household that did not fit into the colonizing public-private binary.

Ultimately, the longhouse research is part of a much larger project, which I would basically call a typological reading of architecture. The main theme of all of this work is to revive the idea of type, and the idea of using typology as a framework to discuss, teach, and research architecture. We believe that, despite all its problems, typology remains a fundamental tool with which we can transcend authorship, technology, or other singular and limiting readings of architecture. Type is understanding that architecture is a constant transformation and evolution of certain forms, and that these transformations register specific historical conditions. So it's not typology in the sense of essentializing architecture to its structure, but to understanding the structure in its historical context, how it evolves and how it transforms.

SMW: I was struck in the lecture by your sensitivity to Indigenous peoples, a sensitivity to other forms of living that are outside our Western norms – your "bad walls make good neighbors" example, and others. That's a significant transformation of a formal methodology in our discipline that stretches from Wittkower to Rowe to Eisenman to you. Is that coming partly from the pressures of the day? And is it landing differently in Lausanne than it did at Yale? And, in light of the questions after your lecture last night, how will your method continue to transform?

PVA: Ten years ago, when I was tasked to teach the survey of architectural history to first-year students at the AA, it became clear to me that it was important to include in my syllabus case studies that were beyond the traditional survey of Western architecture. This inclusion allowed me to challenge many Eurocentric assumptions about what architecture is about, which was also motivated by personal interest. Regarding the longhouse research, our point of entry was very straightforward. We were fascinated by the longhouse, and fascination is often the impetus to research a certain subject. We were interested in how the term *longhouse* is used by archaeologists and anthropologists to address dwellings built by cultures that had little or no contact with each other, and that similar forms of life emerge in longhouses built in very different conditions. We were also fascinated by the sheer beauty of some of these buildings. Only after studying them did we realize that the ways in which these longhouses are built and operated are so different from the logic of the projects I describe in my book on abstraction. Indeed, they represent almost its opposite. In the book, I understand the project as an undertaking based on the division of labor, specifically the separation of manual and intellectual labor. Longhouses are the manifestation of the opposite condition, a unity between design and construction.

Many longhouses present imposing forms that are very regular and symmetrical, forms that put forward a precise idea of spatial logic – even more, I would say, than a Renaissance church. And it shows that self-sufficient communities and Indigenous people have produced something that is more consistent and often more sophisticated than what architecture, in our canonical version, has produced. We just want to make that known and visible.

SMW: I was fascinated by the examples, but I have to admit that during the lecture – and also, at times, in reading the book – I felt a little anxiety about essentializing. There's a point in the book where you talk about experience, and I felt like Heidegger was lurking somewhere in the room. All of the sudden, it feels like there's a different voice – different from Benjamin, from Meyer – coming in from some side door. And here, when you say that we see all these cultures and an innate understanding of this form, it makes me nervous.

PVA: I don't think there can be an innate understanding of this – or any – form. Form, for me, is historically produced and has its roots in context-specific political relationships and their spatial translation. It is interesting to see how some communities in Borneo still build longhouses, sometimes using concrete and steel plates. These longhouses are simple structures, as generic as any other contemporary dwelling. Yet what survives of the older tradition is a form of social organization, a spatial diagram, so to speak, which is carefully adapted to contemporary needs. I don't see any Heidegger in this, I only see cultures that use architecture as a way to give form to a social organization that they have decided to commit to.

SMW: But even as we have been talking this morning, you are not talking about the longhouse as if it's generic – you are elevating it to the status of a Renaissance church. Isn't that a demonstration of looking at it through decidedly Western eyes?

PVA: As I said before, these buildings are extremely sophisticated and do not need to be "elevated." They should simply be held in equal regard as canonical examples of Western architecture. If we don't recognize their worth, architectural scholarship will be stuck on Western tropes. Indeed, we are very aware that there is a risk that we could exoticize or somehow fetishize contexts that were destroyed by the culture to which I belong. The purpose is not to fetishize them, it's just to show architects and students what types of domestic life existed, or still exist, that are constantly repressed or forgotten so that our understanding of domestic space is reduced to just that which is familiar to us. These are all attempts to open up the imagination of what domestic space could be, while acknowledging all of the historical, political, and social problems that looking at this legacy implies.

SMW: To go back to teaching, and you having taught in these different global contexts, what does it mean to bring something like the example of the longhouse to your students?

PVA: It means allowing students to study things that have never been part of the survey of architecture, even if it's very architectural material.

In my courses my approach is very architectural. For example, I always work with specific case studies, whether buildings or projects. I always try to contextualize, but I insist on case studies – concrete artifacts. For the past few years, most of my teaching has been about the history of domestic space. This is an interest that I share both with my practice and with my partner, Maria Shéhérazade Giudici, whose work on domesticity was an important influence in my decision to devote myself to this topic. When I moved to the EPFL, I decided that I would only focus on this topic, and right now, I'm teaching a history of domestic space, starting from prehistory and arriving at the contemporary. Last year, I covered an arc that went from, let's say, the complex and nonlinear transition from nonsedentary to sedentary forms of dwelling, to antiquity. I realized that my syllabus's bibliography did not include many texts written by architects or architectural historians. This is because domestic space prior to the rise of modern domestic space – let's say from the Renaissance villa and palace – is seldom discussed in the historiography of architecture. Most of the literature I've used so far comes from anthropologists and archaeologists. What is amazing is that they describe buildings in a very precise way, sometimes in a more precise way than architects or architectural historians do. Oftentimes architectural theorists and historians talk about everything except architecture. But because anthropologists and archaeologists are so precise, they discuss plenty of interesting details, like the positions of doors and windows, or why doors were in the center, or why they were built on the short side and what that implies in the organization of space. You get a level of precision that is often missing from architectural literature.

SMW: Let's cap this interview on a big note. Where do you think teaching needs to go right now, broadly speaking?

PVA: My first suggestion would be to drastically reduce the complexity of school curricula in order to prevent too much fragmentation, which often means dispersal of focus and attention. Looking to current architecture school programs feels like reading those never-ending restaurant menus with hundreds of different dishes – which always makes me wonder where they store all the ingredients to serve such an infinite variety. I always tell students that we have to be focused. We should be careful to not treat the university as a kind of social condenser, where anything can happen and where we are supposed to have an opinion on everything.

My second suggestion would be to increase the teaching of the history of architecture so that both teachers and students are more literate about the architecture of ancient, modern, and contemporary times, not just the latest project by *X*, *Y*, or *Z*.

My third suggestion – which follows from the previous one – would be to encourage the study of architecture as building, and not just architecture as "ideas" to be projected on everything. Once you study architecture as building you inevitably study how the production of architecture involves issues of economy, politics, labor, etc. For me, the study of architecture in its most material and concrete terms, as both project and building, is the only way to connect architecture to politics and the economy in rigorous terms. Once you are literate about how architecture concretely works, it becomes easier to understand how it works in its larger social context.

Sarah M. Whiting guest edited, with R.E. Somol, *Log* 5 (2005). She is dean and Josep Lluís Sert Professor of Architecture at Harvard's Graduate School of Design and partner, with Ron Witte, of WW Architecture.

Elisa Iturbe &
Maria Shéhérazade Giudici

Carbon Modernity's Domestic Typologies

Maria Shéhérazade Giudici's work offers a critical dissection of domesticity, typology, feminism, and subject formation. Giudici leads the history and theory course at the School of Architecture of the Royal College of Art in London while also coordinating the PhD Program of the Architectural Association. Giudici is also founder of the research platform Black Square and editor of AA Files. *This conversation took place online in November 2023.* – EI

ELISA ITURBE: In *Log* 47 [Overcoming Carbon Form], I argued that there's a specific spatial order that corresponds to the carbon age and published, for the first time, the idea of *carbon form*. Since then, I've noticed that the concept is easily graspable at the urban scale – I only have to show an aerial view of a suburb or a plan of the Ville Radieuse to give a clear example – but the larger argument is that architecture is an instrument used to organize and choreograph an industrial society. It's spatial scripting, and that, of course, applies at the building scale. I think your writing and research make this extraordinarily clear. Even though you don't use energy as a framework for your scholarship, you make an explicit link between space and power, not only at the scale of the building, but also at the scale of the room. I believe this is essential for the concept of carbon form because it shows that architecture can be used as an instrument of subject formation at all scales. In my classes, I always assign your political critique of the domestic interior, "Counter-Planning from the Kitchen: For a Feminist Critique of Type." Can you talk about the Henry Roberts house? For me, that's a very important precedent of carbon form.

MARIA SHÉHÉRAZADE GIUDICI: Absolutely. Henry Roberts's *Model Houses for Families* was published in 1851, and a four-unit prototype was built at the Great Exhibition in London, right next to the Crystal Palace. I see this prototype as the climax in a process of crystallizing models of domesticity that we have been replicating since then. We are essentially talking about 170 years of proliferation of the same model for living, a model that Roberts didn't invent per se in 1851, but

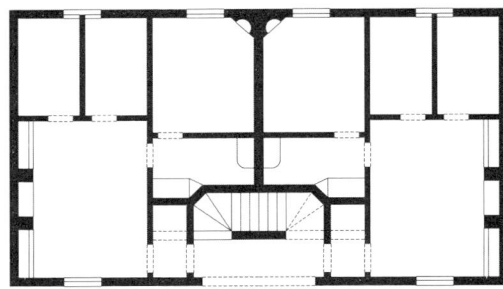

Henry Roberts, plan for two single-family units, from *The Dwellings of the Labouring Classes* (London: SICLC, 1850). Redrawn by the interviewee.

was probably the first to publish and to build in such a clear diagrammatic form.

The model comprises a living room, two smaller bedrooms right off the living room, and a scullery, which gives access to the primary bedroom. Today, we tend to think that this "package" is an unavoidable recipe for housing – a living room, one bedroom for the parents, bedrooms for children of each gender, plus a kitchen and a bathroom. Of course, the bathroom was technologically not yet fully developed in Roberts's time, but his project did include a water closet.

I was in practice as a commercial architect for quite a few years, and I mostly worked on apartment buildings. I was basically asked to produce that model, squeezed into different building envelopes. Sometimes it could be a bit bigger and you would add more square meters, sometimes it had to be a bit smaller so you would lose one bedroom. But the type of rooms that a home should include was unavoidable, and the sequence in which these rooms are deployed is something I never questioned as a commercial architect, or even – at least initially – as a teacher.

In time, I became interested in understanding how such a ubiquitous pattern was not, in fact, a "natural" way of using space, as it didn't necessarily correspond to the way people lived until the late 1800s. Indeed, it was so counterintuitive that Roberts could actually claim he had *invented* this model.

His authorial pretension looks almost funny today, as we take this home recipe completely for granted and few architects know of Roberts himself. Much as Auguste Perret thought it was ridiculous for Le Corbusier to want to patent such a basic model as the Maison Dom-Ino, it is hard for us to see what a radical proposal *Model Houses for Families* actually was. On the one hand, these models were not invented overnight, they emerged from the coagulation of existing practices. On the other, those trends crystallized thanks to a specific project, person, or office. That's what Roberts did. If I had to think of a domestic diagram that corresponds to the concept of carbon form, this is it. In fact, it's the only domestic diagram we are still using today – everywhere.

If we go back to your point about energy consumption, it would be really interesting to add a perspective on the environmental performance of architecture to the work I've been doing in the past few years, which started with "Counter-Planning From the Kitchen." Roberts's model houses were not particularly well-insulated. They needed to be warmed from within, which access to fossil fuels made more feasible than in premodern times. Premodern dwellings, especially in Northern or Central Europe, had very thick walls that could keep the house warm during winter. Roberts's model, however, is a modern type of construction. It relies on a relatively thin outer wall, perhaps a couple of bricks thick, and a rather complex system of flues and chimneys that allow the heating of every room. Obviously, cooling was not yet an issue in Britain at that time. The influence of this technological choice is enormous and it impacts all aspects of life in Roberts's model, down to the different social and gender roles.

I find it quite incredible that, after almost two centuries, with access to new technologies and with a different understanding of gender, so many of the Roberts tropes are still here. For instance, the fact that it's a common architectural choice to force inhabitants to throw a lot of money at unsustainable heating and cooling, rather than building a thicker wall. Until the 1800s, the vast majority of people built their own houses, therefore, they paid attention to how they would perform over the years. Most people building a dwelling were thinking, *When am I going to do maintenance work on the roof? How long until I'm going to need to replace this balustrade? How much wood am I going to have to burn to heat the house in the winter?*

I'm not advocating a return to self-building, but if we want to overcome carbon form, I think the mandate for an architect should be to think in terms of time and performance. All things that, clearly, were not Roberts's concerns. The architect played a crucial role in shortening the life cycle of a building, as well as in choosing unsustainable strategies for heating. Importantly, in Roberts's model houses, the architect's role is one of social engineering, individuating the inhabitants in specific spatial pockets. The architect divides the children of different genders, who should not sleep or even play together. The architect dictates that the parents are not going to sleep with their children, and the architect forces couples to sleep together, which is something that we take for granted but, until that moment, wasn't necessarily a given. The architect also scripts the role of the wife, who is supposed to use the kitchen – or scullery – as a site of control, as in a panoptic diagram.

The Roberts model is almost like an incunabulum, if you want, of carbon form. It is a perfect carbon form diagram from the point of view of social, gender, and age roles. It individuates the nuclear family as this constitutive brick of the society of carbon form. The very technologies it deploys, its strategies to heat, cool, and ventilate the house, conform perfectly to an idea of carbon form.

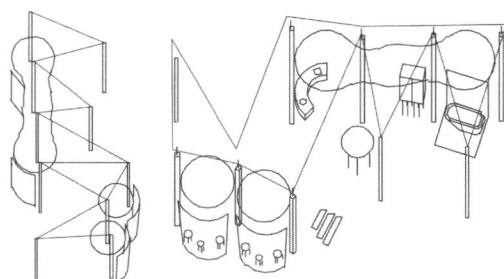

Kazuyo Sejima, Schemes for Platform House I and Platform House II (1987–1990). Redrawn by the interviewee.

EI: You're basically saying that you can make an argument about carbon form by looking at a wall section – not only because it says something about energy use, but because the question of performance is a way to interpret attitudes toward time, maintenance, energy, and sociospatial organization. In your essay about the Roberts model, you also talk about how women have basically been shaped – you use the word *coerced* – by residential architecture, and that typological thinking has become a container for subject formation. Then you give, as a counterexample, two houses designed by Kazuyo Sejima, Platform I and Platform II, which are not partitioned but are open to many arrangements. You suggest that this is anti typological in the sense that the interior spatial arrangements resist typological categories through looseness and openness.

In the way you describe this, it seems that the main ingredient in the making of types is the wall or the partition. How do you think about type? Do you think it emerges through the making of partitions or through the repetition of other elements? The Sejima house, the Platform, is a strong and replicable form. When does architecture become typological?

MSG: There are as many definitions of type as there are architects, but, for me, type is not necessarily confined to the layout or partitioning of space. The root of what I see as type is a specific set of spatial relationships that describes an attitude toward the subject. As such, it could also be embodied by something that is not necessarily a wall. For instance, two apartments could have exactly the same layout but very different ways of handling heating. I've lived in my fair share of studios throughout my life, but I only once had a studio with a heated floor. I behaved completely differently in that space. You tend to sit much closer to the floor because it's really comfortable, and the type of furniture you choose is different. You use the space in a more homogenous way somehow, rather than following the obvious discontinuities that occur in a space that is heated by one radiator.

So there's definitely more to type than walls. However, walls are obviously a powerful tool. When architects, like Roberts, want to put forward a new type, they usually rely on specific plan layouts. But the modes of inhabitation that a plan can generate are not always controlled by the architect, as they depend on a range of other factors. I think that's why Roberts's model was so successful. Its diagram includes far more than walls. It starts with partitioning space, but it also relies on technological choices and the use of specific appliances, down to the fact that there is a kitchen in every apartment.

I ultimately see the concept of type as something that does not address architecture per se, but rather the type of person that is going to inhabit it. In this definition, walls and partitions play a part, but they might not be the only defining element. Obviously, the technology of ventilation, heating, and cooling plays a part, but lighting and even decoration also matter. We often think of decoration as something that is applied, that is irrelevant to the basic performance of a space or a building. But there are many cases where decoration is fundamental to the spatial subjectivity within a house.

Think about the difference between being in a house with wallpaper and a room that has just whitewashed walls, or between an apartment that has carpet everywhere, as we find in many mid-century British apartments, and a dwelling with tiled floors. I think that the linings, even down to the colors, and the use of curtains are really quite crucial. Type is a coagulation of all of these features, features that keep shifting.

Type can be a conceptual quicksand, because one can never quite define it. My personal way out of this issue is to address the inhabitants of the space rather than the space itself. For instance, in the case of Roberts's model houses, the type is not the apartment, it is the heteronormative nuclear family. The idea of using type as something related to subjectivity rather than boundaries allows one also to discuss spaces that look nontypological – families of buildings that cannot easily be grouped through the analysis of their layout alone. The typological potential of these spaces can easily be discussed if one focuses on their performance, on the practices they foster, and through the subjectivity of the people who occupy them.

Now, Sejima put forward the Platform project, both through theoretical drawings and a couple of built houses. The translation from radical drawing to house is quite faithful. Although Sejima needed to deal with the constraints of building, the form of life is translated in a clear way. The house has an enclosure and a roof, but it embodies the qualities of flexibility and openness that the drawings projected, letting the furniture float in a space that the inhabitant can choreograph. This might lead us again to question what role walls play in the creation of subjectivity. I still think that walls are the most powerful instruments we have to define forms of spatial subjectivity, but they are not the only one. Type definitely starts in the physical layout that we record with a plan, but it might not stop there.

You mentioned earlier the almost violent handling of gender hierarchies in the Roberts model. It's an incredibly repressive model based on the individuation of the nuclear family and the creation of the figure of the housewife as a house manager who does not have an opportunity to share laboring tasks with her neighbors. Sharing the burden of cooking, washing, and childcare – a practice that was common in premodern dwelling – is difficult in the Roberts model. This is a deliberate choice Roberts himself explains in the texts published with the plan prototypes. The strategy is enacted through the way the party wall and the staircase are designed. The party wall between two units cannot be pierced to create direct communication between units. Every staircase serves only two apartments on each floor, minimizing contact between neighbors.

It's physically, technically impossible for neighbors to share what materialist feminists' term "reproductive labor" – that is, taking care of the life of the inhabitants of the house. Cooking together, washing clothes together, collective child-rearing, which had been popular before the Roberts model, are explicitly rejected by the patriarchal elites of the mid-1800s.

When I work with students, I often illustrate my research through plans because, at the end of the day, drawing a plan allows us to understand the most basic way a building works. But I don't think that the plan tells the whole story. Two plans might look exactly the same and then perform very differently if their environmental qualities are different. And again, even the surface quality of things can change the perception or the performance of a type.

EI: What I really like about what you're saying is that carbon form is not defined by its geometric specificity. Rather, it can be found when form is deployed in a particular way to *give form* to a social and political condition that's intimately tied to fossil fuel use, or to the logic of an industrial society, which, in turn, is built on dense and abundant energy. We're not going to have an energy transition unless we change our relationship to energy, which requires redefining our ways of life.

The reappropriation of typological thinking requires that we ask what forms of life are being scripted. People ask me all the time, What's the next thing? What is the anti-carbon form? What does it look like? And I often say that questions of building performance may be part of it, but underneath that there is a larger question of how we live, a question that architects can address via typological invention. The Roberts house offers a great example of how building types can do that, and we see it in the 20th century as well. That said, in some ways, modernists had it easy because their energy transition had already happened. They already knew that they needed to give form to an industrial society, so they provided new types according to a social model that had already come into being. But in our case, it's not clear what we need to give form to, which makes the position of the architect today very different than it was in the 20th century. Where do you see the potential for counter-planning, or what are examples of the ways of life that we might give form to in order to counter carbon form?

MSG: This is a crucial question, and it's the most difficult one because, as you mentioned, historically, architects rarely write their own project briefs. There are two preliminary questions I try to use as mental exercises.

One question has to do with rethinking relationships between individuals beyond the nuclear family. The idea of the nuclear family is already dead, if it ever existed in the first place. And if developers started to listen to the demands of the people we design for, I doubt we would still be producing so many Roberts-like units. Single inhabitants, short-term tenants, networked families, and people who work from home are all demanding different forms of housing.

How can we start to design places where people can live in conditions of social solidarity that go beyond the nuclear family? This seems very banal, but it requires architects to rethink at least two conditions that have been unquestioned for over a century. One is the condition of individuality. How do we address the scale of the individual? How do we enable the individual to both survive and be with others while maintaining their individuality? Dwellings for a single person have only become a mainstream architectural product in the last half-century, and making this condition socially and environmentally sustainable is definitely a challenge. The other condition is that of a collectivity larger than the nuclear family. How do we come together in configurations of solidarity that allow individuals to help each other and care for each other? Translating this hope into architecture is not easy, as it requires rethinking most of the parameters, methods, and design strategies that we've learned in school – a lot of the strategies that I myself have taught my students. For instance, this means unlearning the average size and shape spaces to sleep, eat, and work. The ambition to rethink society beyond the nuclear family is an obvious one, from a social point of view. It's very tough in terms of architecture, though, because it puts into question a number of technologies we routinely use by default.

The second question has to do with the temporal performance of space in general – not only of buildings but also of cities, streets, and public space. If we start to think of architecture as a process, not as something that creates static objects, but as something that creates human processes that involve the built environment, then we'll have to start designing in very different ways.

We've made steps forward from that point of view. Architectural practices that are more conscious of the ecological challenges today are open to thinking about how a building performs through all of the seasons, for instance. But I still haven't seen a lot with the consciousness to design a building to work well not only throughout the year but also for 100 years.

EI: I want to ask about the article that you and Pier Vittorio Aureli published in *Log* 47, which was about the history of private property and land subdivision. You make clear that one of the most important developments in the history of settlement patterns was when property became a top-down organizing force orchestrated by the state. That, in turn, displaced other priorities that had previously driven settlement patterns, such as the local management of subsistence.

You identified the rise of centralized and hierarchically organized institutions, the evolution of which was a long trajectory that the history of carbon form fits into. Carbon form doesn't just begin with fossil fuels. This has become very important for me to clarify when I speak about this idea, because the context into which fossil fuels were inserted matters. Its affordances met the desires of a society in which reorganization was already underway. I would argue that it's really only by looking at that longer history that we get a sense of what alternatives to carbon form today might be. In your *Log* essay, you talk about alternative ways of organizing settlement patterns, including a beautiful description of Moisei Ginzburg's Green City. Why is that project important, and what role does the individual play in it?

MSG: The problem is not necessarily private use per se, nor the fact that people might have a specific relationship with a piece of land, but the translation of that use into a rigid

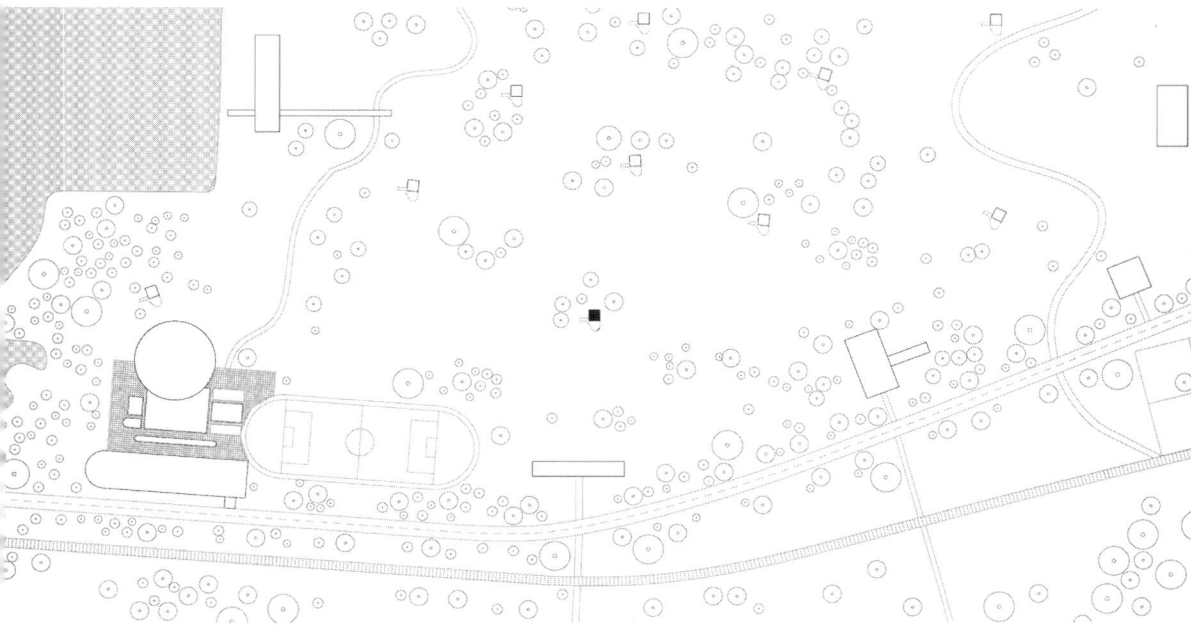

Redrawing of Moisei Ginzburg and OSA, strategic settlement plan for the State Planning Committee, 1929. From Dogma, *Loveless* (Milan: Black Square, 2019). Courtesy Dogma.

exclusionary right, which can eventually lead to misuse, including speculation and uses that harm collectivity and natural resources. When norms, rules, and laws guaranteed by the state protect the narrowest definition of private property, it becomes difficult to think in terms of social and environmental sustainability. Interestingly, such a radical take on private property does not exist in many cultures, and is not necessarily a default attitude of humankind. Nevertheless, the conditions in which modern architecture developed were invariably conditions of private property. This has stifled the imagination of architects toward what can be done if this parameter is altered.

The case of Disurbanism is interesting. A group of architects and planners active in the USSR between the late 1920s and early 1930s, the Disurbanists found themselves in a unique historical condition in which they could think beyond private property. It would be difficult, and it has been historically difficult, for architects living and working within a state founded on the protection of private property to think beyond that condition.

The Disurbanists worked in the early years of the USSR, when actual experiments in collective stewardship and others forms of commoning did take place. This was a rather extraordinary conjuncture, as just a couple of years later such experiments came to an end in the USSR. We cannot really equate the presence of a socialist or a communist regime with the true rethinking of private property because, in fact, that ambition failed pretty quickly in the USSR. The Disurbanists operated in a unique context, where the dismantling of private property not only influenced new forms of housing but also large-scale projects for potential cities. The name Disurbanists itself suggests the group's ambition to "undo" the historical city and search for new patterns of dwelling. In 1930, the group, led by Ginzburg and Mikhail Barshch, put forward two projects that develop a similar idea of posturban development. One of the projects is a plan for Moscow, the other

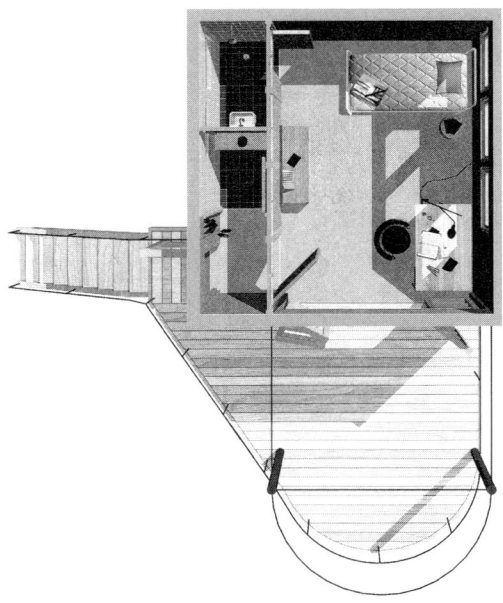

Perspectival reconstruction of a one-person living pod from Moisei Ginzburg and OSA's proposal for the State Planning Committee, 1929. From Dogma, *Loveless* (Milan: Black Square, 2019). Courtesy Dogma.

a theoretical model for linear settlements. Strictly speaking, Green City was the title of the Moscow plan, although it's often used to refer to the second, more radical territorial proposal – which is, in fact, very much a Green City. One might think that the absence of private property would lead to a much more communal lifestyle, however, Ginzburg and Barshch understood that the land being state property didn't necessarily have to mean that people should live clustered together. It could also mean that the individual would be afforded unprecedented forms of freedom of movement.

The Disurbanist model – let us call it Green City for simplicity's sake – is a low-density urban plan based on a linear infrastructural skeleton that was very advanced for its time – something we can still learn from because providing smart and well-designed infrastructure is an important first gesture of settlement. Green City's infrastructural backbone not only offers means of movement but also other kinds of infrastructure, such as education, services, healthcare, and production. The backbone is complemented by a range of housing types, either clustered close to the spine or scattered in the forested area around it. One of these types, interestingly, is individual pods. These pods were designed for single dwellers, not for families or couples, although they are generous enough to host more than one person and therefore allow for moments of conviviality. Moreover, they can be dismantled and remounted in a different location. Theoretically, one can move their pod around and decide how close or how far they want to be from other pods. The pods, as such, demonstrate that the cliché that links the abolition of private property to a 100-percent communal life is shortsighted. In fact, the pods leveraged the public character of the land to allow more opportunities for self-determination of one's place of residence.

Obviously I'm oversimplifying the project, but it would not be wrong to say that Green City included a plea for individual freedom. That didn't mean communal solidarity wasn't an important part of the design – the pods were ultimately scattered around a communal spine where moments of care for each other could still take place.

I think this project is still incredibly innovative for a number of reasons. The first is that it conceived of architecture as starting from a void rather than from the built. In proposing a range of housing types that one could try out at different times of their lives, it highlighted the fact that sedentism is not necessarily a default mode for humankind. Green City implied that a certain degree of nomadism, be it seasonal or covering periods of a few years, could be beneficial and not necessarily entail a breakdown of social cohesion – contrary to the European long-held belief that settling down is a crucial act of any functioning society.

The Western idea of stability, linked as it is to house ownership, creates incredible psychological friction today. Those who have the stability of a fixed house often feel chained to that property, chained financially and mentally. Those who don't have that stability often feel stressed because society tells them they should settle down.

On the contrary, Green City is still today quite inspiring because it shows how settling can be temporary. This feature alone can help us think beyond carbon form, as it posits the relationship between man and territory in a dialectical way – the very temporality of the project forces humans to listen to the territory. Depending on how the forest grows, inhabitants might decide to move the pods or to choose a configuration that better fits the way in which the environment develops.

That being said, it's a project of the early 1930s, so it does conform to a number of parameters that fit into the carbon form mentality. For instance, the idea that being able to move faster is necessarily good. The core of the design is, after all, the railway, a major sign of czarist colonization if we look at the context of the USSR.

Moreover, some of the projected building materials were undoubtedly part of the carbon form lexicon. The design mentality still leans heavily on processes of industrialization and standardization, so I wouldn't say that Green City is necessarily completely innocent of all the pitfalls of carbon form. At the same time, Green City is still an inspiring case study, as its rejection of private property opens up imaginative new ways of living.

EI: Something about our current way of organizing things creates a mandate to settle. This is one of the biggest contradictions of carbon form, because often one of the first things we think about in an energy-intensive society is mobility. We drive a lot, we travel long distances for both work and recreation, commodities travel all over the world. So we think of contemporary society, or fossil fuel society, as premised on high levels of mobility, but it's all also premised on the sedentary imagination. Even if you are a digital nomad, you rely on vast infrastructural networks that bring commodities to wherever you might be. You expect to find furnished apartments and grocery stores wherever you go. You rely on sedentary communities to provide resources and services as you move from place to place. So, although we are mobile, the entire environment is nonetheless organized so that goods and commodities can flow to fixed points, which, at its core, is part of a sedentary model of organization.

The Indigenous societies that you bring up in the essay had totally different relationships to land that are important. They show a fundamentally other spatial organization in which neither boundaries nor domestic spaces are fixed. Instead, settlements are situated in ever-changing ecosystems, moving and rotating as humans interact directly with available resources. This history becomes really important for starting to imagine alternatives, which is so difficult to do because we – those of us that have grown up in industrialized countries – have always been in carbon form.

My last question is, What are you thinking about right now?

MSG: I am now writing and lecturing, in my various courses, on a critique of the idea of care. This can come across as something surprising because *care* is widely seen right now as an unambiguously positive term. Let me first say why care is still a relevant concept to me, notwithstanding the fact that the word has been overused in the past few years, especially after Covid. I still see hope in trying to reclaim its political agency, because it's one of the very few categories that can help us see the need for social change as coextensive with the need for environmental change.

Most of the other theoretical buzzwords tend to accent either social or environmental sustainability. I think that the two perspectives are dangerous because the environmental narrative can be used as an excuse not to deal with social and racial injustice, in the name of humankind's unity in the face of extinction. Care, on the contrary, posits the need to address both questions at the same time. It's not an either/or question. We are going to survive together by being fairer with each other. There's no other alternative.

From this point of view, I think that *care* is still an incredibly valuable term. However, the way it's been conceptually constructed in the West is highly problematic because it's been morphed on a paternalistic idea of care – essentially the type of care that parents have for their children. That becomes the primary relationship of care, out of which all the other relationships of care, be they for your neighbor or for the environment, are nothing but a ripple effect from that primary form of care. Care tends to be a unidirectional relationship between caregivers and care receivers. If we start criticizing the forms of care that we see in the home as essentially dysfunctional because they are gendered, because they are asymmetric, because they are hierarchical, because they construct a set of relationships that I would say are not healthy and not balanced, then it stands to reason that we should analyze the ways we think we have taken care of the environment until now and see if we are making some of the same mistakes. And we *are* making some of the same mistakes.

I am conscious that it's always dangerous to translate a concept from one sphere to another, or from one scale to another scale. Obviously, here I'm making a slippery conceptual shortcut between the intimacy of the patriarchal home and the environment at large. There's a risk in this conceptual jump, but it's a risk worth taking because it's helping me to think through forms of environmental settlement that I was not quite able to criticize until now. Once we understand why the Western concept of care is problematic, why and how it was born as a paternalistic approach that strips some subjects of agency, it becomes easier to criticize not only the architecture of our homes but also that of our landscapes. Essentially, I'm trying to learn from the domestic dynamics we discussed earlier and to use the same tools to understand larger-scale processes.

I also have to disclose my own bias. Being an anarchist, my never-ending concern is understanding how individuals can self-determine their lives while developing mutual relationships of care, friendship, and love with others. It's this conundrum that pushes me to be interested in those architectures that suggest how hierarchies can be rethought to ultimately give equal dignity to all the actors in the process of making our world.

Elisa Iturbe guest edited *Log* 47: Overcoming Carbon Form (2019). She is assistant professor at The Cooper Union and cofounder of the architecture practice Outside Development.

*Ann Lui
& Juliet Sorensen*

Building Justice

Juliet Sorensen is a clinical professor of law at Northwestern University's Pritzker School of Law, where her teaching focuses on international criminal law, corruption, health, and human rights. I first met Sorensen, in 2019, through her work at the Bluhm Legal Clinic representing victims of mortgage fraud in Chicago's West Side. Previously director of the clinic, she is now executive director of Injustice Watch, a nonprofit newsroom whose mission is the examination of issues of equity and justice in the court system through investigative projects. From 2003 to 2010, Sorensen was a federal prosecutor with the US Attorney's Office in Chicago, focused on fraud and public corruption. While there, she co-led Operation Crooked Code, which investigated bribery and bribery-related crimes involving architecture, development, and construction work, ultimately charging over two dozen individuals, including employees of Chicago's building and zoning departments. We talked via Zoom on September 19, 2023. – AL

ANN LUI: How did your perception of the building industry in Chicago change when you worked on Operation Crooked Code?

JULIET SORENSEN: At the time, my vantage point on the building industry was through the lens of a federal prosecutor, and the job of a federal prosecutor is to enforce federal criminal law. So I approached this case through the web of anti-corruption laws that apply to state and local actors at the local government level, which includes Chicago's Department of Buildings – then the Department of Construction and Permits – and the Department of Zoning. The situation that presented itself to me was indeed an ecosystem, a way of doing business, you could call it a *culture*. What was for sale? Everything. Everything could be assigned a value. The reason for that really came down to the notion that time is money in the construction industry. If one could reap savings on the ground by paying a bribe, and thereby sell condo units faster or get an approval that one otherwise wouldn't, or simply get approval more quickly than one otherwise would, then that, irrespective of what was legal, was optimal from the perspective of these contractors, builders, and developers, as well as the city officials and inspectors who accepted their bribes in exchange for things that were mutually identified to be of value.

AL: What were the most egregious examples of bribery and corruption? On the flip side, were there processes or procedures involved that you perceived as unfair but that didn't rise to the level of illegal behavior?

JS: So, I was reflecting on this a bit because of our conversation about building codes. I was thinking about their social purpose and the public policy behind them. The most obvious purpose of a building code is public safety, but not all of these bribes necessarily went to public safety. In fact, it was quite common for an individual who was being interviewed by the federal agents on this case to say, *But nothing ever happened. Sure, I give these bribes but it was all okay. There never was an electrical fire. It wasn't my property in Lincoln Park where the porch collapsed.* But those folks are missing the point for a number of reasons. One is that it's a question, frankly, of statistical likelihood. If you circumvent the building code when it comes to your electrical wiring, no, that's not causative – it doesn't mean that ergo a fire will break out in this unit. But does it increase the chances? Absolutely, which is why the building code exists in the first instance.

There was a property we identified where bribes had been paid literally at every turn in the process of rehabbing this multi-unit building on the North Side. An architect had drawn up fake plans to show basement units as preexisting because, otherwise, the zoning ordinance would not permit them. The zoning inspector himself was bribed when he came out to do an on-site inspection, and he, in exchange, said he took "creative photography" to make those basement units look like they had always been there. It's kind of scarred me for life when it comes to so-called garden units in Chicago. If I ever know somebody who's moving to the area and I can give them one piece of advice, it's to be very leery of the garden unit.

I think that arguably the least egregious bribes, but still bribes that violate 18 U.S. Code § 666 – the provision that addresses state and local bribery – were those bribes that were paid to "jump the line." One might say, in another context, that's not a bribe, that's a tip. Actually, under the bribery law that applies to federal officials, the corollary to state and local bribery, there's a carve out for what is called an illegal gratuity. And I see both sides of that. I see why one is arguing that it's not a payment for a public official to take a decision that they wouldn't otherwise take based on the merits. On the other hand, the challenge with corruption in Chicago is not just these quid pro quo bribes but the long-term, insidious effect on the city's morale and solidarity and sense of what is fair.

I was quite struck by our discussion of equity and inequitable urban and built environments. I think the biggest social problem of corruption in the building and construction industry is that it places a premium on who can pay and it totally discounts equity and social policy.

AL: If we think about, in the abstract, all the value that was associated with those bribes – say, a condo that went to the market two months early or the basement units that were rented illegally or the certificate of occupancy that was issued faster, and the business license that was associated with that – do you also see that as contributing to an inequitable built environment in Chicago as a whole?

JS: Very much so. One individual, Beny Garneata, a successful builder, was ultimately charged with two sets of related activities. One was paying bribes across departments at City Hall on an almost continual basis, but the other was defrauding union pension and benefit funds. He had two companies that were both union shops, electrical and plumbing, subject to collective bargaining agreements. The law requires that if an employer enters into a collective bargaining agreement, they have to pay into union pension and benefit funds – it's one of the most foundational benefits that union membership provides. Garneata was essentially keeping two sets of books, submitting false records to the union and paying his workers off the books. It's a very consistent approach. It's savings on the ground, but a complete disregard for any type of equity or social policy as the basis for the structure in which one works as a contractor or developer.

AL: It's interesting to hear that the people giving bribes were also disregarding the welfare of workers. So in addition to the benefit on the development side, there was ultimately a negative impact on tradespeople, on laborers, and the people who rely on those folks, like material suppliers and the teams that work with them.

In *Log* 54, on coauthorship, my coeditor Ana Miljacki and I critiqued the idea that the architect is a sole genius figure. In fact, it is *all* these people – including those who were found guilty in Crooked Code – developers, inspectors, tradespeople, contractors, who work together to make a project happen. How can we cultivate a culture of working together without entering into the complicity and bad relationships that you found during Operation Crooked Code?

JS: David Johnson, the building inspector who ultimately became a cooperating witness, once told me a story about his first day on the job at the buildings department. He had reported to work and his supervisor sent him out with a more senior inspector so that he could learn the ropes and go to on-site inspections. He got in the car with this guy and, to his surprise, they drove to this other man's house. The guy said, Wait here, and proceeded to go into his house. Johnson sat in the car for three hours, I don't know if [the senior inspector] was taking a nap or watching TV or what. The next day, he shared this with his supervisor, who had assigned him to go out with this other person. He told me he was excoriated for being a tattletale, for being a snitch. Well, Johnson ended up being point zero for corruption in the Department of Buildings. But this was because he experienced the culture, he lived it on his very first day.

We know that culture is difficult to change. That said, I do believe that because the built environment is so highly regulated and there are so many steps, there are some relatively simple interventions that can at least help to shake up culture, keep a culture of collaboration, and maintain a level of accountability and transparency. Some changes were put in place as a result of Crooked Code that I believe were needed. I'd be naive to think that Crooked Code spelled the end of all bribery in City Hall, but I'd like to think that it might have helped.

Everything used to be relationship based at the Department of Buildings when it was time for an inspection. Your area might have been the North Side and my building might have been on the South Side, but I could still call you and say, *Hey, friend. I'm ready for the inspection, and let's grab a beer afterward.* Today, all requests for inspections have to be submitted online, and then they're assigned randomly. Budget cuts to the Department of Buildings also affected the culture. The building inspectors were going out solo, but after Crooked Code they reverted to doing inspections in teams, so there is both mutual support and mutual accountability. Those are just a couple of changes that were put in place. But in terms of coauthorship and the architect, I'm interested in your thoughts on how the architect can be part of the team.

AL: I read a lot of the work of sociologist Robin Bartram, who went on ride-alongs with the conservation building inspectors responsible for issuing building violations. Apparently, many of them saw themselves as "Robin Hoods" who were tough on landlords and went easy on single-family homeowners as part of a larger class battle. Whether or not that was actually reflected in their actions, it *is* clear that they felt they had to make many discretionary or subjective judgments, which they learned to make through a value structure that they learned from their peers. So while there is law about how inspectors need to enforce code, there is also a gray area for subjectivity, which in the best-case scenario allows for discretionary judgment when it's needed but in the worst-case scenario allows for corruption.

There's a land-use attorney in Boston who has advocated for a form of zoning review that is impact-based. If your project has a positive impact on the community, you might receive a more favorable zoning change or expedited zoning review. This proposal, to me, is the opposite of corruption. It incentivizes people to make their projects positive for the community through the same kinds of benefits that Operation Crooked Code found folks paid bribes for. Were there structural or large-scale reforms that you've come across or thought of in the wake of Crooked Code that could have a positive impact on Chicago?

JS: We know that zoning is sometimes code for systemic racism. We know it's code for being exclusionary. Because what is the stated purpose of the zoning ordinance? It's to preserve the character of a neighborhood. That can be a type of NIMBY attitude, keeping out the riffraff. Anyway, notwithstanding the original motivations, yes, there are those who are still committed to finding a workaround, in this instance paying bribes to, essentially, sneak in multiple units.

One of my favorite lines from a judicial opinion is actually from a corruption-related case, but totally different. It's from the United States v. Nixon, over the Watergate proceeding. The Supreme Court said, "Courts must look behind names." In other words, it's our job to not just be formalistic, but to consider the equities. I feel very strongly that that's the case when it comes to the building code, to code violations, to remedying them, and to enforcing the code. And to representing victims of, for example, Mark Diamond's reverse mortgage fraud scheme, which revealed to me the sort of hopelessness of a built environment in which there is no remedy and the violations keep multiplying. It's like a force multiplier where the underlying fraud continues to aggravate everything about the homes of these fraud victims.

AL: Is it true that when Diamond initially approached some of the homeowners, he said he represented a city-sponsored program?

JS: I don't know if he said it was city-sponsored. But at times he said it was an Obama-sponsored repair program.

AL: Ironically, when you and I were trying to find actual city-sponsored repair programs that could help resolve violations, we found out that in the past few years they have all but evaporated. The Department of Buildings' Single-Family Homeowner Assistance program is no longer available, the Department of Housing's emergency roof, porch, and heating repair programs are on pause with no schedule to return, and Neighborhood Housing Services' affiliated home repair programs are the same. What do you make of the situation that many of the reverse mortgage fraud victims find themselves in now? And can you also summarize a little about the Diamond case?

JS: Diamond and his co-schemers approached at least 120 homeowners whom he had specifically identified. They were all older Black owners, mostly on the West Side of Chicago, and some on the South Side. They persuaded them to apply for reverse mortgages, telling them that it was a way to access cash for needed home repairs. Two things then happened. First, Diamond and his co-schemers would arrange for the loan proceeds to go directly to him. He would pocket the loan and drain the equity out of the home. Second, sometimes, as a form of lulling, he and his co-schemers performed some half-baked home repairs. But either they didn't perform them at all or the repairs were so shoddy that over time the situation that existed at first had greatly worsened. I'll give you an example. One of our clients needed a handicap-accessible shower for his mother. The result was a bathroom that was utterly unusable for months for a woman who couldn't navigate the stairs to get to the other bathroom. And the handicap-accessible shower was never installed.

What has happened since then? Well, all of these fraud victims were on fixed incomes, so the fraud robbed them of an asset that was real. Often it was the home they had grown up in and regarded as the family home. It was something they were stewarding, that they were planning to pass on to their children, which we've all been taught is a core aspect of the creation of generational wealth. Now, not only are they unable to pass on a home that's owned outright, but they've applied for these bogus reverse mortgages that come due, which is to say, the lender can move for foreclosure when the original applicant passes away. So the longer that justice is not done, that these mortgages remain valid, the worse are the effects of the fraud on these victims and their families. There are a couple of legal actions pending. One is a federal criminal mortgage fraud prosecution in federal court in the Northern District of Illinois. One of Diamond's co-schemers has pled guilty, and I expect the others will as well. So that's appropriate in my mind. However, realistically, it is unlikely to translate into meaningful economic justice for these victims. Completely separately, my colleague in the Bluhm Legal Clinic and I have filed a lawsuit in the Circuit Court of Cook County – so, state court – seeking a declaratory judgment from the court to void the reverse mortgages on the basis that they were invalid, that they were entered into because of fraud, and that, therefore, the mortgage, which is a form of a contract, is invalid. It's a very challenging litigation that is still pending.

AL: In the opinion that you sent me, it stood out how, in a very evil way, Diamond took advantage of the homeowners. People who were incapable of making decisions about signing contracts were targeted for just that reason. It seems there was a very strategic selection of the people who were the most vulnerable.

JS: Absolutely, that was part of Diamond's strategy. It's another example of the need to look behind the names. That case is an all too rare instance when the Illinois Appellate Court said, *Wait a second. Yes, there is sufficient evidence that this person had dementia, we're not going to stop at this procedural roadblock. We're actually going to take a minute and look at the facts and the equities.* Without that, when it comes to advocating on behalf of homeowners fighting foreclosure, or tenants fighting an eviction order, the court often seems to default, in the former, to favoring the lender, and in the latter, to favoring the landlord without taking a moment just to pause and look behind the names, to consider the facts and the equities.

AL: I was thinking about what you shared with me on the corruption that follows in the wake of natural disasters, which will increase with the climate crisis. While the South and West sides have not been subject to a lone extreme weather event, we can argue that systemic disinvestment is like an ongoing natural disaster. Do you see the Diamond cases also as a form of profiteering in a disaster condition?

JS: That's a great analogy. Low population density, weak institutions, and systemic disinvestment have left homeowners, which everybody, including City of Chicago elected officials, touts as pillars of the community, vulnerable to fraud and scams. This would not have happened in another neighborhood.

This brings me to what you mentioned a few moments ago about the city programs that have been discontinued. There are only so many hours in a day, but if I had a few more hours in a day, I would really make a point to do something about this. It is quite shocking to me that those programs appear to have died on the vine and nobody's written about it, nobody's complained about it. You and I only learned about it because you made the time and effort to try to track down a live body. Do city officials think they can simply implement budget cuts where nobody cares and no one's looking? Where it's going to hit hardest, in neighborhoods that have experienced years of disinvestment and systemic racism? Apparently so. That's the only conclusion I can draw, and it's very disappointing.

AL: This is one of the ways that your perspective inspires me. When we initially found out about the loss of those programs, you were shocked and surprised, while I had taken it in stride as par for the course, thinking, of course, this is just what happens. Those are gone. Now what? I didn't stop to be angry. I really admire the way you see structural issues as sites of potential change rather than foregone conclusions. In the Diamond cases, if you had a magic wand, what would you see as being fair justice for the victims?

JS: Sadly, the magic wand doesn't exist. Step one would be voiding these reverse mortgages so the owners can remain in their homes. And step two would be an actual measure of economic justice in the form of restitution for damages. A magic wand would be to make everybody whole again, to undo the mortgages and restore the equity in the homes, to undo the exacerbated home repair issues and code violations. But that's the thing about issues that produce these sorts of force multipliers. It becomes impossible to go back to square one. You have to start thinking about what remedies can be helpful and meaningful even if they aren't a perfect cure or solution.

AL: The word *multiplier* really stands out to me. Can you talk more about how you've seen those multipliers play out in individual cases?

JS: Some of the Diamond victims obtained their reverse mortgages from a lender who, a few years ago, filed for bankruptcy. Those individuals are getting a comparatively small settlement out of the bankruptcy pool of funds set aside for so-called consumer creditors – that is to say, homeowner borrowers. It becomes quite interesting for an attorney-client relationship at that stage. Ethically, one can never tell a client what to do, one can only give advice. In this instance, because the circumstances are so extenuating, I can advise them to put that money toward the sort of reverse mortgage fraud scheme universe, but I have not walked a mile in their shoes and they may have other debts that are just as important, if not more so.

AL: In one case, we are talking about $2,500 needed for home repair, for outstanding building violations on electrical issues, which is compounded by the additional need for resources to navigate housing court and the permitting process. From a certain point of view, it is not very much money. Compared to Operation Crooked Code, let's say, it is less than some of the bribes that were paid, which developers chalked up to the cost of doing business. Seeing these two construction ecosystems in parallel is interesting to me because Crooked Code reveals how many people and resources you need to get a project done – and how limited those professional and financial resources are for homeowners in disinvested communities. There's very little recourse for folks who don't have access to the ecosystem of architects, builders, and tradespeople through traditional, and costly, routes. Can we pivot to highlighting one of the good actors in the Diamond cases, Reverend Robin Hood?

JS: Reverend Hood is a community organizer in North Lawndale, and his work tends to focus on two issues. One is as a violence interrupter, working with young people on anti-violence initiatives, and the other is with older people. He learned of the reverse mortgage fraud scheme because a family member was a victim. His aunt, who is now deceased, was duped by Diamond into applying for a reverse mortgage. His niece lives in the home today, and we're representing her as she fights foreclosure on the family home.

It was Reverend Hood who brought the reverse mortgage scheme to the attention of federal agents. He called, he wrote, he visited until a federal criminal investigation began. He is oftentimes a liaison to the community where we sometimes find client relationships to be challenging. And understandably so, people may feel embarrassed, feel ashamed, and not want to engage even at a psychological level. Someone once said to me, Oh, I saw your letter offering to represent me for free, but I figured that was a scam too. There's an understandable skepticism in the community. Reverend Hood has been an invaluable bridge to clients and other community stakeholders. He is tireless, and his dedication to peace and justice in North Lawndale is single-minded.

AL: I met him once through the context of the Diamond cases. What stood out to me was his fighting spirit. In one case, he marshaled the news media. One of the Diamond victims was being evicted so he made sure there were cameras on the sidewalk because he recognized that what was happening needed to be acknowledged, that it was unfair, and that there was no other recourse.

You also are the executive director of Injustice Watch. Former Mayor Rahm Emanuel implemented a landlord scofflaw list in 2014 that was used to identify people who had multiple code violations but didn't address them. But, for some reason, that scofflaw list just stopped being updated. It's a data-driven measure that would be very easy for us to bring back into play. How do we stay vigilant and amplify some of these exploitive conditions that we're seeing in Chicago around injustice in the built environment?

JS: I really believe that transparency leads to accountability, whether it's investigative journalism or open courtrooms. But it's not just transparency alone – that can be a tree falling in the woods. It is an engaged society and an informed society. Then you optimize democracy. You do it from the ground up, which is more challenging in neighborhoods that have experienced systemic disinvestment like Lawndale than in other more well-resourced places. But making one's voice heard, being treated with equal dignity, is critical for this sort of structural recognition.

AL: I have one wonkish question and then one abstract question for you. Have either the Diamond cases or Operation Crooked Code required any out-of-the-box legal thinking or procedures that you had to implement in order to seek a fair outcome for the victims of fraud?

JS: Once a grand jury investigation has been initiated, the federal government has pretty significant powers to undertake an investigation. And those were leveraged. In Crooked Code, there was a wiretap; there were multiple cooperating witnesses who consented to recording on their phones. They wore body wires with transmitters and recording devices, and more. That said, that is part of the toolbox of a federal criminal investigation, which is a considerable toolbox. Frankly, it has been much more challenging advocating for the victims of Diamond's reverse mortgage fraud. We determined legally that they did not qualify as a class, so we could not file a class action lawsuit because there were multiple lenders. Instead, we sought this declaratory judgment from the court.

In the criminal case we have run into the immutable fact that, in the United States, our system is an adversarial one. In a criminal case, in federal court, there are the individuals they've charged, the defendants, and the victims, who are remote third parties. There is a federal victim witness statute, which includes a list of rights or entitlements, but a victim is not a party to the case. And twice now I've actually submitted filings pursuant to this victim's bill of rights, but it's done so rarely that the clerk in the federal courthouse didn't even know how to accept it. We said, We're entitled to do it, we represent victims, here's the statute, and she said, But you can't file anything, you're not a party. The judge figured it out. In any event, the adversarial system was designed with an eye truly toward fairness and getting to the truth, but I can tell you, having represented these folks for several years, that it's increasingly urgent that their voices be heard.

AL: It strikes me that right now, under the new administration in Chicago, there is no Commissioner of Housing and there is no Commissioner of Planning & Development. With the lessons from Crooked Code and from the Diamond cases, what do you feel we, the citizens of Chicago, should be advocating for in the next four years around housing, zoning, and development?

JS: I do think that the twin issues of patronage and systemic racism cannot be ignored. I would hope that those critically important positions be filled by somebody who is, number one, selected on the basis of merit, not political clout, and, number two, has lived experience, personal, and professional, with all of the facets of the built environment and the unique challenges that we face in Chicago's neighborhoods. That would be my wish.

Ann Lui guest edited *Log* 54: Coauthoring (2022) with Ana Miljački. She is a founding principal of Future Firm, a Chicago-based architecture and design research practice, and assistant professor of practice at the University of Michigan's Taubman College of Architecture and Urban Planning.

*Darell Wayne Fields
& Milton S.F. Curry*

This Is a Time For Manifestos

Appendx 1: Culture / Theory / Praxis, edited by Darell Wayne Fields, Kevin L. Fuller, and Milton S.F. Curry, 1993.

Milton S.F. Curry produces creative work and scholarship on the role of architecture in shaping social consciousness and on the intersectional role of race, class, and urban geography embedded in modern and contemporary aesthetic practices in the Americas. He is professor of architecture and senior associate dean at Cornell University College of Architecture, Art, and Planning. He uses architecture as a medium from which to form new imaginaries about the American subject and American society. He is working on two books: Optic Black: Essays on Architecture Race Theory *and* Citizen Architect: Designing Democracy. *Curry founded* CriticalProductive Journal, *a peer-reviewed academic journal focused on culture and spatial practice, distributed by MIT Press, and cofounded* Appendx Journal. *While dean of the USC School of Architecture from 2017–2022, he led the acquisition of architect Paul R. Williams's archive, now co-owned by USC and The Getty Foundation, and is now cocurating several exhibitions on Williams's work in Los Angeles. Professor Curry serves on the Museum of Modern Art's Architecture and Design Acquisitions Committee and the Abode Communities Board of Directors. This interview was held in September 2023 via a video conference call between Ithaca and Princeton. – DWF*

DARELL WAYNE FIELDS: You and I have had collaborations over the years, which, for me, are still in play. One of the most significant, I think, is our venture publishing *Appendx*. You, Kevin Fuller, and I began publishing it in the early 1990s. The reason we started was our failed collective attempt to gain access to architectural theory publications at the time. Those would be *Assemblage*, the *ANY* series, MIT Press, etc. They all seemed closed to our efforts to publish a coauthored text and manifesto. Being acutely aware of *Log*'s publication lineage, I initially was reluctant to guest edit *Log* 57. Cynthia Davidson perceived my initial concern from the perspective of committing to a lot of editorial work. While that's true, it was a lot of work, I was most apprehensive about the appearance of being co-opted by the systemic architectural discourses that *Appendx* critiqued back in the day. I'm also always working on an ongoing Black aesthetic project. So, for *Log* 57, I resolved the conflict internally by imagining that the editing of *Log* 57 was the next issue of *Appendx*. I continue to appreciate Cynthia's ability to deal with me in that ongoing internal creative conflict. The crossout, for example, of the title *Log* on the cover is, among other things, an explicit homage to *Appendx*. Given that framework and your role and your experience in architecture, do you have similar concerns about having this conversation in *Log*?"

MILTON CURRY: It is great to be in conversation with you. You have been an intellectual mentor and friend, and your presence is felt in the discipline through your teaching, pedagogy, exhibitions, creative work, and scholarship. In answer to your question, yes and no. I think I would be more concerned if you hadn't been the editor of *Log* 57, which I think marks an important moment in terms of reckoning with harm that's been done in the past and using platforms that are in play today to rectify some of that.

I see *Log* 57 as an authentic effort to rectify some of the exclusions that have occurred in the past with respect to the various publications. I think that as long as we're open and honest and feel comfortable about what is selected to be printed, I am completely comfortable having this conversation and having it published in *Log*.

DWF: You said yes and no. I'm assuming that's the yes part. What was the no part?

MC: Well, the larger question of what I think you're getting at is the work that we did early on in *Appendx*, in which we were "foraging" for ways to construct something that had not been constructed, a kind of theory of Black aesthetics, or Blackness in architecture, or whatever one would have called it at the time. We had to forage through the humanities, social sciences, and literary theory with little, quite frankly, to help us in architectural history, although that's a forensic project that you and others have taken on. Nonetheless, we had to be courageous and radical to create a pathway then that has now opened up a subdisciplinary field.

I've termed that subfield Architecture Race Theory. I think that we did open up a pathway that has been productive in terms of Black designers and architects, many of them who participated in *Log* 57, *Appendx,* and *CriticalProductive*, and in exhibitions like "harlemworld" and "Reconstructions," having a voice and a seat at the table as new theories of architecture are ideated. The question is, How do we fortify that and how do we institutionalize this important work within the canons of architecture and architectural theory?

DWF: You mentioned *CriticalProductive*. You're the executive editor of that publication. As I recall, it was started initially at Michigan, correct? And is now, formally speaking, an MIT operation, correct?

MC: I started the nonprofit entity, CriticalProductive Inc, in 2008, while I was a professor at Cornell. At that time, I saw a dearth of work at the intersection of cultural theory and urbanism/urban design and city design. In 2011 and 2013, I edited two pilot issues: *CriticalProductive* V1.1:Theoretic Action and *CriticalProductive* V2.1: Post-Capitalist City. We have relaunched the journal with a revised look and feel, and with MIT Press as our global distributor – the first issue, *CriticalProductive* 1: Sovereignty/Populism, is due out in spring 2024.

DWF: Congratulations on that! Given the framework that we're talking about with *Appendx* in relation to some of the things we're now doing individually, are there any strategies or tendencies, aesthetic underpinnings, that are in play with *CriticalProductive* relative to *Appendx*?

MC: There are two specific issues that came out of the *Appendx* experience. One was the importance of articulating the notion of a manifesto, which can be the inaugural moment of a discourse, an intervention or a disruption. Second, I would say there are so many unfinished social movements that we don't necessarily have to start new ones. We can pick up the baton where those before us left off. *Appendx* was an effort to marshal disciplinary and discipline-adjacent talent to pick up the mantle of social movements that were unfinished - initially by producing a kind of manifesto of sorts in a bold articulation of a new subdisciplinary area of Black aesthetics. The role of social movements in informing new trajectories of architecture theory continue to be one of the motivations behind *CriticalProductive*, whether they be the civil rights movement or queer theory and space, feminism, or postcoloniality.

DWF: I completely agree with that. Speaking of manifestos, I think we're currently experiencing real historical conflict in real time. These projects, especially the projects that are incorporating theory, provide platforms for refusing certain cultural misinformation, misappropriation, and for fighting back, I think, against the pervasive historical amnesia that's in play at this moment.

MC: Unfortunately, it's been Black people in this country, in addition to others who have been underrepresented, who exhibit the courage in the face of conflict, in the face of violence, in some cases, to speak truth to power. To articulate our history and our cultural agency with authenticity has fallen on us. I'm afraid it will, again, fall on us to exhibit the courage, in the face of misinformation, disinformation, and overt racism, to create an enduring theoretical momentum that allows us to move through this period and, hopefully, advance the work that we're doing through the difficulties and the resistances that are designed to turn the clock back on the racial progress for Black people in the United States.

DWF: You just used the term *exhibit*. I think that in some of my own work in moving this Black aesthetic project forward, I realized that the manifesto doesn't necessarily have to just be a textual thing, that it needs to be visualized in some way. That was always a challenge. I recall that back in the first issue of *Appendx*, we were so concerned about the reading of the journal and our efforts as being some kind of pseudo-aesthetic project that we precluded the use of any images. So, I think that in my own work, it's been an ongoing project to actually, as you were saying before, fill in some of the possibilities that *Appendx* provided.

In terms of exhibits, you and I were also participants in the "harlemworld" exhibit, in 2004. As I recall, you worked with Studio Museum in Harlem Director Thelma Golden to map out who might be interested in participating in the exhibit. How did that get started?

MC: There were conversations around what a show would look like that focused on Harlem but also engaged architects. I provided some of the names that I think were included – some may not have been – but in general, it was an effort to try to advocate for us, for Black architects who have low visibility and low numbers in the ranks of architecture faculty nationally, as well as registered licensed architects. I'm pleased that the show happened. Exhibiting the work of Black architects in a major museum marked a milestone. As it turns out, this, unfortunately, is a rare occurrence.

DWF: Your own piece in that show, as I recall, was about urbanism. I can see that manifestation of urbanism in the project relative to your notion of *CriticalProductive* also being about urbanity, Black cities, etc. Can you describe your project and what you were attempting to do there?

MC: In trying to link things in terms of manifestos and unfinished social movements, the project looked at housing, retail, and commerce in a somewhat cynical way. The title was NegroCity Housing + Harlem Target. The notion was that Target, the big national retailer, would be the impetus for actually building social housing in Harlem. Within that social housing, the ground floor would be a supersized Target store that would then host recreational activities on a terrace level. A series of towers and horizontal slab buildings would be different forms of housing, which I surmised that Harlem needed, or needs, in terms of building a multi-class set of people who live in Harlem.

At that time, in 2004, Harlem was going through a heavy gentrification phase. The question of who "owns Harlem" loomed over the entire show. I think that the timing of the show helped to engage the community, not so much in a pragmatic conversation about real estate development, but about conceptual frameworks that could guide the thinking about what the new Harlem was going to be and whom it was going to be for.

DWF: Do you think that the use of conceptual design provocations can be effective platforms to convey some of the things that we're talking about? Is that still in play in some of your own work strategies and how you might use design to give a voice to these predicaments?

MC: It is, absolutely. The question opens up a lot of issues that cut across academia, professional practice, the way we build housing in cities today, and urban development strategies. I'm looking strategically at urban development projects that are real estate developments. I worked for over seven years on trying to transform the Oakland Coliseum area into a vibrant urban development that would be beneficial to the Black community in Oakland, as well as the larger community.

Unfortunately, this was back in the '90s and early 2000s. I got an education in politics, money, and corruption, quite frankly, in not being able to move that forward, even though we were producing visuals and models and moving through all the city processes. I think it's truly important to invest in the conceptual. I'll give you one example that sticks with me that I'm trying to work through in some of my current thinking. When I was the associate dean at the University of Michigan Taubman School of Architecture and Urban Planning, one of my early assignments from then Dean Mónica Ponce de León was to figure out what we should be doing in Detroit. Not knowing Detroit very well, I made several trips to meet with different constituencies, nonprofits, and others, and, in the end, developed an idea that we would look at large-scale urban development and partner with nonprofits. That didn't work. The nonprofits really had no faith that we would execute the conceptual work that had been done in a number of urban charrettes with previous administrations of the school.

So we pivoted to developing a high school program in Detroit called University of Michigan Architecture Prep, which launched in 2015 and is still in operation. It has been successful in opening up possibilities for high school juniors to become interested in architecture and to have a pathway, with some expertise under their belt, to apply to and get into architecture schools. But what sticks with me is that during the seven-year period I was in the Detroit metro area, there were troubling instances of squandering resources and a lack of leadership in redeveloping Detroit in an egalitarian way. As Scott Kurashige outlines in *The Fifty-Year*

Rebellion: How the U.S. Political Crisis Began in Detroit and Wallace Turbeville reveals in his Demos report, "The Detroit Bankruptcy," the City of Detroit's bankruptcy was driven by a severe decline in revenues and not an increase in obligations to fund pensions. The series of factual distortions by the city's Emergency Manager (appointed by then Governor Rick Snyder and accountable to no one) and his team precipitated the unprecedented $800 million bailout led by the Ford Foundation.

Here's the problem. Through all of that, one person acquired over 300 buildings in Detroit. At the same time, the discourse in the city was "right-sizing," or "downsizing," Detroit with a series of diagrammed and colored planning maps that were distributed to residents, implying that over time certain neighborhoods would cease to receive city services. But there was no architectural or urban design thinking that would allow people to see what a future Detroit might be and how they might leave a home 30 minutes from the downtown core, a home that had been given to them by their grandmother and that they didn't have any debt on, to come into a more compact and denser centralized city and have greater access to services, jobs, etc.

I believe that that strategy failed, in part, because there was no design concept that people could see and understand or think about conceptually. But I believe it was the right strategy to bring people closer to the city center and core, because it's a very strung-out city in terms of geography, and transportation has always been a problem.

DWF: That's interesting, because I have always believed that design, by bringing together sets of disparate relationships appearing as iconic visual signs, creates a compelling conceptual platform for sustaining place and community. In terms of large-scale operations, although at a different scale, in your role as dean at USC, you became the steward

Paul R. Williams, photographed in 1952. Photo: Julius Shulman. © J. Paul Getty Trust. Getty Research Institute, Los Angeles (2004.R.10).

of the Paul R. Williams Archive at the school. How did the school come into a relationship with that collection and the Getty?

As I understand it, you're still curating the collection. It's a very interesting project. The idea that a unitary archive of a significant Black architect doubles as a refined set of case studies for Los Angeles's building typologies is amazing.

MC: When I became dean at USC, in 2017, I met Karen Hudson, Paul Revere Williams's granddaughter. We struck up a series of conversations that led to talking about acquiring his architectural archives at the school. Williams was the first Black member of the American Institute of Architects and the first to receive both fellow status and an AIA Gold Medal. He was extremely prolific, over 3,000 projects. Most of his projects are in Los Angeles and Southern California, but many are in Las Vegas, the Northeast, and Washington, DC. He also had associations in Colombia and did work in Latin America.

Through the discussions with Karen, the school decided to acquire the archive, but because USC doesn't have the capacity of other large archival entities, I wasn't going to do it without a partner who could ensure that the archive would be stewarded in perpetuity. So I brought in the Getty Research Institute, and began talking with Getty Foundation President James Cuno as well as other Getty leadership. They had just started their African American Art History Initiative and were very interested in this project. And we said, let's acquire it, and we'll be 50/50 owners. As it stands now, I lead a curatorial team made up of several faculty from USC, the Getty Research Institute, and the Los Angeles County Museum of Art, who I brought in to be a curatorial partner.

We're setting up three concurrent exhibitions, in 2026, at the three institutions. They will be slightly different exhibitions, but there will also be the first academic monograph of Williams's work, featuring previously unpublished projects. And I believe these will be the first monographic shows of a Black architect in any major American museum, fortunately and unfortunately.

Williams was a Black architect, but he's one of the most exceptional American architects, period. I think that he doesn't get his due credit because he was extremely eclectic. Architects like Le Corbusier and Venezuelan architect Carlos Raúl Villanueva were stylistically eclectic early in their careers. They did a lot of classical architecture and then pivoted toward modernist architecture and innovated within the Modern Movement. Williams was no different. He just had a great career doing a lot of private homes that happened to be for very wealthy or entertainment-related people, which is what people know about him, but he also did a lot of public housing.

He worked with A. Quincy Jones, Welton Becket, and all the major White architects of the time. He did gas stations. He did 25 churches. He did community buildings. He did public housing, with Hilyard Robinson at Howard University. So he had a very long, established career. And for any architect to be producing work at the scale that he was, to run an office and to manage all that, and to be a Black person who, in some cases, could not visit the construction sites of the projects he was working on, is really truly exceptional. I'm really happy that we acquired it, and I look forward to sharing the archive as it gets digitized and people are able to go to the Getty, where it's physically located, to look at it.

DWF: Well, you were kind enough to invite me to be part of the initial discussion about the archive. One of the most interesting things that I found was what Williams was doing aesthetically. Usually, the eclectic or ad hoc tag is a historical label that diminishes a body of work. At that time, as you know, I was pushing the idea that one could exhibit the work, but that scholars could also examine the formal underpinnings that might be found in the archive. As you have called it, taking a forensic attitude in relation to the design work.

I'm not necessarily pitching something in terms of a road for scholarship, but I do think there is something about Williams's work that could be studied forensically so that we become more aware of the underlying principles of the design, regardless of the aesthetic variation. So I'm encouraging you to put the archive under that kind of scrutiny, because it's a rare opportunity to have a collection of work, particularly the drawings and models, in which you can actually see the architect's concepts underlying and hidden by a variety of buildings.

MC: It's a question of tools. Do we have the tools to do that work? I think there are possibilities in terms of being able to have scholars' eyes on this work, but we also need designers' eyes on this work to do forensic creative analysis. I'm not sure that the academy is

Paul R. Williams, Lucille Ball and Desi Arnaz House, Palm Springs, California, 1955. Photo: Julius Shulman. © J. Paul Getty Trust. Getty Research Institute, Los Angeles (2004.R.10).

equipping students with the tools to be able to look at something like Williams's work critically. It's great for people to read your work, my work, *Log* 57, *CriticalProductive*, *Appendx*, *Race and Architecture*, and many of the other works that are out there. But it's got to be taught and it's got to be pedagogically invested where, when someone is analyzing Williams's work, there's a citation, there's a footnote that is intellectually generous to the frameworks that are allowing that scholar to pursue certain questions. What I fear in the discussion of Blackness and architecture is an empty appropriation without proper citation and reference to those who have taken the time to develop deeply theoretical frameworks beforehand. That's part of my impetus in developing this idea of Architecture Race Theory.

The subfield Architecture Race Theory, as I outlined in my "Toward an Architecture Race Theory" essay in the "Reconstructions" catalog, needs to be named, needs to have an umbrella over it, where it's institutionalized within the corpus of architectural scholarship. Otherwise, I fear that the contributions will be diminished or appropriated without any reference to those who came before to construct that paradigm in the first place. I know you're invested in that, and I'm invested in it, but I think that's important for the durability and endurance of the legacy that has been established and that can also evolve and be productive in analyzing new things that come along.

J. Max Bond's work is going to have its moment in terms of being analyzed, as it should be. And there are many others. Through this project, I've uncovered Black

Paul R. Williams, The Beverly Hills Hotel Addition, Beverly Hills, California, 1950. Photo Julius Shulman. © J. Paul Getty Trust. Getty Research Institute, Los Angeles (2004.R.10).

architects, some of them working in a very traditional modernist ethos, doing exceptional work that has not been recognized. But as you said, with that history comes also a theorization of what they were doing and why they were doing it.

Robert Kennard, another graduate of USC architecture, is the subject of a book his daughter is publishing next year. It's an amazing story as well. I did not know of him before coming to USC. There's a lot that we need to uncover. We cannot count on museums to do it. As I said, "harlemworld," with 18 Black architects, was one show with Black architects. We just had "Reconstructions" at MoMA, in 2021. With all that has been given to this country by enslaved Africans, Black American craftspeople and inventors, and Black architects, it is pathetic that we have had only two major exhibitions featuring Black architects' perspectives on the world as they see it; and not one monographic exhibition featuring a Black architect!

DWF: You have used the term *analysis* a few times. Is the notion of design forensics different from conventional architectural analysis?

MC: It's an interesting question. When you look at the work in "Reconstructions," for example, I think some of that work is forensic and it's also creative and projective. When I look at the work of Amanda Williams, I see both a critical eye toward certain concepts that have been referred to in science fiction or Afrofuturism, and the projective potential to think architecturally about the spatial implications of those concepts. When I look at the work of Mario Gooden or Yolande Daniels, there's a forensic element, but there's also a projective element. Architects have a unique capacity to take the historical, provide an analytical lens, and then move into a projective dimension sequentially or simultaneously. This gives the work additional meaning, and it's different from traditional notions of preservation as well.

DWF: I want to shift to the current predicament, which is the recent decision by the Supreme Court relative to affirmative action, diversity, etc. I want to preface my question with two observations. The first observation expresses a distinction between affirmative action and diversity.

Affirmative action – that is, the use of numerical racial quotas of historically disenfranchised minorities – ceased with the decision in *Regents of University of California v. Bakke* in 1978. In the court's ruling, Justice Powell argued that race consciousness in admissions may be considered for the benefit of diversity. Diversity programs in architecture schools do not guarantee the presence of the historically disenfranchised. Diversity beneficiaries do not have to be historically disenfranchised.

As we speak, the media is still writing articles stating that affirmative action was overturned under the court's [June 2023] decision, *SFFA v. Harvard College*. My point, given my cumulative experience in architecture schools, beginning in the early '90s, is that there hasn't been a problem of Black students or Black faculty being overrepresented. To the contrary, in both cases, the numbers account for perhaps zero to three percent participation. In an introductory drawing and lecture class, for example, that means a maximum of two to three Black students. Ivy League schools tend to be a little better, if I can use that term, than public universities.

Again, I'm speaking of an experience in architecture schools in relation to that recent court decision. Although the schools may be complicit, I'm troubled by the law itself. That said, it seems to me that three students out of 70 dispel the notion of so-called affirmative action quotas continuing to benefit Black students exclusively. Maybe someone can appeal to Chief Justice Roberts to provide the same diversity loophole for architecture schools that he allows for the military academies. I'm not sure.

My second observation relates to a compelling statement, in 1941, by John Dewey. He wrote, "Our anti-democratic heritage of Negro slavery has left us with habits of intolerance toward the colored race, habits which belie profession of democratic loyalty. The very tenets of religion have been employed to foster anti-Semitism. There are still many, too many, persons who feel free to cultivate and express racial prejudices as if they were within their personal rights, not recognizing how the attitude of intolerance infects . . . the basic humanities without which democracy is but a name."

One of the most compelling statements you made in the 1993 inaugural issue of *Appendx* was, "No longer can we easily point to overt practices of racism, sexism, and gender bias. These types of discrimination have become successfully entrenched in a variety of institutional contexts, however, including even the law, and the rule of law is being used to squelch dissent – something I'm sure the founding fathers did not anticipate or desire." I think these prerequisites, meaning diversity as a legal construct, Dewey's comments on the entanglement of race and democracy, and your critique of discrimination are very compelling and crucial at this point. Based on your experience – as an academic, a theorist, a designer, and all of the territory we've covered thus far – do you see a way out of this current predicament?

MC: First, let's start with *Bakke* and move to *Grutter v. Bollinger* [2003]. As these decisions on the use of race-conscious strategies in university admissions evolved, we moved away from a notion of repair for harm that was done and toward a more nebulous term, *diversity*. Certainly, diversity is a compelling interest for many of the reasons that were outlined in the *Bakke* and *Grutter v. Bollinger* Supreme Court cases – that having racially and ethnically diverse universities enables the nation's leadership to reflect the diversity of the nation's citizens, which produces better collaborations, more innovation, and a richer intellectual milieu. But when you move away from the notion of repair and toward one of diversity as a compelling interest, you open the door to where we are now. Trying to define diversity in a country as multiplicitous as the United States leads to including every person and group as part of the polity – you don't want to leave anyone out. Yet the harm done to African Americans, Hispanics, Latin Americans, Indigenous Americans, etc. is distinctively systemic and distinctively enduring, meaning that the physical and economic impediments to overcoming the taking of land and opportunity continue to reverberate and have real-life impacts today.

So, we have to focus on the fact that taking race out of consideration means taking the conversation about systemic inequities that resulted from slavery off the table, especially in terms of creating pathways for those who were locked out of the system and out of wealth creation for generations. We have to continue to put that back on the table, and architecture schools, through pedagogy, can do that. Law schools, through Critical Race Theory and other forms of knowledge production, can do that. And as long as there's academic freedom in the institutions where I teach, I will continue to do that.

Having said that, we have to appeal to a broader set of values. When I look at the founder of Cornell, or the early presidents of the University of Michigan, I keep coming back to the fact that the university has to be a place where democracy and academic freedom are central to its core mission. We have to keep it as such. I'm certainly open to inclusiveness and debates on various aspects of the political spectrum. But we have to assert that one of the values of higher education is to enable students to become more human by becoming more *humane*, by understanding the systems that are having different effects on different citizens in our country and our world.

Those who would ban the use of race-conscious admissions, both in university admissions and in business, don't understand the core intent and desired impact of the Fourteenth Amendment to the US Constitution. Justice Ketanji Brown Jackson was very focused and articulate in her dissent in the affirmative action case that a ban on taking race into account *at all* is at odds with the intent of the Equal Protection Clause of the Fourteenth Amendment. Look at Florida. Unfortunately, K–12 students under the curriculum now being enforced will be the most poorly educated students in cultural studies in the United States. That doesn't bode well for students, whether White, Asian, Black, Hispanic, who want to go to college, pursue a career, and be knowledgeable about the world. It doesn't do anybody any good.

DWF: I think the notion of color blindness in the academy, set against the disenfranchised, is the most cynical misrepresentation of civil rights I've seen in some time. It's getting more and more difficult to get up in the morning. I have to cope with the reality that my concept of the university, the concept and context you described, can cease to exist overnight and be completely legal. Given the current situation, this is the first time, as an academic, I've felt like the Black content of my scholarship would be banned in other parts of the country.

The reality is that I can pursue that here, in Princeton, but perhaps in places like Florida or Texas, given the politics, and even the law, I may not be able to teach a course in the university. The underlying tragedy is that the territory I've always valued in the context of the university, the freedom of intellectual activity it supports, has, in recent circumstances, made me question what I'm doing and supporting. Quite frankly, I'm not sure how to address this political instability right now. These recent court decisions, which seize our lives in some way, mean we have to really rethink the notion of civil rights, personal rights, and freedom of expression, and whether the country or our schools or our states can be on the same page with contested constructions of democracy.

MC: Can the citizens of this country, the US, withstand the assault on democracy and the movement toward authoritarianism and fascism? Creating new forms of otherness by banning certain books, claiming that slavery was an honorable endeavor, vilifying the trans community, and other distortions of information under the banner of rebalancing one-sided speech – these are creating an environment where it will be difficult to sustain the honorable and vexed egalitarian experiment that we call America. Singling out a student's race in university admissions as something that cannot be used in any way to understand that student's place in the ongoing system of racially unequal policies (in education, housing, jurisprudence, business, labor, etc.) is problematic.

At USC we achieved diversity and excellence simultaneously by attracting students to the promise of becoming a "citizen architect" and by broadening the pool of public-school students who were exposed to the work one can do in the discipline and in the profession. In addition to the University of Michigan Architecture Prep, I formed the USC A-Lab, and I can tell you, from firsthand experience, that if we want more Black and Hispanic students we need to go where they are, which is the public school system, and develop opportunities to expose them and all students in the public school system to our profession. Now I'm afraid that the SCOTUS 2023 decision severely limiting the use of race in college admissions will have a chilling effect on universities' attempts to expose a broader number of students to college pathways.

DWF: I completely agree with you on recruiting, and not just recruiting undergraduates for master's programs. I've done similar recruitment activities, even with my own high school, back in Dallas. I established a recruiting platform that identified talented students from the architecture program in high school to participate in Harvard's Career Discovery program. Not to get those students to go to Harvard, but to help them experience academia and the university and campus. These kinds of experiences develop an interest in architecture, and the aspirations of those students carry directly through their academic work. So I completely agree that those activities are critical.

MC: Major top-tier universities will have to invest in the K-12 educational system. Perhaps the SCOTUS 2023 decision can motivate a fresh look at recruitment and admissions. What kind of student do we need to produce for architecture today, and what kind of student is coming in? And maybe we need to shift the way that we educate them. This brings us full circle to our work in the academy, publishing, teaching, and our work on the outside, lecturing, exhibiting. We have to continue to advance with rigorous work and work that courageously challenges our peers.

Darell Wayne Fields guest edited *Log* 57: Black is. . . an' Black ain't. . . (2023). He is a visiting research scholar at Princeton University School of Architecture and the author of *Architecture in Black: Theory, Space and Appearance* (2015) and *On Solitude* (2021).

Entering Cub - Minneapolis Quarry, Minneapolis, Minnesota, 2023. Photo: Arseny Pekurovsky.

I hear that some people dream of going to space. I want to go to the supermarket.

The supermarket is a universalist temple for meditation. An unlikely refuge. Don't worry, the airlock will close behind you and your problems will be left on the curb. Sanitation will pick them up on Friday. Problems don't exist at the supermarket because time has been eliminated. From the cheese aisle, you will see lunch, dinner, and maybe even breakfast, simultaneously. Here, the sun never sets on the bananas. Do you think the temperature and humidity are carefully calibrated to keep the vegetables crisp? Think again, sweet pea: the pleasurable whir of 300 refrigeration units is there to calm your nerves, lower your heart rate, slow your metabolism, and assuage that overactive brain of yours that always gets your ass into trouble. The supermarket is no place to pop your cork. In this perfect hermetic environment, you will glide between the aisles like a satellite. And when you emerge from the airlock once more, you'll feel the heaviness of your feet and the weight of one too many grocery bags. — Arseny Pekurovsky

*Todd Gannon
& Caroline Levine*

Everybody Needs To Breathe Oxygen

Caroline Levine is David and Kathleen Ryan Professor of Humanities at Cornell University, where she teaches in the School of Criticism and Theory and in the Department of Literatures in English, which she chaired from 2018 to 2021. In her books, Provoking Democracy: Why We Need the Arts *(2007) and* Forms: Whole, Rhythm, Hierarchy, Network *(2015), Levine examines the efficacy of the arts and humanities in democratic societies and the relevance of formalist interpretive strategies to understanding the relationship between aesthetics and political action. On August 11, 2023 – a few days after wildfires broke out on the Hawaiian island of Maui – I met with Levine over Zoom to discuss the development of these themes in her latest book,* The Activist Humanist: Form and Method in the Climate Crisis *(2023), and the relationship of her research to architecture and urban design.* – TG

TODD GANNON: In *The Activist Humanist* you take up themes that are pressing not only to every person on the planet but also that resonate strongly in architecture. You ask, How does an individual meaningfully engage the climate crisis and work at a scale that can effect substantive change in the world? Could you provide a little background on why you've taken up these issues and where you hope to take them?

CAROLINE LEVINE: I always feel a little like I'm wandering into fields that are not my area of expertise and then pulling things from them that help me think new thoughts. Wandering into architecture and urban design, which I did when you invited me to teach with you at Ohio State, in 2017, was certainly not something I have any training in or expected to do. But sometimes my own field doesn't have answers to questions I'm asking – or doesn't articulate the answers. The other day, while talking to a fellow literary critic, I said, I'm always trying to cross the gap between art and political action. She replied, There is no crossing. Why would you even try? A lot remains unspoken in that response. Who says there is no crossing? What stands in the way of trying? In my work, I try to get into the real guts of the relationship between art and political action and to articulate the unspoken assumptions about their relationship.

In a way, all of my books attempt to answer the question, What is not being said? As I wrote them, I kept thinking, I'll be persuaded by Marxism this round, or Deleuze and Guattari will get me this time. Instead, whenever I thought about politics, I'd end up asking questions about institutions and infrastructures and the built environment – and that's what kept drawing me to the field of architecture. Architects are obliged to articulate what those in other fields can more easily leave unsaid. There is something obviously more practical and engaged about what architects do, compared to what literary critics do.

I also turned to design and infrastructure studies because I kept running into a wall when I read literary critics' responses to the climate crisis. You hear lots of people in my field saying there's nothing we can do about the climate. We have to give up and start mourning. This seems to reinforce the idea that there is no relationship between art and political action, that there is no crossing the gap. And so I started to think about a theory of inaction and of an incapacity to act. That's what ended up in the book.

TG: *The Activist Humanist* builds on your earlier work, both in terms of subject matter and your methodology. In *Provoking Democracy*, you flip the familiar claim that avant-garde artists rely on the freedoms that democratic states provide to make a much less obvious claim that democracies should not merely allow, or support, or tolerate avant-garde art, but that democracies actually *require* the challenges of the avant-garde, which ultimately propel the cause of freedom. You look at art and its place in democratic political contexts to demonstrate how works of art – and artistic sensibilities more broadly – resist the tendency of democracies, when majorities become too entrenched, to swing toward totalitarianism. Your thesis is that we need wrenches in the machinery of governance for that machinery to work properly. Then in *Forms*, you develop your investigation of the relationship between cultural production and political justice by making another counterintuitive claim: that formalism, the long-discredited close-reading tactics of the New Critics of the first half of the 20th century – Cleanth Brooks, T.S. Eliot, I.A. Richards, etc. – might be recuperated as a method for gaining insight into literary texts as well as for provoking meaningful social change.

Your interest in recuperating old-school formalism to advance contemporary political work resonates in the field of architecture. There is a long legacy of formalist criticism in architecture, and as in literary studies, historicist methods of critique have put significant pressure on older formalist techniques. While this work has opened important lines of inquiry, architectural thinking also has at times been hamstrung by historicist critique, because its predominantly negative formulations tend to foreclose specific focus on the future in favor of laying bare the contradictions and inequities of the present and the past. To borrow a term from *The Activist Humanist*, historicist thinkers like Theodor Adorno, Michel Foucault, Fredric Jameson, and Manfredo Tafuri tend to operate *anti-instrumentally*, and thus tend not to be particularly useful to the act of designing, which, at some level, requires one to instrumentalize. In *The Activist Humanist*, you are determined to find ways to actually get stuff done, and to do so, you adopt specifically architectural vocabularies. Words like *building*, *infrastructure*, *framework*, and *design* appear repeatedly. How do you understand the relationship between architectural thinking and your work?

CL: First, I'd like to toggle to your work for a second. In your book, *Figments of the Architectural Imagination* [2022], I was struck by the argument that the utopian, dreamy possibility that never gets built is still generative, that there is power to do political work invested in designs that were never intended to be built. This is where our two fields talk to each other. There is a value to the thing that doesn't become actualized in concrete form. But you're in a field that does cross the chasm between the dream and the realized material form. We literary scholars are not supposed to instrumentalize. We are not supposed to take the art object as a plan or a program or a lesson. In our field, that constitutes a bad reading. It is seen to destroy the experience of the art object itself. The art object is not supposed to be taken into the world of design. I think a basic tension is happening across the fields of art history, literary studies, cinema and media studies, and musicology. On the one hand, there is a strong commitment to the notion that the dreamy, utopian, imaginative work exists in a realm of freedom, in a realm that opens us to the possibility of what could be. On the other, there is a desire to say we are engaged in these complex cultural and social worlds in which art plays a part. What is missing in so much of what I read in literary studies today is an articulation of what happens when we move from the dream to the material instantiation. Usually, when an art object is actualized in the world, we say it's ideological, we say it's repressed, we say it's historically conditioned, right? And we say the dream is somehow the possibility, the alterity, the opening. This is our current definition of the aesthetic. But some aesthetic objects do get made. They provoke people to make things, they have some material footprint, and they give people ideas for doing things. So what happens if we take that seriously?

What happened to me, which I think is going to be a real problem for me going forward, is that I lost interest in the category of the aesthetic. I loved your point in *Figments* about Grand Central Station, that such spaces transport us to a realm that is different from the everyday world, that they inspire feelings of awe when we walk into them. But to me, everyday design is just as interesting in the sense that all these designed objects that make the world that we live in – all those toothbrushes and coffee cups and subway stations and crosswalks – make our relations to each other possible. Whether we are paying attention to them or not doesn't matter, because either way, they create the possibilities of our collective consciousness and action. That's partly why I lost faith in the aesthetic as a special category while writing *The Activist Humanist*.

TG: How are you dealing with that?

CL: Today, I'm doing more activism than anything else. I teach classes about how we engage in collective action on climate change. In them, we incorporate all kinds of rhetorical and visual techniques, but they don't stand apart as a separate realm that shifts our consciousness in some new way. We just incorporate them into our other questions about the economics of climate change, the politics of climate change, the rhetoric of it, the photography of it. It's all one big set of questions about how we engage the climate crisis. I'm feeling much more drawn to interdisciplinary work and away from traditional humanities work, for sure.

TG: And yet as one moves through *The Activist Humanist*, a lot of conventionally aesthetic objects show up, and they do important theoretical work for you. Whether they be novels or murals or television shows, you corral a wide range of literary and artistic examples to help make the case for instrumentality.

The Activist Humanist: Form and Method in the Climate Crisis by Caroline Levine, 2023. 224 pages. Princeton University Press.

CL: I guess my question, after finishing the book, is this: Take a routine like brushing teeth, which is ordinary and important to our health, and then take the refrain of a pop song that gets us dancing. Is one fundamentally different from the other? Are the patterns they imprint on our daily lives really so different? Does one belong in a category separate from the other? If we look at them in terms of their forms, we can see that both involve bodily movement. Both involve repetition. Both are important to our health. So, I just lost faith in the specialness of artworks and became interested in the potential of everyday objects and activities.

TG: In the book you point out an interesting habit among us theory writers. You call attention to our tendency to focus on open-endedness, on spectacle, on moments of drastic and memorable change, which you characterize as the *pause*, the *rupture*, and the *dissolve*. You demonstrate the way theorists look for gaps and openings in the objects and systems we study and then point out the work that can be done in these breaks with the conventional or the normative. Then you make a case for the opposite approach. You argue that at this moment, when the climate crisis has all of us thinking about issues of survival, qualities like stability, permanence, and predictability seem to require some attention.

While these qualities don't necessarily draw the interest of historicist critique, they are issues that architects must deal with all the time. We tend not to make a lot of noise about them because architects, too, are drawn to the gaps and the fissures and the spectacle of nonnormativity. Like our friends in the humanities, we tend to speak about those gaps and fissures and spectacles in terms of the freedoms that they afford. A break from convention is a move in the direction of freedom. Many of us have worked in that mode for a very long time. But when the planet is literally on fire, routines like brushing teeth, walking to work, or taking the subway, though perhaps less exciting than revolutions, come into focus as the basic elements through which we can recalibrate our relationship to the world, to the consumption of raw materials, and to the distribution of scarce resources. Certainly these are questions that architecture must take up out of necessity, but you show how they have productively been taken up in literature as well. You describe the routines that one finds in Charles Dickens's novels, for instance, or the focus on the bureaucratic institutions of the British welfare state in the television series *Call the Midwife*. This focus on routine, on the repetitive, on the mundane, unspectacular things that we all have to do, is striking. You seem to flip the entire argument without seeming belligerent. It is an instructive model for anyone interested in advocating for meaningful change.

CL: One of the things I am struck by in political philosophy is that when philosophers talk about what is good and fair and just, they often talk about basic necessities as being boring. They will say, *We have to make sure everybody is housed and clothed and has enough to eat. Now let's move on to the more problematic question of education.* This made me realize that I am interested in what is boring because it is actually universal. We have been so allergic to universalisms for so long, but everybody still needs to breathe oxygen. Part of the reason we – the political philosophers and the literary critics, and maybe architects, too – haven't been arguing about that is that we have been able to take breathing oxygen for granted. And it *is* boring, until it's threatened, at which point it's not boring at all. The need to breathe clean air is really urgent today.

I'll give you a related example. In literary studies, happy endings have been out of favor for over 100 years. There are maybe three of us in the field today who have fought for them. And yet audiences lap them up. In response, we tend to say, Oh, they're just ideological dupes. They're just enjoying something that's bad for them. We're the ones who really understand freedom. What if that is a mistake? What do we miss when we routinely assume revolutionary disruption and excitement to be more interesting and more valuable than the ability to look forward to a predictable future? Doesn't being able to look forward to enough material goods to keep on going constitute its own sort of aesthetic pleasure? Isn't there value in that?

Questions like these made me realize that I was bored with revolutionary disruption. It wasn't giving me anything to hold on to. What's more, all the attention it had been given didn't seem to be producing any actual revolutionary disruptions in the world. The people on the side of disruption in the humanities sound an awful lot like people in the business world, which is all about innovation and disruption. These biases are everywhere, not just in this rarefied world of avant-garde thinkers in the arts. So I began to think, what happens if we understand disruption not as automatically productive but rather as ideologically neutral? What if disruption is sometimes useful and sometimes not useful at all? In other words, what if the breaking of form is sometimes good and sometimes not good? Sometimes, if you've got a good form, you don't want to break it. If you've got a bad form, maybe you do want to break it. The important thing is to realize that it's not the act of breaking that's good or bad. Too often, criticism seems to lose sight of this.

TG: Throughout your work you consistently separate ideology from form. In *The Activist Humanist* you question the critical impetus to "burn it all down," a battle cry one hears across cultural fields. Any architect knows that it's a lot easier to knock a building down than to put one up. And yet we as a culture tend to valorize critical demolition: Smash the idols! Drive the money changers from the temple! In *Toward an Architecture* [1923], Le Corbusier has a famous line, "Architecture or revolution. Revolution can be avoided." Critical culture lambasted him for this. Tafuri, for instance, wanted the revolution. "There can never be an aesthetics, art, or architecture of class, but only a class critique of aesthetics, art, architecture, and the city," he wrote ["Toward a Critique of Architectural Ideology" (1968)]. "Any search for an alternative within the structures determining the mystification of planning is an obvious contradiction in terms." Where does that leave architects? Burn it all down.

Whatever the shortcomings of his position, at least Le Corbusier held out hope that he could design his way out of the problem. We don't need to go to war, he seemed to say.

We just need a plan. Of course, Tafuri argued that Le Corbusier's plan was identical with that of capital, that Corbusier best demonstrated how to absorb all these pesky, revolutionary, avant-garde artists (and everybody else!) into the machinery of capitalist exploitation. Tafuri's argument is convincing, but it is not clear to me that his solution, revolution, not architecture, is the best option.

CL: Why does it have to be either smashing or planning? Surely the two go together. You break something and then you put something in its place. I've never understood why it's only breaking. I get that there's this idea that somehow a whole new consciousness would emerge that would allow one to think some thought or have some relations that are unthinkable now. But I keep coming back to two thoughts. First, as Raymond Williams pointed out, though the French Revolution lasted just a few years, the revolutionary work of displacing the aristocracy with the bourgeoisie took another 100 years. And we still have a king of England, right? It's not altogether gone, even now. We don't have any historical evidence to support the idea that revolution will somehow suddenly produce a completely new consciousness.

Second, we actually know a lot about what humans need to survive. There are not infinite ways of organizing human societies. You've got to get clean water to people, and you've got to take wastewater away. Every culture has had to figure that out in some way. I think the Corbusier example is great. Yes, I can see how saying that we can design our way out of this could feed right into the hands of the worst actors right now. But could we as citizens think about what makes a just society and start building right now? I think we could do that. I think we should do that. Right now. Even if we fail, it's still worth doing.

TG: And yet, as we can see in all those T-shirts with Steve Jobs and Che Guevara on them, our culture tends to celebrate revolutionaries. There are moments when revolution is the right move, but there are also moments when intelligent mundane changes are the right move. A lot of the work you are doing is looking for those literary examples that can help make the case for mundane changes. How can we, reading Proust and immersing ourselves in the everyday, find different ways of engaging the world?

CL: The artwork that first got me thinking about mundane changes was the television series *Mad Men*. Part of the shock of watching *Mad Men* is seeing everyday life 50 years ago, kids without seat belts, pregnant women smoking. There's a picnic scene where the family dumps their litter on the lawn and then just walks away. It's shocking. There was a big debate among academics and people reviewing *Mad Men*. It makes us feel complacent, was one side. We've solved these problems. Weren't they so backwards then. Look how far we've come, was the other. Most of the people in my world were on the complacency side. But I was fascinated by how, in 50 years, our habits as a culture have changed. How did people change so many daily habits from the 1960s to the 2010s? In the case of seat belts, not only did the rules and regulations change but the way we experience getting into a car changed dramatically as well. Getting into a car is different from what it would have been 50 years ago. I'm going to feel incredibly anxious every second that I don't have a seat belt on. My body has incorporated the habit in some way.

In recent years I've expanded my thinking beyond the question of habits, because I think it is part of the tool kit of the fossil-fuel industry to say, *It's your fault, because your carbon footprint is big. You're driving your car; you need to change your habits.* They have deliberately waged a campaign to put the blame for climate change on us ordinary people. Of course our habits are contributing to climate disaster, but we don't have a lot of choices. Not having a car is a big problem in a lot of places in the US, right? So the question has to do with habits, but it also has to do with infrastructure. And it is through the combination of the two that we can make substantial change. Public transportation could produce a huge new range of habits that expands beyond how we get to work in the morning to how we interact with each other. If everyone was waiting at the bus stop, relations between us would be very different than if everybody was getting in their cars. And so new habits learned around new infrastructures can lead to new relations with one another.

Take Cesar Chavez. He was a great leader and organizer of people, but the people also were organizing each other. There wasn't just the grape boycott; there were also strikes and unions. Together, they produced a huge infrastructure on the ground. We don't usually hear that collective version of the story because our taste for revolutionaries has overshadowed all the other work that needs to take place to actually produce a revolution. We want individual charisma and leadership so profound that it can change the world – but that's not actually how it happens. So, what is our theory of social change? It turns out, a lot of people think there is no social change. They think, I can't do anything. I have no power. I have no agency. I can recycle. I can bike to work, but that's it. And my individual recycling and biking won't be enough to have any impact, so what's the point? That kind of reasoning, which is all too common today, is really troubling to me.

TG: We seem to have inherited some of these attitudes from the 20th century, which instilled in us a strong cultural interest in revolutions and in individual protagonists. We love singular heroes in whom we can consolidate all the energy of a massive movement. Che Guevara, Le Corbusier, Steve Jobs, Zaha Hadid, the list goes on. This long-standing interest in the unified subject as the sole agent of change seems to be something you are explicitly arguing against.

Your aim seems to be to locate literary examples that shift attention away from works that valorize the single protagonist who solves all the problems, gets the girl, and rides off into the sunset and to pay more attention to the infrastructures at work. David Simon's television series, *The Wire*, which you write about at length in *Forms*, operates like that. When you and I taught *The Wire* together, we spent a lot of time with the students looking at Baltimore – the institutional structures, the bureaucratic structures, the social structures, and the neighborhoods. It was interesting that, even with so many amazing actors on screen, with so many great protagonists to root for, what made *The Wire* go was the web of relations, the network that tied all those protagonists together.

CL: People think of the novel as the consummate art form of the 19th and 20th centuries. A novel is good at a lot of things, but it is not good at thinking collectively. You have to think outside of the traditional novel to find works that are not protagonist-driven. So, what forms capture collective life better? I think photography is much better at giving us a sense of the crowd, for example. Think of the pictures of Tahrir Square in Cairo in 2011. You saw huge masses of people coming together. A novel just can't give you that. This sort of medium specificity is what has made me interested in affordances. What possibilities do some forms afford that others do not? How can we link together multiple forms to think the thoughts that we need to think? Most novel critics say, I want to think about climate change. I'm going to look at the novel. This may be fine, but it is also important to think about what the novel does not do. What do we need other forms to do when we're thinking about climate change? The collective piece is the crucial one. It is also something that takes me very far from my earlier work. Lyric poetry and the novel, the two great 19th-century forms which I've worked on for many years, are both individual-centered forms.

TG: I want to put another concept on the table that I think plays a role but is not a focus in *The Activist Humanist*: irony. In addition to our interest in outsized protagonists and revolutionary events, academics of the last 50 years have invested heavily in ironic critique. We use irony to wag a finger and point out problems. But when we do this, we also tend to valorize the omniscient narrator. In ironic critique, there is always a narrating subject who sees everything that's going on in a way that no one else does. Tafuri, of course, is a prime example, but he's far from the only one. You challenge us to disperse the protagonist, but another part is to disperse the tendency toward ironic detachment that we associate with the omniscient narrator or the know-it-all critic. Every generation seems to have its pet theorist who can do no wrong – in my lifetime, Foucault, Derrida, and Deleuze each played this role. Citations of their writing in critical texts functioned like gospel quotations in a sermon. Such rhetoric can rally us around an idea, but it can also distance us from the issues at hand. This sort of critical distance isn't doing anyone any good. Part of what we need, I think, is a new way of asking questions that is conscious of our tendency toward irony and critical detachment. I suspect that this sort of detachment is at least a symptom – but maybe it's a cause – of these claims of being unable to do anything other than what we've always done.

CL: You're right. Ironizing gives one the illusion of an outsider's take on the situation. But one of the problems with climate change is that we can't get outside of it. And if we can't ironize climate change, do we then just have to let it happen? Are detachment and capitulation the only relations we can have to it?

TG: I feel like those are the typical choices offered by a lot of criticism, and you provide a host of examples in your introduction to *The Activist Humanist*. We hear a lot of pronouncements about the horrific state of affairs today, but few specific proposals for how to change things. We are simply told that "further study is required." And when we do hear proposals for change, they often get picked apart by ironic critique. That said, I have to admit that I really enjoy ironic criticism, even if I've become impatient with its shortcomings. There's an extremely seductive music in a well-delivered quip. It can cut to the heart of a matter with devastating precision. Ironizing, I am convinced, still has its uses. Even so, my students today don't seem to share our generation's taste for irony. They seem much more earnest.

CL: What I struggle with in today's students is not earnestness but the other side of detachment, which is perfectionism. You're not going to get a perfect building, right? It's always going to be compromised by all kinds of other pressures. Can we live with the "good enough" building or the "good enough" university?

TG: In that sense, Dana Cuff's new book, *Architectures of Spatial Justice* [2023], is a great example. She describes her work with CityLab to implement zoning legislation in Los Angeles that allows for accessory dwelling units in the city. The ADUs increase density and available housing stock, provide revenue streams for homeowners, and provide affordability for renters. Of course, they also increase traffic, place strains on local infrastructure, and can hasten gentrification. In other words, ADUs are not perfect. But they are, Cuff argues, a step in the right direction. And if, to mitigate traffic problems, we also incentivize the use of public transportation over private cars, and to reduce strain on infrastructure we couple ADU construction with improvements to municipal services, and to guard against gentrification we develop fiscal policies to throttle rapid increases in rents, then we might be able to realize – or at least move toward – that still-utopian dream of a less car-dependent Los Angeles. ADU legislation is not glamorous. Iwan Baan probably won't show up to photograph it. But some of those ADUs that the legislation makes possible, by firms like Sharif, Lynch: Architecture, ByBen, and JK & Co, are also interesting as aesthetic objects. This wasn't the point of Cuff's research, but it is certainly a welcome side effect.

Cuff's book is filled with other examples – the work of Hitoshi Abe's ArchiAid in post-quake Japan, Alejandro Aravena's Half-Houses in Chile – that offer case studies in turning attention away from the singular architect and toward more collaborative modes of design and construction. These projects aren't revolutionary, but they are making more of an impact than revolutionary rhetoric alone could ever do.

CL: Right. It's not fancy or dramatic, but it's happening all over the place and could fundamentally change the way that architects work.

TG: I don't think we do a good enough job celebrating these incremental improvements, and it's time to change that. It's worth noting that we as a culture are more than capable of significant and rapid change. As you said, 50 years ago nobody wore seat belts. Now everyone does. Fifteen years ago, none of us had iPhones. Today we're addicted to them. Under the right circumstances, we are happy to adopt new ideas practically overnight.

CL: I know it was a politicized experience and patchy, but a number of us stayed home and changed our lives completely under Covid. We parented differently. We educated differently. It was clear a lot of people could transform their lives overnight. But there were a lot of us in the environmental movement who thought Covid would be a chance to regroup and to try new things. Instead, there was this huge push to go back to normal, which I think is too bad. I don't love Zoom, for example, but it's much better, in terms of carbon footprint, than flying somewhere and flying back, which is what people were routinely doing. I do think we're capable of change. And I think huge government programs have changed us. Not that I would endorse it at all, but certainly the Federal Highway Act changed our lives fundamentally. No one is the same as they were before that. The landscape was transformed. So, I agree. We're changing all the time. And some of these high-level actions could really save us if we have the will to implement them.

Todd Gannon is a *Log* protagonist and a professor of architecture at The Ohio State University.

*Michael Meredith
& Alex Da Corte*

A Conversation Pit

Michael Meredith's copy of *The House Book* by Terence Conran, 1974. 448 pages. Mitchell Beazley Publishers. Opposite page: Alex Da Corte, detail from *The Conversation Pit*, part of THE DÆMON, Matthew Marks Gallery, Los Angeles, September 24 – November 4, 2023. For color photographs of Da Corte's work, see pages 132–133.

I fell in love with Alex Da Corte's installation Rubber Pencil Devil *(2017). Maybe because it is set within a freestanding neon-lit structure based on Robert Venturi and Denise Scott Brown's Ghost House. In 2022, we met at the American Academy in Rome. I learned more about how he works. Alex is constantly constructing work with things around him, equal parts thoughtful and playful. There are references, some obvious, some less obvious. They're not references as quotation, but references as material. Everything is physical, in space. Each work is totalizing. All over. And there is color. A lot. For some reason, his combination of purples and reds have stuck with me. There is a general attitude that maybe some would call postmodern or pop, but I don't see that. His work is something else. This conversation happened as he was preparing a new exhibition at Matthew Marks Gallery in Los Angeles, titled* THE DÆMON. *His installation sets a group of colorful flocked sculptures in an all-white conversation pit that evokes Eero Saarinen's Miller House in Columbus, Indiana. Our conversation was about and around a conversation pit, and about the importance of conversation in general, to be talking with, listening to, and learning from others. – MM*

MICHAEL MEREDITH: Wow, a conversation pit! Looks wonderful! Your new show in LA is about Terence Conran's *The House Book*, is that right?

ALEX DA CORTE: It is! In my mind, every show is architectural and everything is sculpture. Even paintings. I'm always thinking about the word *installation*. A painting on the wall is an installation. How about you, do you know *The House Book*?

MM: We have that book, bought it a long time ago. It's actually on the shelf across from me in the studio. How do books end up where they do? We are constantly surrounded by them. It's next to a book on concrete construction details and another on theater design. It's large, beautiful, and outside of typical architectural discourse. It's more commercial, about decor, interiors, lifestyles, like an encyclopedic catalog of interiors that you can pick and choose, or sort of a decor version of the

"Transformations in Modern Architecture" exhibition at the Museum of Modern Art. In my architectural world, Conran's house book is probably considered anti-intellectual, but I've always been both repulsed and fascinated by interior design and lifestyle stuff.

ADC: The book encourages you to build your house a certain way. But who actually built their house like that? I wonder who, if anyone, actually employed all of its ideas. The book is a manual for creating an environment – they don't quite say a "safe space" – where everything is warm, carpeted, and tailored to suit you and your ego. It's all about you. To me, that's not architecture.

MM: The conversation pit was definitely a big part of *The House Book*. It was a space for a certain kind of social lifestyle. Do you want your installation to be a place for hanging out and having a conversation?

ADC: I don't know if there's a conversation. When I was making *THE DÆMON*, I kept referring to Thomas Eakins's painting *The Gross Clinic* [1875]. Everyone was confused because it isn't a picture of a conversation pit. It's a painting of a surgery in a medical theater. These spaces were set up like arenas – think of the Colosseum. It's a space between what is being looked at, the body of the patient, and the spectators. The surgeons have cut open the patient's leg. It's a surgery on a femur.

MM: Inside and outside simultaneously, literally.

ADC: But is there a conversation happening in that arena, in the show, in the conversation pit? Sure. There is a dialog on color, form, history, etc., but it's also about absence. No one's there, no one can go there, there is no body. What do you make of a conversation pit without a conversation? It's just a hole.

MM: Sealed off in its own world.

ADC: Well, maybe this is a question for you. When an architect makes a conversation pit now, is it understood as kitsch or pastiche or nostalgia or irony? I'm not interested in those registers at all, but how do you think about architectural tropes when you're not trying to make a stylistic gesture?

MM: I don't know what it means to do a conversation pit nowadays, regarding style. We try to avoid style, but work is always interpreted. We are usually starting with the things around us, looking, listening, reacting. If the conversation pit seals the inside and outside together somehow, we might try to expand it to include other things, other conversations. There is never just one conversation. We work with both noncompositional, art-historical models, vernacular construction traditions, and material economy – concepts that weren't part of our formal education. We are also working with things as taught to us. There are many little games that we play out in our work as a project evolves. Usually those are informal conversations in our studio about if and why we like or dislike what we're doing – things like proportions, use, economy, material, composition, effects of movement, or stability. We used to be more explicit about those games as part of our process, but now we talk about it less and we're more focused on being in the world, part of a community, and working with other people. Architecture is always a conversation with others. It is not something that happens on its own or through just one person. This is what makes it difficult. Do you feel like you're reacting to things around you?

ADC: I'm always reacting to something. My work transgresses some kind of inner thing from an outside space and pokes holes or disrupts things. I'm interested in a certain violence against a typical process or a standardized way of thinking about or seeing the world. Convention is irritating to me, the expectation of what something is supposed to be annoys me. I just think that people get lazy, they settle into routines, and they get stuck seeing the world in a fixed way. I'm interested in pushing the limits of how we hold space and how we navigate a place that's always changing. I'm thinking about how architecture can shape a space, or a site, and make you feel things.

MM: We're all Alice in Wonderland, inhabiting other people's constructions, their fantasies, sometimes tall, sometimes small, although someone's fantasy is another's nightmare.

ADC: Smaller or taller or more religious in Wonderland, or maybe more interested in spending money. A few years ago, I read this series of essays by Ralph Rugoff about art in the '80s called *Scene of the Crime*. The premise was that artists were working with the idea of "evidence," almost an invisible material or space. Like a forensic investigation, the subject of the art was not what was there but what was absent. The crime scene is another kind of site for discourse that is not necessarily *about* the crime. To me, *The Conversation Pit* is not about a conversation that happens in it, it's just a site for something else.

MM: I have never thought of your work this way. I see the violence, the horror of the world we are all born into, the attempts to work against the perception that everything is settled – history, meaning, conventions. But there is always beauty, too, and humor. I'm sure you know the image from the 1931 Beaux Arts Ball, with William Van Alen dressed as the Chrysler Building. It reminds me of the costumes for an opera in Venice, *Il Corso del Coltello*, that Claes Oldenburg made

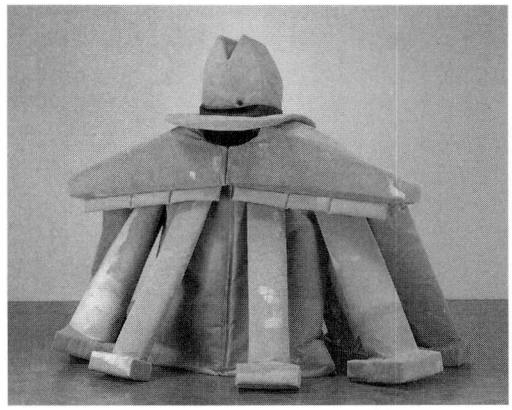

Claes Oldenburg & Coosje van Bruggen, *Frankie P. Toronto Costume*, 1986. Canvas filled with soft polyurethane foam, painted with latex. Courtesy of Pace Gallery, New York. © Claes Oldenburg and Coosje van Bruggen.

with Frank Gehry. This one is a kind of alter ego for Gehry himself: *Frankie P. Toronto*.

ADC: That is incredible. I had no idea about this project. I just looked it up: *Il Corso del Coltello*, the course of the knife. I've always wanted to make a video where four guys dress up like famous buildings, maybe even four New York museums: The Met, Breuer's Whitney, MoMA, and the Guggenheim. And then they wrestle WWE Smackdown!–style. The Beaux Arts Ball is where that idea came from, actually.

MM: Count me in, if you're looking for performers. Is architecture often a point of departure for you?

ADC: I always start a show thinking about the space in terms of the architecture but also where it is located, what was there before. Venturi, Scott Brown's "ghost" architecture appealed to me because it explicitly conjured an image of something no longer there. But, say, for my show on the rooftop of The Met – which was related to a single factoid about the site of the museum in Central Park – as soon as I realized that the only other significant architecture in the park is the zoo, I had defined my problem. It's not a problem

Alex Da Corte, *As Long As the Sun Lasts*, The Metropolitan Museum of Art, New York, 2021. Photo: Anna-Marie Kellen

at all but rather a set of ideas that shape how people exist and perceive things in a place. I began analyzing the problem, and I began to wonder whether the way we had been living in this place was the best use of the land and of our resources. And that's how I made *As Long As the Sun Lasts*.

MM: Every place starts out as a crime scene. Every place has already had something happen there. We can never escape history or ourselves.

ADC: That is the case for any work I make. It always relates to the house or the idea of the home and the body within it and outside of it, on the street. I did a show of reverse-glass paintings earlier this year that began by thinking about Venturi, Scott Brown's writings on Main Street and the city of Philadelphia. The gallery was on Broad Street, which is where the city's Mummers Parade is held on New Year's Day. It's the oldest recurring folk parade in the country, and it's freighted with very problematic ideas about minstrelsy. I began thinking about newer, radical parades and performances in the street, like Oldenburg's *The Street* and *The Store*. Then I began creating a space that could move between an internal site, like a home, and the outer street. When I began dissecting those binaries, I kept landing on glass and the window as my transitional space, a nonbinary space.

MM: You were working on *The Glass Age* project with Prada then?

ADC: Right. I was thinking about that metaphor for when your parents pass away. They say when your parents die, it's like a sheet of glass comes down. Eventually you'll walk into it, it'll break, and then you have to just walk through it. But you can't ever prepare for when you're going to walk into that sheet of glass. You just know that eventually you will. I have happened to walk through it twice – not with my parents, but with a serious illness falling out of the sky – so I started thinking about that.

MM: Like you said, there is a conversation about form, color, and history in your installation, but there is also an ongoing conversation about being human that runs throughout your work.

ADC: The question for me is, What is it to experience things in a double way? One mode is to experience form, color, and history as aesthetic dimensions of culture, but the other sense is more fundamental, physically in space. We're experiencing and perceiving the world that way all the time because we have our bodies and are inside our bodies. Even if we are "posthuman," my body is still falling apart – I contend with it every day. For me, the image of the constant grappling with this binary of being both inside and outside is glass. It is ambiguous, both material and transparent, clear but unclear, solid but fragile. I am exploring that unresolved state of being. That goal isn't unique to me. Years ago the Pictures Generation showed us what it was like for people to relate to the world in an age of television. Before that, pop artists explored how people related to extreme capitalism, advertising, and so on. It just makes sense to me that 100 years after the invention of plate glass and this way of looking, glass has profoundly influenced how we live and who we are.

MM: Hilary [Sample] and I are always looking and listening, and we're constantly responding by writing, making books, creating videos, or making more generally. We were once asked to talk about our favorite space for an exhibition on housing, and we chose the window. For us, it's a space where inside and outside meet, but it's ambiguous, nonbinary, interior, and exterior. Color is another ambiguous space. It doesn't have dimensions in the way that architectural space has depth and volume. Color is a consistent element in your work. Even though the work can be violent or strange, it's always beautiful because you're a great colorist. And even when the colors change, as in some of the video works, there's an attitude about color that seems constant.

ADC: I would say that color holds space in particular ways that evade fixed meanings or qualities. Even if it's color on a wall, it can hold memories and be fluid in how it relates to light or to the taste of the viewer. But, really, my color is not remarkable. I'm literally just copying what I see. Sometimes it's a blue that Walt Disney decided to put next to a certain shade of purple or green. For me, that was just recognizing a kind of intelligence about color. It's what you would do if you were an animator working for Disney. It's the same color logic, somewhat related to opponent colors.

MM: It's a kind of color theory, but it's not coming from high culture. It's not Josef Albers, it's not Goethe's color wheel, and it's not even complementary colors, exactly.

ADC: It's not complementary colors, no, but opponent colors. When they get together, they make white light, or an even light. Opponent colors ground each other, neutralize, or cancel each other out, in a way. This can happen with all sorts of different colored light. That's why when you're in a dark room, say, and see light coming in underneath the door, it seems to have a certain color, even though you know it's "white." Oftentimes, it seems yellow because dark rooms are generally blue. It's not that the light is yellow, it's just that your eyes are adjusting for difference between these opponent colors. I'm not so interested in actual specified color, but in its effect, or even evidence. To put it very bluntly, I care about what color does.

MM: Are there certain colors that recur or echo in your work? In *The Conversation Pit*, for instance, the Castiglioni-designed Lampadina Table Lamp and the potted plant are both green, but are they the same green?

ADC: They're all bespoke. The colors are specific to each piece. In *The Conversation Pit*, the red pot is the heart of the whole show. The heart's been kind of sabotaged. The pot has been knocked over, so the heart is positioned in the center and everything else is around that, positioned in relation to it.

MM: Did you pick the red as a result of that idea, or did the idea emerge as a result of the color? The knocked over pot is where I noticed something's awry, and because the hue is so bright, it demands your attention. Many of Gustave Caillebotte's paintings have a single dot, or daub, of red in them that directs your eye in a certain direction.

ADC: The idea came first. That red on the pot is the blood. It's the heart, the center, and everything else ripples out from there. I use red and red-orange quite a bit. It's like a brick red.

MM: We like red bricks. We like colorful objects floating around in our projects. But color has been a fraught subject in architecture for a long time and is hardly discussed in any serious way these days. There's a common misconception that modern architecture was all about white walls, glass, concrete, and maybe some chrome. But the modernists were obsessed with color. Le Corbusier published several books on color, and Bruno Taut even dreamed up utopian cities and structures filled with color and polychromatic light. That started as early as 1914, when Taut designed this pine cone–shaped Glass Pavilion for a trade fair in Cologne. Ironically, photographs of the building are only in black and white, but it was a riot of colored glass. For Taut, a world made full of color would be a world full of free spirits and endless creativity. He enlisted his friends and colleagues in the idea, and they circulated letters and drawings between them, calling themselves a circle of "imaginary architects."

ADC: Wow. This is incredible. I am an "imaginary architect." Taut's idea of connective tissue between ideas reminds me of a thing my friend Kim once said and I repeat often. She said, "Our lives are not our own." Our lives are like Legos – reliant on each other in wholly good ways, ways that suppress ego and promote conversation, collaboration, and progress for a whole.

MM: I totally agree. Artists, architects – anyone, really – we are a group of people. Life is a collaboration, and work is a collaboration. There are no other models of architecture. There is no single heroic architect and there never was. That's another modern misconception. Architecture always relies on others. Maybe art is different, but I have a sense that you run your studio like we run our architecture practice.

ADC: My studio is very collaborative. There are many different skill sets and many projects progressing simultaneously. It's everything from music videos and film to sculpture and installations. At the same time, teaching is also a big part of my work. I'm constantly researching and feeding the studio's thinking at the same time that we are producing. I know that you and Hilary teach as well. What are you working on now?

MM: We're doing many things, a mix of real projects for buildings, objects, academic research, imaginary experiments, and personal creative things – ceramics, music, or cutouts. We work across multiple formats. We make a mess. I don't try to make sense of it at this point. For better or worse, we don't neatly follow the logic of capitalism. There's no bread-and-butter professional project for us. Right now we are designing apartments, furniture, a greenhouse, a few small houses, some interiors and additions, housing, a winery, and also some rugs that we're irrationally excited about. If nothing else, I think what matters most to us is who we are in conversation with. Hilary and I are lucky to be in constant dialog with one another, and at the same time, constantly engaging with the people around us. Those conversations evolve and build on one another, like stacking blocks, and in the end, these friendships and conversations with different people and with histories, technologies, ideas, buildings, inanimate objects, furniture, artworks – basically the world as we experience it – matter more to us than any single project.

Michael Meredith guest edited *Log* 22: The Absurd (2011). He teaches at the Princeton University School of Architecture and practices architecture, with his partner Hilary Sample, at MOS.

Peter Eisenman & Valerio Olgiati

Making Sense of The Non-Referential

Since the publication of George Baird and Charles Jencks's collection of essays, Meaning in Architecture, *in 1969, the best theoretical works on the discipline of architecture and its transformation from modernism to postmodernism have been concerned with the evolution of meaning and the nature of signing. Today, as architecture faces another transition, from postmodernism to the digital, and more specifically to artificial intelligence, one book strikes a chord in the struggle for disciplinary renewal. It is a small book titled* Non-Referential Architecture, *"ideated" by Swiss architect Valerio Olgiati and written by architectural theorist Markus Breitschmid. In it, seven principles, not unlike Le Corbusier's five points, are articulated in a straightforward manner: Experience of Space; Oneness; Newness; Construction; Contradiction; Order; Sensemaking. In an attempt to open Olgiati's thinking to examination, I asked him to talk about the idea of non-referential architecture. Olgiati and I agreed on a dialog via email. What follows are my questions to Olgiati and his replies. – PE*

PETER EISENMAN: First and foremost, I am interested in what you mean by *non-referential*. I am working on what I assume to be a similar theme: what I call the becoming unmotivated of the sign – that is, that there is no one-to-one relationship between the sign and the signified, or in Derrida's terms, a free play. Is non-referential something similar?

VALERIO OLGIATI: I can only speak from my perspective as a thinking and building architect who tracks down social issues and tries to incorporate them into his work. What I call non-referential could be something similar to free play. In my opinion, the fact that there is no one-to-one relationship between the sign and the signified, as you say, is no longer a utopia that we strive for and hope for, but rather a fact.

    Since the 1960s, some leading architects have made many attempts to destroy the valid one-to-one relationship. This was, so to speak, an attempt at liberation. The free and individual interpretability of form, and also the making of form, has become more and more a reality during postmodernism. I am convinced that we have reached the end point of modernity, or postmodernity, in this regard and have now exceeded it. We live in a heterogeneous world, a world characterized by polyvalence, pluralism, and diversity. We are drowning in a shoreless ocean of lack of intention and a thousand desires. With the seven principles in *Non-Referential Architecture*, I want to explain how buildings can be done today with a certain degree of universality. The question we architects face is no longer, as it was in the postmodern era, how we break out of conventions, but rather how we break in. Into a contemporary world without conventions and valid agreements, into a world in which we can and should be a part. In my book I describe how architecture can be freed from the extra-architectural in order to free itself from interpretability – to be freed from everything that determines a building as an expression of an individual's view or of the beliefs of a specific group. But this does not mean indifference to the ideas of buildings. In any case, global society can no longer understand views and beliefs in a universally valid way. I am convinced that in our day and age, a building can only be grasped and positively experienced if its spatial nature, and not its message, is determined by a meaningful idea.

PE: What is the difference between non-referential – that is, no longer symbolic and reliant on images – and buildings that have to be significant? Does non-referential equal significant?

VO: The question is how we define significance. I understand significant as something that is essential. To your question: yes, if a building successfully and skillfully follows the principles of non-referential architecture, it will be essential. Buildings today that base their core message on projected narratives cannot be essential. By projected narratives I mean what you mentioned – symbols and images that determine the expression of a building or even become buildings themselves. Such buildings may be able to reach the masses but they cannot achieve essentiality because they ultimately imitate something that is defined and imposed from outside. They have no being of their own and they don't make us creative. We see this in the contemporary architecture of icons which try to speak of themselves through the expression of assembled images and bore us after a short time. The Eiffel Tower, the Sydney Opera House, and the Guggenheim Bilbao, some great icons, derive from their own and inherent reasons and still do not bore us today.

I think the use of symbols and images to define the essence of entire buildings was mainly introduced in parallel with the emergence of product marketing. While it was still practiced as advertising in the 1960s, marketing was practiced from the 1980s onward. Since then, this sales technique has been used by architects, sometimes very successfully, to promote themselves, mainly to laypeople, to secure market shares, and to create identities. The new basis from which we must start today is the new society. Our global, polyvalent society functions differently than it did in the second half of the 20th century, when there were only two sides of the Wall and people understood each other. The people who determine what is happening in the world today grew up in different cultures and different political systems. They read images in different ways and associate their meanings in divergent ways. This means nothing other than that a building that tries to explain its existence primarily through its images can no longer make a meaningful, essential, and recognizable statement, because, as I said, as imitations buildings have nothing essential to say and because there is no longer any real consensus about what such images and symbols want to say.

PE: You suggest that buildings must be "of their time." Isn't "of their time" an ideological construct – that is, historicizing?

VO: You are right, that could be understood as ideological, but this is not my intention. Actually, at this point in the book I just want to say that non-referential architecture cannot refer to historical models.

PE: You say that there is a demand for newness in a non-referential world. Why? Buildings "of their time" are not necessarily new.

VO: I use newness not as a categorization but as a compositional tool. With this topic, I am speaking to architects who want to design and build buildings today. Everything I explain in the book about generating the actual architectural form is aimed at the human sensory experience of a building. Newness has the power to engage and move people who are standing in front of or inside a building. The question is, How can a building make people creative? Everything we already know provokes us only a little and does not stimulate our curiosity. Newness, however, provokes and challenges the senses and the intellect. If we look at the history of art, even today, we are only fascinated by those artists who created something new. I would say a good artist is one who says or does something that no one has said or done before.

PE: In the book, you say that ordering systems imbue buildings with a coherence and that coherence is the "sensemaking" in our non-referential world. Coherence, for me, is not new. Also, order is not new as a means to sensemaking. Help me here!

VO: I say ordering systems imbue a building with a coherence, but I am not saying that coherence alone has the ability to make sense. A building needs coherence through ordering

Peter Eisenman's copy of *Non-Referential Architecture*, ideated by Valerio Olgiati, written by Markus Breitschmid, 2018. 141 pages. Park Books.

systems for it to be able to develop sense. I understand your confusion. In today's world, which I describe as non-referential, it no longer makes sense to work with ordering systems alone. At a time when agreement and its corresponding ordering systems are disappearing, such systems, applied in isolation and however defined, can no longer create a comprehensible understanding. They float in a vacuum, so to speak. I would like to emphasize here that I consider any form of architectural classicism, applied today, to be outdated or irrelevant. The consequence of all of this is that it is impossible for further deconstruction of any system to make any relevant statement. We have arrived in the deconstructed world and now live in it.

PE: So in a non-referential world, the only way to conceive of buildings is through making sense! Why? Is this another form of rationalism?

VO: Because the world is divided and a common understanding is nonexistent. By *sense* I do not mean questions of being as such. In my book, when I talk about how a building should make sense, I mean that a building should trigger understanding and inspiration in the people in that building. In my opinion, it is precisely this new society that is the biggest challenge for us architects. We architects create spaces. My focus is on that. Experience in space is universal. Spaces have the ability to be universal. Humans have the urge to find sense in basic experiences. And sense organizes the world and connects people. Regarding your question about rationalism, perhaps my point of view can also be described as a type of rationalism. However, my view has no connection to the historical rationalisms, the ideology of classical or functional tectonics.

PE: The word *sense*, in English, has two meanings: To make sense of something is to understand it, and to have sense is to experience something physically. I think you are talking about the latter, while I am more interested in the former, or at least in both meanings. My idea of unmotivated signs is of empty signs, signs without meaning, like the words and letters in Ed Ruscha's paintings that don't mean anything other than their objecthood. To experience their full objecthood without meaning (or sense, in your terms) is what I mean. I realize we mean the opposite, because I thought non-referential meant without necessary meaning.

VO: I also like doing something that doesn't make sense. Something that doesn't need to be understood. This is very rebellious! Especially in a society driven by restrictive morals, it is a great and divine feeling to be able to make pure objects without meaning. In my opinion, however, this feeling when reaching an object without meaning is only possible from a nostalgic perspective. For my part, I have great feelings when I create an object that is itself coherent. Ruscha is, of course, wonderful. I understand why you like him, but I like Mark Rothko the most.

PE: In the book, you say sensemaking saves form from formalism. Why?

VO: Architects didn't have to explain themselves until the 1990s. Our discipline had fixed and well-known rules. Architects could either build with them or against them. An architect who then created form, whatever form, without intention and without a goal, worked according to the general and agreed upon rules of architecture. Buildings that today determine their appearance solely for formal-logical reasons are ultimately self-referential and can neither reach society as a whole nor move an individual person. As I said, I am of the opinion that we no longer just dream of the polyvalent world but that it now fully exists, and buildings that have no sensemaking aspect disappear in the flood of images and opinions. People are no longer willing or even able to perceive such buildings. So, what is our basis for working without a consensus on shared values? Even a conceived and constructed building of our time, which is designed exclusively methodically in terms of form, cannot develop any meaning in the conscious experience of the inhabitant. That is why I would objectively describe a building without any aspect of sensemaking as formalism.

PE: Ultimately you suggest that architects like Rem Koolhaas and Frank Gehry have left the modern project behind. Koolhaas and Gehry are very different! Koolhaas is an ideologue, Gehry a form giver. Both are critical, one as a form maker, the other a sensemaker… difficult to sustain your argument if they are the same!

VO: I think they are both at the transition from modern to new era, and I didn't say they are the same. I appreciate both very much, otherwise I wouldn't have mentioned them in my book. What connects the two is that they are exponents of architectural modernity. By *modernity* I mean more or less the 20th century. Gehry was the first to dismantle the classical order and to create something that was fascinatingly new. Of course, he didn't have to explain himself because at some point, during his time of shared values, everyone understood what he was doing. Gehry is a successful brand today, but the roots that support his work no longer exist. Koolhaas is a great thinker and has built decisive things. In his projects he actually dealt with questions of quantity. He practiced the functioning of architectural structures to the extreme. His buildings are imbued with scientific passion. But they also need to be understood so that they can develop their meaning. Whether someone like Koolhaas can continue to inspire architects today depends on how far our individualized society will turn away from reason.

PE: One last thing. Mirko Zardini, whom you know, wrote an essay titled "Toward a Sensorial Urbanism" to introduce an exhibition at the Canadian Centre for Architecture called "Sense of the City." I believe his idea is more like what you intend by non-referential. I was thinking your project was also signs without meaning, but this is not your project. This is particularly true when it comes to your references to Christian Norberg-Schulz and Peter Zumthor, who are close to phenomenology.

VO: I can only give a reduced answer here, because I don't really see the connections you are making. Do you believe that a physical object, even one that only represents its objecthood, can be experienced and understood without phenomenological consideration? I cannot imagine that. Even Ruscha's work can only be perceived coherently as an appearance. However, I can confirm that my project is not signs without meaning. *Non-Referential Architecture* describes a set of considerations on Experience of Space, Oneness, Newness, Construction, Contradiction, Order, and Sensemaking.

PE: The last of your seven points, sensemaking, is the most challenging for me. We will have to try to understand our differences regarding its meaning in the future.

Peter Eisenman, an architect and teacher, guest edited, with Anthony Vidler, *Log* 28: Stocktaking (2013), in which they presented a series of interviews on the state of architecture – exactly 10 years ago.

One day we woke up and realized we couldn't care less about what happens in Paris.

We do what they told us not to do. Our way of doing things seems suicidal to business schools:

> Our garments smell of smoke—they are woven and embroidered next to the stove. We create few of them, and we do it slowly.
>
> We're like grasshoppers in the field: small but rambunctious.
>
> We work in a country in which 68 different languages are spoken. Textiles are our lingua franca. Among ourselves we speak in fingers, palms, and cubits.
>
> We use fabrics that were woven to be treasured. A huipil is an open book.
>
> Its brocades tell the story of how a caterpillar morphs into a butterfly. The same rectangle that is a skirt in the morning becomes a mat in the afternoon and a blanket at night.

It's up to us to put an end to fashion as trash. We don't design garments to end up rotting in a dump.

We say no to bloodsucking transnational corporations and to the mass production that is so detrimental to our planet.

Anonymous assembly is for the plunderers of souls.

No to the false neoliberal urgency that season after season prioritizes volume over care.

No to the uniform. No to malinchismo—to the vile automated consumerism that favors all things foreign.

Let's not fool ourselves. We all participate in fashion.

Yes to insubordinate creativity.

Yes to work free of distress.

Florencia Pita & Carla Fernández

Ephemerality Will Kill Us All

Manifesto of Fashion as Resistance by Carla Fernández, 2017. 62 pages. Opposite page: The introduction to the manifesto. All images courtesy Carla Fernández.

Designer Carla Fernández and her eponymous fashion house, based in Mexico City, are dedicated to preserving and revitalizing the textile heritage of Indigenous and mestizo communities in Mexico. The brand's vision of the value of manual methods proves that ethical fashion can be innovative, avant-garde, and progressive. Carla articulated her approach to fashion in her 2017 Manifesto of Fashion as Resistance, *which contains 10 points. The first five are about our relationship to nature, and the second five points deal with issues of labor and society. Our conversation took place over Zoom on October 17, 2023. – FP*

FLORENCIA PITA: Carla, I would like to focus on the first five points of your manifesto, as I believe they relate conceptually to environmental thinking and our relationship to nature. In your manifesto the notion of "fashion" is shifted away from the idea that garments are commodities and instead thought of as natural objects. Here, garments are cultural artifacts that are made and fabricated with the environment and not on the environment. Could you talk about why you wrote the manifesto? Then we can go through those points.

CARLA FERNÁNDEZ: Yes. Well, I am an art historian as well as a seamstress. I couldn't study fashion in Mexico because there was no degree for it. While I was studying art history at the Universidad Iberoamericana, I was learning how to be, and also working as, a seamstress – how to sew, how to create garments from scratch. Not designing but making them. I've loved fashion since I was very young. I was born in a country that at the time [in the '80s] was looking to the United States and trying to be part of this "neoliberal" culture, even though Mexico is very culturally diverse with Indigenous communities – we have 68 different living languages in my country, plus, of course, the Spanish.

So I was born in a country where I was told we didn't have fashion. But I traveled a lot around Mexico, and I saw that we have the most amazing fashion one could ever dream of being worn by Indigenous women and men. It was interesting how blind we were to that cultural expression. I think that fashion is one of the major cultural expressions of humanity. We have made clothing since the beginning of time, not just for survival but to express ourselves and our community.

When I started being interested in fashion, in high school, I dressed very extravagantly. The administrators would call me in – and this was a contemporary and open-mind school. I didn't understand why they were so afraid of my attire. I used to wear pink skirts and neon colors because that was the trend, and I couldn't understand why it was unacceptable for the teachers. So I learned the power of clothing, that something as simple as color could have an effect on people.

After traveling with my parents and seeing the complexity and beauty of Mexican traditional attire, I understood that we live in a country of textiles. And I wanted to work with the best designers and artisans from Mexico, from the mountains to the deserts. These artisans have a history of 3,000 years of making garments, a knowledge that has been transferred from mothers to daughters in a continuous exchange. As a designer I come to these communities not as somebody from the city to tell them what to do but to learn with them. At our fashion house, we decided early on that we would all collaborate in these creative processes

At first, I think I wrote the manifesto just to clarify in my mind what we believe is the way to make fashion. It's also understanding the Indigenous knowledge of textiles and this equilibrium with the land and with community. That's how we make fashion. I wanted everyone involved in our fashion house to understand what we are working toward and what we are proposing as a fashion system.

FP: The first point in the manifesto is the idea that "to be original is to go back to the origin." This doubling of original/origin puts into question where ideas come from and how they can be made anew. How do you work with Indigenous communities and yet create original work?

CF: Well, it's not me who makes it original. The origin of all these textiles and beautiful attires is what makes it original. One of the biggest misconceptions of people from cities, those who are more attached to the Industrial Revolution, is that Indigenous communities are static. No, they evolve.

Let's think about the backstrap loom, which consists of sticks, rope, and a strap that is worn around the weaver's waist. The sticks are taken from the mountains, and for the rope, you can grow your own cotton so you are completely independent [of markets] and do not devastate the earth, as you only use what is necessary. Here you are relying on your human capacities and your environment.

It's very interesting to say that it's not original because it's static, when it's completely the opposite. It's thousands and thousands of years of generation after generation developing one technique that allows us to live in accordance with our environment instead of making many identical, soulless objects that are designed to be thrown away.

It's important to understand that to be original is to go back to the origins because there is nothing more beautiful than a handmade process in which the artisan sees what is in the environment, takes it, and processes it in her mind. They have these mathematical minds. Then it goes through the heart because it's made with a lot of love. You will take care of that garment and the knowledge that comes with it.

When you make something slowly, it's like walking. When you walk somewhere, you notice what's happening around you. It's the pace that we're given as humans – our legs. We walk slowly and see the sky, see the flowers. Even with a bicycle, you don't get that – and even less in a car. That is the

Serafina Ruiz Arias using a backstrap loom, San Pedro Chenalhó, Chiapas, Mexico. Photo: Ana Hop. For color photographs of Carla Fernández's work, see pages 138–139.

origin I am talking about, the complexity and beauty of being original that comes from these origins. One hundred years ago, even my grandmother was making her own clothing. It was clothing meant to last, made with love, and not meant to be discarded.

FP: I understand that for you what makes something original is not necessarily the concept of novelty but rather of longevity, of garments that are meant to last. This brings me to the second point in your manifesto, the idea that "fashion is not ephemeral." We can think of ephemerality in abstract terms. For example, fast fashion is ephemeral in terms of trends and styles, but is nonephemeral once it goes to the landfill. Here, longevity is parallel to the long life span of nylon and polyester, two staple materials of fast fashion.

I believe your work is both nonephemeral and ephemeral. In terms of the forms, styles, and processes, your work can last forever, each of your garments can be collected, cherished, and passed on to future generations. But it is also ephemeral because it is made of natural materials, the textiles and fabrics can go back to the land and disintegrate.

CF: Well, I was referring to fashion as an industry. Fashion is always changing. When you say something is fashionable, it means that it will only be around for a few moments, and another fashion will replace it, and then another. It's always replacing itself. That's why I think it was important for me to say that it is not ephemeral, because when your mind is connected with these fashion systems, everything seems like it has to change as fast as it can. New clothing arrives at the style racks, I think, every 10 days or less. The replacement of fashion and the replacement of trends – it's so fast and incredibly sick.

I understand what you say about the textiles and the fabrics, but in the terms of the manifesto, I was saying that fashion is not ephemeral. We have to relearn clothing. It's not disposable nor should it be. Fashion is one of the most polluting industries in the world because of that sickness of replacing and replacing. And then what do you do? Not even the vintage movement or recycling will end it. Ephemerality will kill us all. It's killing us already. The fabrication, water contamination, production of cotton – cotton needs a lot of water, even more if it's organic – and the issues of labor and production around clothing are all devastating. That's why we need to start thinking of fashion as something that you will use and cherish.

And I like what you said, and we say it in another part of the manifesto. When you use fabrics that are made naturally, of course, you can discard them. For example, these buttons are made of shell, and this is linen and cotton. So when you dispose of these, they will be absorbed by the earth, but still, we cannot think that way. I did a very important study to see how many times you need to use a tote bag made of cotton to be sustainable. It's around 70,000 times. So you have to be very careful of that.

FP: The conversations regarding the role and mechanisms of industrialization in fast fashion apply to architecture as well, maybe we can call it fast architecture. It is a question not only of the life span of buildings but also of the sourcing of materials and the design process. Parallel to what is called the fashion industry, we say the construction industry. The meaning of *industry* relates to production and manufacturing procedures. In both cases, once the designer is detached from manufacturing, removed from material sources and fabrication, then our labor as designers becomes industrialized. Your work is a reminder to think beyond industrial production and to engage traditional manufacturing techniques as a way to connect back to the things we build.

The third point in your manifesto is "tradition is not static." Today we look at something that is traditional in opposition to what is contemporary or new, yet your point is that tradition is constantly being remade.

If I look back at my own history, growing up in Argentina, I question what would be an Argentinean tradition. The answer would bring hybrid results because what we call Western culture is so ingrained in the customs of the country that notions of local and nonlocal become mingled. Yet, if we think about your point on transmission, then these constantly evolving traditions become our current cultural references.

In Latin America, the fact that tradition is not static means that there are things that are the combinations of Western and pre-Columbian cultures, which can enrich or erase traditions. How does the concept of the nonstatic evolve for you culturally?

CF: It's important to demonstrate what we talked about earlier, that people tend to think that all of these beautiful processes, like making clothing that looks similar to what we have seen before, are static, but they're not. It's a process of observation in accordance with nature and believing that we humans are part of a whole, not that we are on top of the world. This is why these processes can be similar to what they were 3,000 or 5,000 years ago. And that is why the Western world has tried to erase these knowledges.

There are trends even in these communities – things change and evolve. In some ways, that fashion changes even more than ours. For example, if you compare how people in cities dressed in the '70s to today, it's the same pants, the same colors, the same jeans, the same T-shirt. But if you look at traditional garments, you see that the flowers are completely different, that there are more birds, that there are contemporary messages on their attire, and so on. And that it's very different in the motives they are exposing. Maybe it's not the silhouette that has changed or the technique but a text that is read on the textile.

I always say that textiles were the first language we communicated with. It's important to understand the textile as an evolution of the world because textiles and weaving are one of the models of human evolution. Technology today still uses the same language for making, the same binary language that comes from the loom. The Industrial Revolution started because of the loom. The Aztecs started their empire because of cotton. The importance of textiles for humans is in how we solve problems in order to wear them, the complex cultural significance they have for us, and now, of course, their ecological, political, and social impacts.

FP: I was trying to point out that the idea of tradition does not belong to a single country or culture. For example, looking at your collections, the Diego Denim Trousers are made out of denim. Denim was first produced in the 17th century, in Nîmes, France. It was popularized in the 19th-century California Gold Rush, with Levi Strauss & Co. We can say that demin went global. The loom itself is also global, is something we all share. There is some kind of loom in every culture around the globe. So the question of where things "belong" is a tricky one. Your fourth point in the manifesto is quite relevant in this examination of cultural references.

This point is titled "square root." Its mathematical meaning describes the value that, when multiplied by itself, produces a given number. If we think of this not as mathematical but as a compound word then it can be thought of as what the writer Bruna Mori calls an open compound word, because the two words sit side by side. One word is *square*, a geometry, and the second is *root*, or origin. Both geometry and origin come together here in a kind of "original geometry."

I know that in your research, the square form is rooted in Mexico's Indigenous garment culture, which is in clear opposition to the human-centric profiles and silhouettes of Western garment pattern designs, which are based in curvature. So how do you combine the two forms, the two cultures?

CF: Well, for me, understanding the way of making clothing in my country was the starting point of our work. About 30 years ago, I started working with artisans because of a program by the government to establish liaisons between artisans and designers. The artisans were trying to please a market that was foreign to their culture – we all, of course, want to sell. If we are merchants and craftspeople attending to a foreign market, we need to hear and to understand what they're asking us. They would ask us for new designs because they didn't like the silhouettes of Indigenous clothing. Indigenous garments are very geometrical because they depart from squares and rectangles.

Are you familiar with huipiles? They're like kimonos, which is why people think our clothing can be very Japanese. Kimonos and huipiles are pretty similar because they depart from the same union of squares and rectangles. When we started trying to make Western designs with the traditional techniques, it was a disaster. You can't put a buttonhole through something woven on a backstrap loom because it unravels, and you can't cut a curved armhole in a square huipil. Trying to cut seams like that is a disaster because the textiles are very thick and difficult to sew by hand.

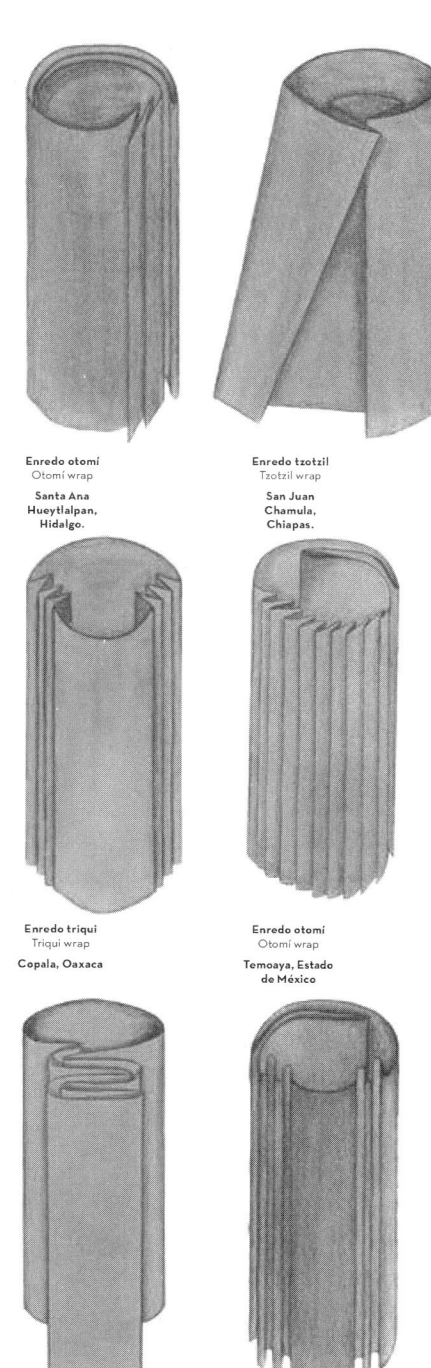

Carla Fernández, diagram of folding and pleating techniques for various *enredos*, wraparound skirts found across Mexico.

So I started to understand the endemic way of making clothing and how we could depart from that to make these designs that belong to our own language. This is what we call the square root. It's a play on words because, of course, it's the square root in mathematics and also the roots of our clothing, mixed with squares and rectangles. When we changed our design strategy to relate to the forms of the Indigenous weaving patterns, it was very successful.

One of the most terrible things imposed on us as humans is uniformity. Everything looks the same. Every single chair in the world looks the same, every smell smells the same, every store looks the same. These things don't come from handmade processes or artisanal projects. When you can use your own tools as a design statement, while still being handmade, you can make new things. It's very cool because you have this diversity. That is the meaning we took from the square root. You have to find your own local ingredients and use them as tools of design.

FP: I am interested in your description and embrace of the square figure. It's such a strong geometry and it comes straight from the loom, an endless rectangle with grids of squares. In Western fashion, patterns with curves and shapes are cut out from the fabric but in your work the surface of the fabric is what is shaped, folded, or pleated, so there is no need to cut, there is no waste. In architecture a square form is a very stable figure, but each surface of the square can do a lot to challenge its robustness. Your garments also defy the mighty square with texture, material, color, and frill.

CF: In Mexico, and for Indigenous communities, the square represents the earth. It has the four points – north, east, west, and south – and the center, which is what they call a God's eye. So the square, in pre-Hispanic cultures, is everything. You see it with the Greeks and you see it in grids and the pyramids. You see it everywhere. Now, I have a mind that's very schematic. It's much easier for me to design and create using those patterns. As I show in the diagrams, you can fold it, and if you pleat it on top, then you can have a circle. You can have a triangle. You can have any shape that you want by making pleats and folds. The beauty of this figure is that it can be very static or not. It can be the most nonstatic of all depending on how you work with it as a textile.

FP: One example of this link between square geometry and local history would be the work of Josef and Anni Albers, who, starting in the 1930s, would bring their students from Black Mountain College and then Yale to Mexico to visit pre-Columbian archaeological sites. The goal of these visits was to see pyramids, sanctuaries, and landscapes as material objects describing square profiles. Josef's series of paintings, *Homage to the Square*, is a clear representation of the idea of the flatness and depth that coalesce in the sequence of flat cubes.

The Alberses came from Germany to America, and then visited Mexico. So, again, there's a weaving of cultures in which you start to see all kinds of potential. But what connects those three cultures is the abstraction of the square.

I love the fifth point of the manifesto, "the origin of the textile is the earth." When Bruno Latour describes his hypothesis that we have never been modern, he talks about the fact that our relationship to nature has been broken by our modern mind. He created this beautiful diagram in which he defines the idea of culture and nature, or human and nonhuman, as a separation created by modernity – by the modern mind, the Cartesian mind, the scientific mind. He thinks that cultures that are premodern had a different relationship to nature, a more intrinsic relationship to nature. He calls it the premodern mind, not a primitive mind, but a mind that understood earth in a continuum. He talks about the need to move away from dualistic thinking and into hybrid works of translation. I think that the way you look at textiles as belonging to the Earth brings up Latour's idea of this hybrid thinking.

If you look at any garment you buy today, you are so detached from wherever that garment came from, where the textile originated, the fabrication of it, its composition, etc. So I think that your way of looking at premodern cultures isn't historical, it's changing our mind about how we see that relationship with nature.

CF: I think what you're talking about and what Latour is saying are exactly what the Indigenous communities have been telling us for thousands of years. That's why it's so important. When you understand how a textile is made by a weaver and an embroiderer in San Juan Chamula or in Tocuaro or in Michoacán, then you understand that idea – not thinking of humans as extractors but as part of a whole.

Every single Indigenous community in the world is trying to teach us that we are not above the earth. We're not saving the earth, we're not killing the earth. We are part of it. That's why it's important to understand the processes humanity has developed for all of these thousands of years of evolution – the most intelligent ones are the ones that follow that thinking of not being above nature. These handmade objects understand that relationship.

So, yes, we have to change and we have to understand. I don't know what is going on with humanity. Like with Covid, the people in the urban areas are the ones who suffered the most. In the manifesto, I ask, if tomorrow the petrol is gone, the light is gone, who will suffer? A little bit like what happened in Covid. It was us – we were not capable of living with Mother Earth. We were not capable of growing our own food, of making our own clothing, of educating our own kids. We were completely in the hands of what they call modernism or technology.

We have to stop and think to reevaluate what humans are made of and what we're here for. We're not here to destroy the planet, destroy other peoples, or destroy countries. We're here as a community to help each other and to live in communion with others – and not only humans. That is what handmade textiles and working with communities has taught me.

FP: Yes, this is why you say that "the future is handmade." I have one of your tote bags, and I'm going to use it 70,000 times.

Florencia Pita guest edited *Log* 17: Superficial (2009) with Mark Foster Gage. She is an architect and educator based in Los Angeles and Argentina. Her practice is Florencia Pita & Co., and her upcoming monograph is titled *Curves and Lines*.

Observations on the Year of Barbie

Architect Barbie slips into the brown woolen cardigan of the Log Lady, who, in David Lynch's *Twin Peaks*, speaks in riddles transmitted from a log cradled in her arms. The newly concocted Log-Lady-Architect-Barbie (LLAB) holds the wise log to her plastic breast. She shows us the beautiful figure of architecture – surely the original Architect Barbie – etched in Charles Eisen's frontispiece to Laugier's 1775 edition of *Essai sur l'architecture*. Looking into our eyes with every ounce of sky blue she can muster, LLAB says, "Look at where I come from!" The log responds, "Look at your reflection and see the mirrored ball. Do you see how it scatters the light, shatters origins?" – Pia Ednie-Brown

Toyo Ito & Associates, Architects + Maki Onishi / o+h, Home for All for Children in Higashimatsushima, Miyagi, Japan, 2013. The three whimsical structures provide flexible spaces for children displaced by the 2011 Tohoku earthquake and tsunami. Top: Maki Onishi, sketch of the mobile structures in a procession similar to those in traditional Japanese festivals. All images courtesy onishi-maki + hyakudayuki architects / o+h.

onishimaki + hyakudayuki architects / o+h, Community Center "Alberobello," Koriyama, Fukushima, Japan, 2021. The assisted living facility is constructed as a small village, providing residents spaces for independence, such as gardens and private rooms, as well as engagement with community and care services. Photos: Kai Nakamura. Read Thomas Daniell's conversation with firm cofounder Maki Onishi, "The Positive Power of Architecture," pages 33–40.

Alex Da Corte, *Rubber Pencil Devil*, film still, 2018. The video is installed in the neon sculptural frame of a "housey" house, reminiscent of Venturi, Scott Brown's Ghost House (1976). Opposite page: Alex Da Corte, *THE DÆMON*, Matthew Marks Gallery, Los Angeles, September 24 – November 4, 2023. The installation includes *The Conversation Pit*, a series of sculptures in brightly colored flocking. Images courtesy the artist. Read Michael Meredith's conversation with artist Alex Da Corte, "A Conversation Pit," pages 108–114.

The Los Angeles Design Group, installation design of "Eternal Medium: Seeing the World in Stone," Resnick Pavilion, Los Angeles County Museum of Art, August 20, 2023 – February 11, 2024. The partitions, pedestals, and tables are painted Dunn-Edwards Black Bay, a subtle off-black. Photo © Marten Elder. Courtesy the architects. Read Anna Neimark and Andrew Atwood's review, "Stone on Stone," pages 41–46.

Lacol, La Borda, Barcelona, 2018. Left: Simple, standardized materials, such as wire mesh, cross-laminated timber, and a polycarbonate roof, are used to economically create community spaces while also reducing the overall carbon footprint of the housing co-op. La Borda received the 2022 EU Mies van der Rohe Prize for Emerging Architecture. Photos: Institut Municipal de l'Habitatge i Rehabilitació de Barcelona. Opposite page: Lacol, La Balma, Barcelona, 2021. Through passive cooling strategies, energy costs for the housing co-op are half those of similar multi-unit buildings. Bottom: The entrance to the ground-level communal kitchen and dining room. Photos: Milena Villalba. Read Ana Miljački's conversation with Lacol cofounder Cristina Gamboa, "Housing Makes a Community," pages 47–57.

Carla Fernández and Pedro Reyes, "Think Twice," SCAD Museum of Art, February 12 – September 1, 2019. Photo: Humberto Moro. Courtesy SCAD. Top: María Elena Vázquez Guzmán using a backstrap loom and modeling her shawl, San Pedro Chenalhó, Chiapas, Mexico. Photos: Ana Hop.

Carla Fernández, Fashion in Motion: Carla Fernández, Victoria and Albert Museum, London, October 19, 2018. © Victoria and Albert Museum, London. Read Florencia Pita's conversation with fashion designer Carla Fernández, "Ephemerality Will Kill Us All," pages 120–128.

Zaha Hadid Architects, AI prompt: "Headquarters designed by Zaha Hadid Architects," 2022. Produced with DALL-E. Right: AI prompt: "Museum designed by Zaha Hadid Architects," 2022. Produced with DALL-E.

Zaha Hadid Architects, AI prompt: "Group of towers with exoskeletons designed by Zaha Hadid Architects," 2023. Produced with Midjourney. Read Cameron Wu's conversation with ZHA principal Patrik Schumacher, "Form, Words, and Artificial Intelligence," pages 203–214.

Ursula Biemann, *Forest Mind*, 2021. Performance of Mamita Rubiela Mojomboy in her lush territory in Piamonte, Colombia. Opposite page: *Acoustic Ocean*, 2018, in "À bruit secret: Hearing in Art," installed at the Tinguely Museum, Basel, 2023. Top: Sci-fi performance of a Sámi marine biologist channeling vocalizations of marine species. Her scientific instruments are presented in the video installation. Bottom: The changing water chemistry of the oceans disrupts the microscopic shell-forming lives of the sea butterfly. Biemann's project, according to Sanford Kwinter, is to simply reveal the mysterious emergence of worlds beyond the distorting bias of geometry. What replaces geometry in her system of unveilings is the action of intelligence that is seen to ceaselessly animate matter and to drive our universe to expression. She not only documents how this process operates at every level and scale – photons, DNA, geochemistry, images, thought – but how it includes us as well and embeds us inextricably in the Earth System as an intimate and transpersonal relay whose pure purpose is to generate knowledge and meaning, and hence consciousness itself. Read Kwinter's discussion with Biemann, "*Sentipensar*; or, How to Become Earth," pages 224–236.

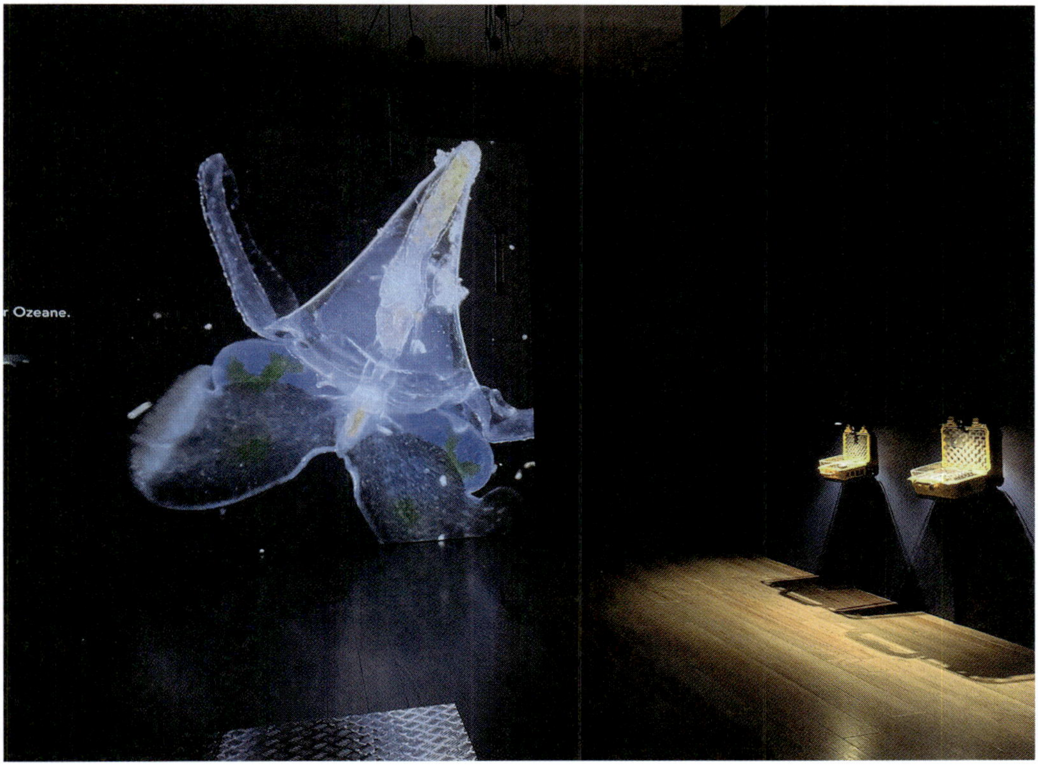

Ozeane.

Louise Lawler, *Portrait*, 1982. Silver dye bleach print, 19 by 19 inches. Courtesy the artist and Sprüth Magers.

Sylvia Lavin

Birdcalls; or, Criticism in The Environment

Log has been recording "observations on architecture and the contemporary city," accommodating shifting points of view, modes of observation, and types of inscription, for 20 years. This is a remarkable achievement for many reasons, including the fact that it is 20 years, not 4.2 or 18.7, that provokes historical reflection. Twenty years is the length of time typically used by social scientists to demarcate a generation, a term of art for creating historical cohesion and fabricating periodicity. This deeply entrenched historical structure gains its authority from the on-average 20-year human reproductive cycle, an imaginary time frame that, in fact, depends to a significant degree on the material condition of women: access to health care and reproductive health care in particular, the degree to which their work both in and outside the home is recognized and compensated, and their reproductive freedom. The conditioning environment of reproduction, in other words, not only directly shapes reproductive behaviors in highly volatile and often unrecognized ways, but, in so doing, also invisibly undergirds how we organize history and what we consider to be its proper domain.

Almost exactly 50 years ago, 2.5 human generations ago but 1.6 generations of African forest elephants and 25 generations of some species of parakeets, questions of reproduction and history were asked explicitly by *Birdcalls*, a work by feminist conceptual artist Louise Lawler, a member of the so-called Pictures Generation and an artist well-known for working across media and situations, from photography and installations to ephemeral formats such as napkins and matchbooks. For *Birdcalls*, sometimes referred to as "Patriarchal Rollcall," Lawler recorded herself sounding out the names of male artists then dominating the art world, using the chirps and peeps of birdcalls.[1] The humor of the work was tinged with urgency as it attested to how the constant repetition of these names assembled a generation of men into a canon that excluded women and artists of color, relegating their productions to a noncultural status

1. The history of *Birdcalls* is not straightforward and the dates accompanying the work, as well as the materials that constitute it, vary. The event said to have triggered the work's ideation occurred in 1971. However, the first documented performances of the work took place at St. Mark's Church in New York and at Pierre et Marie in Paris in 1983. At that time, the work was composed of a sound tape, 7:01 minutes long, mixed by Terry Wilson, and a series of names printed on yellow card stock in a red/green code that indicated which parts of the name were being uttered (in some cases, Lawler only squawked an artist's surname). In subsequent performances, the means by which the names were printed varied, ranging from wall vinyl to matchbooks. In 1982, Lawler produced a photograph titled *Portrait*, showing a parrot against a red background, that frequently travels with the work, which is now composed of a digital audio file and instructions requiring the list of names be legible within the acoustic space created by the sound and in the appropriate color code, but otherwise leaving the particularities of their publication unrestricted.

while simultaneously relying on their reproductive labor to maintain the genealogy. On the one hand, as we observe architecture and the city today, it is important to underscore the ways in which these issues of representation have still not been adequately answered.[2] On the other hand, it is equally important to recognize that the very conditions of possibility that prevailed in 1972 have radically shifted: reproduction is now digital rather than mechanical; feminism has gone through multiple generations, waves, and intersections; and both sound and animal studies are now distinct interdisciplines. In other words, the elemental ingredients of *Birdcalls* are not what they once were. As a result, considering this work today raises questions not only about the inner workings of critical reception but also about how works of art, of structure and of form, change in relation to changes in their environment and about the role such circumstantial externalities play in critical interpretation.

Birdcalls was always deeply entwined with its environment, if by environment we mean the milieux of the New York City art world of the 1970s and '80s. The Pictures Generation was based in New York, and *Birdcalls*' first "showing," in 1983, was at the Danspace project at St. Mark's Church, itself a performance venue and landmark of "alternative space," a geographically defined mode of critique. If the historical avant-garde was both metaphorically and actually rooted in Bohemia, *Birdcalls* was a quintessentially "downtown" work. Not only was Manhattan's downtown shaped by various real estate and art market economies, first those of SoHo, then of the East Village, it was also shaped by the discursive and theoretical work of writers associated with the art criticism journal *October*, also a downtown institution. Indeed, the rich literature on *Birdcalls* uses the work to explicate a set of interrelated concerns that dominated the historiography of the 1980s: feminist critique, theories of repetition and substitution, and institutional critique.[3]

These thematics not only are the key concerns of the literature on Lawler but also constitute the principal coordinates of what Rosalind Krauss, a founding editor of *October*, in 1980 called the "map of distinctions" that delineates a space for art that is "uninhabitable, occupiable or enterable," a space in which the medium of physical immediacy is "replaced by that which is conceptually marked." In such a space of rigorous abstraction, the multiplicities that inhere in the environment cannot exist. "Pluralism," Krauss wrote, "does not obtain in art."[4] This is to say that during the long

---

2. In a November 2023 panel discussion on *Birdcalls* that I organized for the Princeton School of Architecture Media + Modernity lecture series, Gavin Steingo called attention to the way in which the distinction between birdcalls and birdsongs, a distinction that arises in the literature on *Birdcalls*, is highly gendered and to how competition and aggression dominated ornithological understanding of avian communication until women ornithologists entered and reshaped the field.

3. As a literature, the writing about *Birdcalls* focuses on feminist critique, not only in the biting send-up of the male canon, but also in the use of the parrot portrait to resist the woman artist becoming subject to the male gaze; on the problematic of repetition, both because Lawler had initially intended the work to be distributed as an LP record and to address the ways in which art historical repetitions reinforce hierarchies of power (the canon gains authority by repetition but the parrot loses authority by repetition because its mimesis lacks human intellection); and on institutional critique discussed in relation not only to Lawler's interest in alternative spaces but also to her centering of marginal media, from napkins to paperweights, and ancillary activities that are typically merely art adjacent, such as rearranging, curating, etc. Perhaps in keeping with Lawler's practice of repetition, many of the texts on her work have been repeatedly republished and anthologized, including one of the first, Andrea Fraser, "In and Out of Place," *Art in America* 63, no. 6 (June 1985); Rosalyn Deutsche, "Louise Lawler's Rude Museum," *Transversal Texts* (June 2006); Helen Molesworth, "Louise Lawler: Just the facts," and Lawler's own "Arrangements of Pictures," *October* 26 (1983): 3–16. These can be found in Lawler and Helen Molesworth, *Twice Untitled and Other Pictures (looking back)* (Columbus: Wexner Center for the Arts, 2006). See also Stacey Allan, "Role Refusal: On Louise Lawler's Birdcalls," *Afterall: A Journal of Art, Context and Enquiry* 20 (Spring 2009): 108–13; and Wendy Vogel, "Louise Lawler's Bird Calls," https://wendyvogel.net/portfolio/louise-lawlers-bird-calls/.

4. Rosalind Krauss, "Architects' Drawings/Artists' Buildings," in *Drawings, The Pluralist Decade* (Philadelphia and Chicago: ICA University of Pennsylvania and Museum of Contemporary Art Chicago, 1980), 33–41.

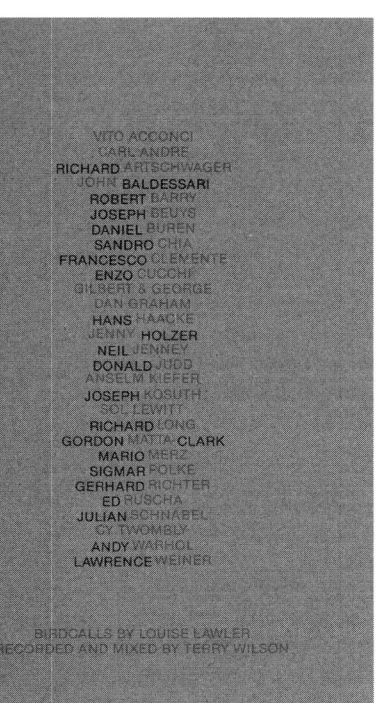

Louise Lawler, announcement card for *Birdcalls*, The Danspace Project, St. Mark's Church, New York City, 1983. Printed card, 5 1/4 by 3 1/4 inches. Courtesy the artist and Sprüth Magers.

5. This narrative is repeated in nearly all of the literature on *Birdcalls* and was documented, I believe for the first time, in an interview with Douglas Crimp in *Louise Lawler: An Arrangement of Pictures* (New York: Editions Assouline, 2003). It reappeared as Louise Lawler and Douglas Crimp, "Prominence Given, Authority Taken," *Grey Room* 4 (Summer 2001): 70–81; and in Helen Molesworth, ed., *Louise Lawler* (Cambridge: MIT Press, 2013).

6. See John Durham Peters, "Bird, Schedule, Name: On Some Media in Borges," in Daniel Balderston and Nora C. Benedict, eds., *The Oxford Handbook of Jorge Luis Borges* (Oxford: Oxford University Press, 2023).

decade of the late 1970s, the specificities and contingencies of historical and environmental particularity were not available as art theoretical concepts and that the then dominant conceptual frameworks were designed to exclude and protect the work of art from the bobbing vicissitudes of experiential flotsam and jetsam, the unpredictable temporalities of commodification, and the banal fluctuations of the weather. From a logical point of view, the environment did not, and could not, exist.

There is one exception to the cartographic rules that situate *Birdcalls* within the domain of art, which is suggested by *Birdcalls*' often repeated origin story, according to which *Birdcalls* was born late one night, in 1971, near the Hudson River. Lawler had been asked to assist (but not to exhibit) in the installation of what became known as the "Pier 18" show, an exhibition of only male artists that took place in a disintegrated city edge populated almost exclusively by male artists and gay men. Leaving the pier in a state of exclusion and vulnerability, Lawler and fellow artist Martha Kite began to squawk the curator's name, Willoughby Sharp, to produce the sound effects of madness they hoped would dispel the interest of any potential attackers. This instinctive sonic defense, so the narrative goes, was eventually disciplined into *Birdcalls*, a work rigorously composed of three parts: bird sounds, a schedule, and names.[5]

In his recent essay "Bird, Schedule, Name," media theorist and elemental philosopher John Durham Peters considers the role of the environment in the interpretation of works of art.[6] His focus is on what he calls circumstantial details, traces of apparently random externalities, the nonhuman bystanders and indeterminate coincidences that enter a work even if only peripherally. Birdcalls, evidence of other lives and agencies; train schedules, reminders of the ineluctable force of time; and proper names, distillations of innumerable prior human efforts to organize the world into language but as such unauthored and inchoate, are in themselves collections of such circumstances. Fundamental to Peters's argument is that this kind of "external" detail necessarily impinges on and shapes human action in ways that inevitably leave traces in works of art. These residues of the flotsam and jetsam of context in a work's apparently primary content, not context in the sense of the political conditions or economic constraints coincident with a work but in the sense of more elemental phenomena such as the rotation of the Earth or the sound of a passing bird, scramble expected

Earth Day, Union Square, April 22, 1970. New York Police Department photograph collection. New York City Municipal Archives.

hierarchies and establish a correspondence between a work's center and its periphery. Critical attention to these reorganizing interferences with imagined forms of autonomy therefore makes evident an environment full of parts one would not expect to belong together.

It might seem that none of the bird, schedule, or name components of *Birdcalls* are arbitrary details. The names are internally consistent with the canon, the schedule is motivated by the temporal facts of recording, and the birdcalls are determined by the long history of the parrot as human companion and mime. But even cursory attention to the sounds made in *Birdcalls* makes it plain that they are not imitations of the sounds of a single species of bird and that critics have too easily accepted as fact Lawler's account of squawking like a parrot as a natural and instinctive response to urban vulnerability. Further, the repetition, not of the work, but of this origin story about the work, begs the question of why *Birdcalls*, of all possible works, needed an origin story in the first place, especially one rooted in biographical experience, tied to the artist as person and to life in downtown New York City. Why, in other words, did criticism feel the need to attach *Birdcalls* to a form of authorial authenticity, and to the forms of reproduction traditionally considered proper to human history, that both criticism of the era and the work itself were otherwise trying to subvert? *Birdcalls* may have eventually been converted into parrot mimicry by what Manfredo Tafuri called criticism in the boudoir, but it seems important to consider if this type of response to the work was triggered by, and constituted an attempt to discipline, the way in which its birdcalls were evidence of unruly and unanticipatable externalities, pointing not only to conceptual marks collected together as art but also to a cosmos full of parts that could not be expected to belong together. Such circumstances require criticism not in the boudoir but in the environment.

During the 1970s, the environment we call New York City had what it thought was a bird problem, more precisely, a monk parakeet problem, because large numbers of these birds, like the Jackson Pollock and Jasper Johns paintings that Lawler photographed ill at ease in the domestic decor favored by their collectors, were finding themselves living in unexpected places.[7] The sudden flocking of monk parakeets around New York City is said to have been caused by the accidental opening of a crate at John F. Kennedy International Airport containing Uruguayan imports to be sold to exotic bird collectors.[8] This global trade converted, or, to use Peters's term, transubstantiated, what were considered agricultural pests in South America into objects of domestic display. The parrot problem was caused less by their escape than by the fact that they turned out to be quite amenable to living in New York and, like other immigrants, settled in, multiplied, and eventually became subjects of a developing political ecology. For some, they were an invasive species, terrifyingly robust, that would no doubt devastate the natural/native environment. For others, the birds were natural objects, and hence intrinsically beautiful, valuable, and innocent. The birds, in other words, generated discourse and debate about how to define the environment and what kinds of beings should have standing in it.[9]

Close observers of the contemporary city know that monk parakeets, like many artists and architects, moved to Brooklyn and designed great roosting architectures where they established forms of reproductive freedoms not readily available to women. Their success required the ability to thrive in hostile environments and was a surprise to ornithologists who anticipated they would fare poorly in a cold climate. This robustness led the US Fish and Wildlife Service to yield to nativist genocidal impulses and call for their total eradication. The technique deployed in this effort was to lure birds into traps by playing tape recordings of their calls.

7. Ann Goldstein's essay "In the Company of Others," in *Twice Untitled and Other Pictures* (133–43), pays particular attention to the series of Lawler's photographic works that confront how collectors arrange their personal belongings, from monogrammed bedspreads to paintings by Jackson Pollock, pets, and other domestic accoutrements in private spaces, and compares this domestic work to the work done by professional curators in public spaces.

8. Other explanations include that some birds escaped domestic cages or that private collectors deaccessioned their birds by deliberately putting them outdoors.

9. For responses to the presence of the birds in New York during the 1970s, see Douglas P. Kibbe and Noel J. Cutright, "The Monk Parakeet In New York," in *Bird Control Seminars Proceedings* (October 1973); John C. Devlin, "A South American Bird is Found Thriving Here," *New York Times*, December 16, 1970; and Harold Faber, "State Acts to Wipe Out Monk Parakeet," *New York Times*, April 7, 1973.

Monk parakeets nested in the Gothic Revival spire of the main entrance to Green-Wood Cemetery, Brooklyn, New York, 2020. Photo: Ryan Mandelbaum.

10. A complete exhibition history for *Birdcalls* has not been established, but it seems that, during the 1980s, it was mostly seen in alternative spaces and university museums and then moved into larger museums and art fairs in the '90s and aughts. It was installed outside in the gardens at Dia Beacon in 2005 and again in the Pantentuin Meise in 2021. In 2019, *Birdcalls* was also installed in the Museum of Contemporary Art Cleveland, a building designed, in 2012, by Farshid Moussavi, and one of a series of museums designed by women architects in those years. (Diller + Scofidio designed the ICA/Boston in 2006 and Zaha Hadid the MAXXI in Rome in 2009). Just as Lawler had centered marginal activities typically surrounding and supporting art proper, several of these architects reorganized museums such that hallways, elevators, and other services were intermingled with and sometimes indistinguishable from spaces for art. In Cleveland, for example, *Birdcalls* was in the "sound gallery," which is also a fire stair.
11. This designation appears in an announcement for the Danspace Project performance of 1983, which featured a series of dances that were collectively titled, "In order to get a job you have to get experience, In order to get experience you have to get a job."
12. Molesworth, "Louise Lawler, Just the Facts," 148.

Sylvia Lavin is Professor of the History and Theory of Architecture at Princeton University.

Recorded birdcalls of birds-out-of-place thus wafted through the airwaves of the city just as Lawler was squawking her way around the canon. Like Uruguayan parakeets, *Birdcalls* also migrated and found modes of survival despite the hostility of the New York art world to what it saw as an invasion of women artists, at least initially. Each iteration of the work is distinct, not merely because like any installation or performance the work depends on the particularities of a given site, but because it is in the nature of this work in particular to change the conditions that encircle it. First performed along urban margins, *Birdcalls* found its way into museum and gallery spaces where it could not be properly displayed or contained, hence it eventually headed off and into institutions that were actively reorganizing their approach to edges and centers. *Birdcalls* now moves about in stairwells and botanical gardens, drawing institutions and their visitors into novel spatial ecologies.[10] Proleptically digital, *Birdcalls* arrives in each venue with an installation code that produces necessarily inexact duplicates and draws other agents also typically on the edge of art – curators, catalog designers, and birds – into its formation. Each 7:01 minutes of its sonic unfolding is a life span, the irreducible finitude of which does not obviate survival.

These various circumstances at the periphery of *Birdcalls*, or what with typically understated irony and prescience Lawler once called *Birdcalls of the North American Artist*, suggest that the work explicated the emergence of environmental ideation before it could be conceived in art theoretical terms, even by Lawler.[11] The shape of this episteme can only be gleaned at the edge of *Birdcalls*' native habitat, an environmental periphery that is inevitably the center for something else, and by criticism that has left the boudoir to model the field not as a bounded rectangle, even if it is filled with the mass timber and carbon neutrality of good intentions, but as a gaseous structure that can be observed and logged, but not read. *Birdcalls*' entanglement in these contradictory understandings of the environment and its openness to being remade by unpredictable externalities goes a long way toward explaining, as Helen Molesworth has argued, why Lawler's work has become more difficult to read over time but, in its avian call for criticism in the environment, I would suggest, more salient as a result.[12]

*Bryony Roberts
& S.E. Eisterer*

Expanding Embodiment

S.E. Eisterer is an assistant professor of architectural history and theory at the School of Architecture at Princeton University. S.E.'s research focuses on spatial histories of dissidence, feminist, queer, and trans* theory in architecture, as well as the labor of social movements. She is working on two books: the interdisciplinary history and translation of Memories of the Resistance: Margarete Schütte-Lihotzky and the Architecture of Collective Dissidence, 1918–1989 *and the edited volume* Living Room: Architecture, Gender, Theory, *which illuminates methods and theories in writing about feminist and queer spaces. This academic year she is also a senior fellow with the Alexander von Humboldt Foundation at the Munich Documentation Center. This conversation took place over Zoom in September 2023.* – BR

BRYONY ROBERTS: Given your attention to lived, bodily experiences as intertwined with research and knowledge production, I thought it'd be interesting for us to have a dialog in which you reflect on embodiment from the perspective of architectural history and theory and I bring some perspectives from practice. There has been growing interest in embodiment in recent years across social justice movements and fields of cultural theory, and increasingly in architectural practice and research. Many of these emergent discourses are connected to longer lineages of intersectional feminism, queer theory, and postcolonial theory, among others, which have confronted and transformed discourses of phenomenology and affect. Can you describe the landscape of writings on embodiment that influence your work?

S.E. EISTERER: One of the beautiful things, both in scholarship and in teaching, is the move toward embodiment across a number of fields. Ideas in feminist and queer theory, as well as border and migration studies, African American studies, Indigenous studies, and certain branches of the environmental humanities have been really inspiring. To start with queer theory, as an example, I admire the work of Susan Stryker and Jack Jen Gieseking, who bring an embodied approach to architecture and the city. In the recent book *A Queer New*

York, Gieseking illuminates lesbian, queer, and trans* spaces and the people who enliven them through the concept of "constellations." The writings of Audra Simpson, bell hooks, Gloria Anzaldúa, José Esteban Muñoz, Saidiya Hartman, and others have transformed entire fields and created new ones. With my students, I have been reading about the perspectives of queer and feminist Indigenous scholars. In 1988, Midnight Sun wrote a foundational essay titled "Sex/Gender Systems in Native North America," published in the anthology *Living the Spirit*, that I wish more architectural historians would discuss. The point I would like to emphasize is that there are multiple approaches and historiographies pointing to why scholarship that both centers and produces embodied ways of knowing is needed, while responding to specific disciplinary formations and concerns.

If I had to say why a type of situated approach to architectural history and theory is needed specifically, it would be because there is a way of embodied knowing that actually exceeds what can be stated "objectively." This is specifically important for a field that has too long relied on "neutrality" as an attainable position from which to speak. Attending to embodied ways of knowing expands architectural history and theory not toward details or the anecdotal but toward larger social and political questions and solidarities.

BR: Absolutely. In wrestling with these topics with my students, we often discuss the interplay between individual experience and larger solidarities – how Donna Haraway talks about not just partial situated perspectives but the fact that they're overlapping. So it's about seeing the rich knowledge of an individual's embodied experience, but then asking how to find solidarity, or community, that works toward collective knowledge. What can it look like when knowledge comes from community building and the sharing of individual embodied experiences instead of supposedly universal or objective knowledge?

SEE: I think Haraway's perspective on this issue has been key. She marks the idea of "a view from somewhere" when she writes that "the joining of partial views and halting voices into a collective subject position . . . promises a vision of the means of ongoing infinite embodiment, of living within limits and contradictions – of views from somewhere" ["Situated Knowledges: The Science Question in Feminism and the Privilege of Partial Perspective"].

The idea of living and writing from a position of "limits and contradictions" is not about everybody having an individualist perspective but that there is a solidarity of concerns. That distinction is critical, and sometimes it gets missed. Haraway is not advocating for hyperindividualized perspectives.

The poet June Jordan, who I really love, said that when she read her poems aloud, she always listened for the moments that resonated with the audience. When she heard resonances, she knew that political and personal arguments had larger lives. If the poems did not resonate, they needed more working through. C. Riley Snorton theorizes active listening in a beautiful lecture he gave on what is understood as trans* pedagogy. Snorton defines this type of listening as an instructor assisting students to come more fully into their own authentic voice. I found it eye-opening to ask what architecture pedagogy could look like from that perspective.

BR: The act of listening is actually a very embodied experience of knowing what resonates collectively. Your use of the word *limits* is also interesting, reflecting on the history of discourses around embodiment and phenomenology in particular. If we look back at the writings of Husserl or Merleau-Ponty, there's always this question of how to bracket the frame of awareness of experience. Many of the powerful critiques of that work, such as Sarah Ahmed's *Queer Phenomenology* or Jos Boys's "Cripping Spaces? On Dis/abling Phenomenology in Architecture" [*Log* 42], ask, What are the bounds of those brackets? Since those brackets are very narrow in the canonical works of phenomenology, what if we zoom out to see the social or political or cultural contexts that situate individual experiences? But, like you're saying, even when you do see all the cultural, political, and economic forces that have brought your individual self into this position, there are inevitably limits to that viewpoint, right? Some of those conditions themselves are the limits, and they can make it difficult to see beyond the individual perspective.

SEE: So, I want to ask you, why do *you* think embodied knowing or an embodied practice of architecture is important?

BR: For me, it does still feel like a necessary form of resistance to the disembodied ways of researching, teaching, practicing, and writing that are so prevalent in the field of architecture. The expectation of impersonal neutrality denies the particularities of marginalized experiences. To ask people to be disembodied is to ask for production and to ignore the fact that that comes with labor that is situated in a very particular life, place, and story. I think it's a lot more interesting when you do look at all those stories. I'm drawn to that complexity. But I also think it is political. Foregrounding embodied experiences is a kind of political and epistemological empowerment because it says that those are experiences that matter and that listening to them could actually change the kinds of knowledge we have and the way we work. If we make those changes, then so much more is possible in both research and practice. How about you? When you're teaching, or even writing, how do you think about addressing those limits in the act of creation? How do you work through the situatedness of your perspective and its limitations?

SEE: For each project, the answer is slightly different. As a historian, I have always liked that the material gives you something back, that it warrants a specific type of treatment. By this, I mean if you are trying to write a situated essay about the history of modern architects in Germany in the 1920s, the techniques you might apply will be different from writing, say, an embodied piece about being a queer person working in architecture today. These topics, but also the respective historiographies, archives, and silences in and around them, will point to different limits and contradictions. Secondly, the form of writing itself can signal a type of open-endedness or fragmentariness, again contingent on subject matter. There are many examples from theorists, some of whom I mentioned earlier, that use the structure and form of the written document to remind the reader that theirs is a methodology that acknowledges limits. So, for example, you can use vignettes or shift perspectives moving between different historical subjects. Especially if you work toward a politics of difference, some scholars choose to weave more personal writing together with their inquiry into archives, objects, buildings, landscapes, ecology, etc.

BR: Can you say more about how certain subjects prompt a different kind of embodied approach in your work?

SEE: This year, I am finishing a book on Austrian architect, resistance fighter, and women's activist Margarete Schütte-Lihotzky (1897–2000). In taking up this relatively well-known figure, I am attempting to write not about an individual, but rather networks of people and to center their collective life alongside their political work. Alongside a critique of the gendered hierarchies, systems, and institutions through which Schütte-Lihotzky came to design kitchens and kindergartens, I stress the defiance of her resistance labor. I also see her life as a prism to write about friendships, at times love, and forms of political and artistic refusal. This aspiration prompted methodological interventions that describe not just an individual but groups, shifting perspectives and viewpoints between various persons who worked both in architecture and in resistance groups with Schütte-Lihotzky.

BR: It seems like a key part of your project is actually epistemological. The work is probing ways of knowing dimensions of the past and present that are not as documented and are therefore not as easy to know. How do you develop the tools for knowing this kind of material? Do you have to use other types of source materials that might not be typical?

SEE: Methodologically, the main intervention is to look at types of archival sources that are not necessarily the most common in architecture. In the realm of organized resistance, there were many material artifacts and textual documents produced in internment that I felt need discussing, such as clandestine writing, crossword puzzles with pseudonyms, and knitted or sewn objects that were gifts of solidarity among dissidents. A main question for me was, How can you read archival materials that document such unthinkable oppression in conjunction with materials that we look at more conventionally in the history of architecture? There is, of course, not one answer, but for me, by looking at the labor of women who were interned and who produced these objects of solidarity for each other, knitted from the threads they had smuggled and given to each other, I began to see the architectural work

otherwise. Many of these women had an embodied knowledge and experience with crafts that they used to make these objects. When centering these clandestine objects, they emerge clearly as examples of resistance art. And then, when you look back at Schütte-Lihotzky's Frankfurt Kitchen, arguably her most famous work, you see it cast in a different light.

BR: How is the kitchen different when you look back at it?

SEE: I think it is a pretty conservative, single-authored architectural object that makes no secret, even aesthetically, of wanting to introduce the professionalization of housework into the domestic. Susan R. Henderson has written that it was implemented in Weimar Germany with the effect of redomesticating women at a time when they were entering the workforce in large numbers. Viewing objects of resistance art – those crafted clandestinely and in solidarity to fight against the Nazi regime – shows that they stem, by contrast, from a collective with a more radical politics and from the embodied knowledge of women. All of these facts challenge conventional notions of provenance and made those objects stand outside the fields of art and architectural history for so long.

BR: Earlier, you mentioned the writing structure itself being a way for grounding these issues and thinking differently. In your essay "Spatial Practices of Dissidence: Identity, Fragmentary Archives, and the Austrian Resistance in Exile, 1938–1945," published in *Aggregate* as part of the collection "On Collaborations: Feminist Architectural Histories of Migration," you experimented with the formatting of the essay so that the stories of different figures in the Austrian resistance appear side-by-side, interspersed with artifacts from their lives. This seemed to

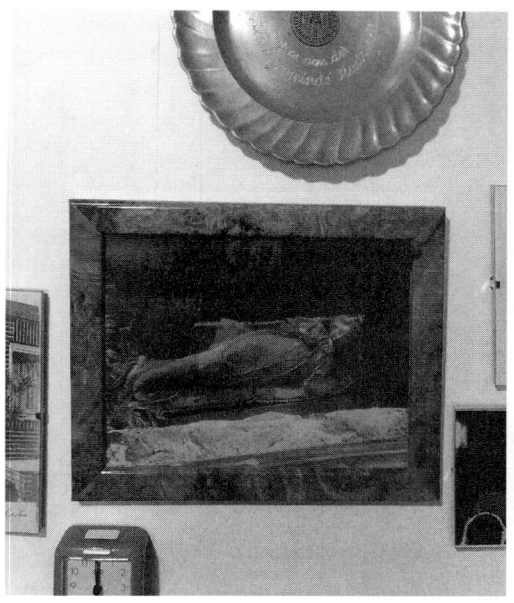 

Family photos of Margarete Schütte-Lihotzky in her home in Radstadt, Austria, now owned by her great-grand nice. Photos: S.E. Eisterer, August, 2018.

be an intentional effort to foreground partial but interconnected voices. You mentioned that you've also asked students to play with this approach by bringing their own embodied experience into the work. How do you ask them to do this, and what kind of results has it had?

SEE: I believe we can allow other forms of knowing and writing to enter the classroom, while, to go back to the Haraway quote, acknowledging that there will solidarities around these issues. Glimpses of personal experience in writing can and should translate to others who share similar, but also very different, paths. It has been useful to think through this with students in a course I am teaching at Princeton that is in conversation with feminist and queer theory. We usually start from writing about a place in short forms of free writing and in conversation with thinkers the students select. Over the duration of the course, all of the assignments become iterative – to get away from notions of completeness as well as the long papers that miraculously write themselves in the last week of class.

Let me give you some examples of projects that, in my view, worked with embodiment in interesting ways. One is by a doctoral student in the history and theory of architecture and the other by two professional students of architecture. Guillermo S. Arsuaga, a PhD student at Princeton, worked with bodies of literature at the intersection of environmental humanities and queer studies to describe Pheasant Island, which, being in the Bidasoa River between Spain and France, changes sovereignty every six months. For Guillermo, this island was a way to interrogate histories of colonization and of European sovereignty as well as environmental history. In the course paper, Guillermo included Euskara poems and free writing using translanguaging to describe the island's environmental history and the story of his grandmother, Maria, who escaped Spain via the island for France with her family during the civil war. Every summer now, Guillermo goes to this island. Sometimes he walks, at low tide, or rows a boat by himself.

 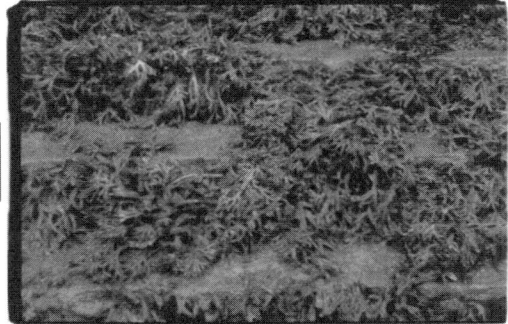

Algae covering the stairs facing the Bidasoa River, on Pheasant Island, between France and Spain. Photos: Guillermo S. Arsuaga.

People can not stay overnight on this island that changes sovereignty (although guided tours are offered). But he rows there in an act of defying this dual sovereignty, which eclipses other forms of belonging that are not recognized by the dominant nation-states or the European Union. In the paper, his poems, interspersed with the narrative of family history and the environmental inquiry into Pheasant Island, he altered this site for the reader. Reading his family history, you get a sense that the environment is both personal and political. Guillermo also emphasized thinking beyond binaries by narrating the entwined lives of the river, plants, and people.

The other example is a project by Sophia Diodati and Daniel Landez, who thought about representational techniques based on queer of color theory. For part of the project, Sophia created embroidered elevations on voile. The central question she asked was, What type of lineages and what kinds of embodied knowledge can one draw upon when stitching an elevation, moving it from paper to cloth? How does this change in medium actually alter what an elevation does, and which bodies of knowledge does it foreground?

BR: I really appreciate how you're asking students to bring their own experience but then find a way for them to see that in relation to other situated experiences and multiple scales of conditions. I think that is key, because it has a built-in counterbalance to a project becoming entirely about a myopic, individual world. Even the topics you're asking them to address – language, geography, histories of gendered making – put the individual in relationship to many stories.

SEE: I know you have been invested in thinking about embodied practice in architecture and what that means for the architectural studio. How do you approach these topics in your own work?

BR: Well, I love that you raised the question of what an embodied drawing is because it's something I think about a lot. I think it's parallel to how you talk about writing history in that both the subject matter and the techniques, or methods, of practice need to be expanded.

In terms of subject matter, it's urgent to find ways of making that pay attention to diverse embodied experiences and then to actually make spaces that support people who are currently marginalized and uncomfortable in spaces not designed with their experiences in mind. To do this requires ways of knowing and understanding multiple embodied experiences, which have not historically been part of the architectural tool kit. I work to bring that kind of knowledge into design practice through interviews and through cocreation and collaboration with self-advocates who can speak to experiences of gender, sexuality, race, and disability in a particular site.

To address that subject matter, you have to change all of the processes of architecture, from start to finish – and change the sequence of the processes. If you're really prioritizing lived experience, then you have to start with understanding people's experiences. For me, that means starting with interviews and conversations, and developing tools to record and gather that information in a way that reflects the nuances of it, which is tricky. And then the design process begins, but it's always a feedback loop with those participants or self-advocates. So it's switching the sequence – you don't start with a napkin sketch, you start with the conversation.

But I think all the steps of the process also have to be questioned – representation, drawing, fabrication. Those are all loaded with different histories. So many of the drawing tools that we use in Western architectural education and practice can be traced directly to the Italian Renaissance and very specific ideas about the role of the architect as a thinker, but not as the person constructing the project. There's a built-in disconnect between the idealism of drawing and the world of making. I've written a little to challenge that idea of drawing and to figure out ways of drawing – meaning both documenting the world and generating new designs – that start with bodies and the ways bodies experience space. I've worked on performance projects and in collaboration with performers to map spaces. I've tried taking impressions of buildings with casts. It's about finding ways of documenting architecture that are incredibly tactile and sensory and not just about a line.

In terms of materiality and fabrication, I'm interested in learning from the long tradition of crafts that have been gendered as female, but then reclaimed by feminists and queer artists. I try to be critical about that, too, because it's important not to be essentialist about the gender of ways of making. So I'm constantly trying to find ways of documenting the world, learning from other people, and making stuff that centers embodied experience and invites other people into the process, both the process of making and then the process of experiencing the work.

To your point, that moment of bridging from individual subjectivity to collectivity, or solidarity, is the most important thing. I find that tactile worlds can invite that kind of experience, and if you start to make those worlds from processes of collaboration and research so that they're also about the cultural histories of a place, then those worlds can bring layered meaning to the act of bringing people together.

I try to bring these different approaches to process into the classroom as well by asking students to make drawings of sensations such as sound and touch and by doing collaborations with community partners. I think it's crucial that students learn the embodied skills of being able to talk to people and learn from them, and to not assume that the architect knows everything in the beginning. That is a big pedagogical shift that needs to happen.

SEE: I totally agree with that. In this group I have been working in for a couple of years, called Queer Space Working Group, one of the core objectives is to collaborate with organizations. Because when I was teaching the course on queer and feminist histories of architecture for the first time, one of the students broke down and said, Now I know all of these theories, and I feel even more pessimistic about practice. I realized that meant I didn't do a very good job highlighting the tactics that I do believe have efficacy and the many ways in which queer subjects have created spaces under difficult circumstances that are inspiring and point ways to practice.

 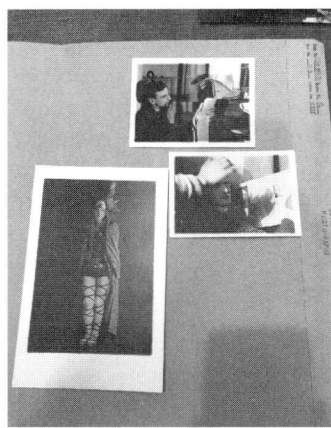

Family photos of H.D., Bryher, and Kenneth Macpherson with baby Perdira. Clockwise from top left: The shadow of H.D. while watching Bryher and Perdita playing in the sand; Kenneth swimming in Lake Geneva with one of the family dogs; test images of Kenneth, including one in Celtic costume; Bryher and H.D. holding Perdita. Courtesy Yale Collection of American Literature, Beinecke Rare Book and Manuscript Library. © 2016 the Schaffner Family Foundation. Photos of photos: Sergio Preston, from the dissertation "Authority and Romance: Queer Histories, Modern Homes," 2023.

I don't believe that professional architecture is doomed at all. Architects are part of many processes in which their knowledge is deeply needed. Queer-feminist journalist and author Michaela Dudley writes, "Dehumanization begins with a word, but so does emancipation." So what we historians do in our corner of the world can also transform the built environment in ways that matter and that are not progress-driven – or that are, at least, less violent and more lively. Thinking about practice may require different perspectives – cooperative, interdisciplinary, municipal. There are so many options. As educators, we can do much to highlight how these practices can be really exciting, engaging, and meaningful – working for a water department, an LGBTQIA+ nonprofit, a school district, etc.

BR: There are so many parallels with work in practice right now among feminist practitioners, with this focus on collaboration and cocreation, on multiple voices, on new forms of representation and communication. It's fascinating to see how that plays out across theory and practice, and how it has historically, too. All these themes have been in the mix for decades, yet they are often uncelebrated or not taught. But it feels like there's a kind of momentum at the moment.

SEE: I agree. The last few years have marked a tidal shift in methods and practices. A lot of projects in the history and theory of architecture have emerged that are thinking quite seriously about these issues. When I started, we debated whether or not you could use the word *I* in your dissertation. Now, 10 years later, whole sets of methods and bodies of literature have opened up, exploding that conversation. In the work of students, I see that they know the bodies of literature. They are eager to enliven and chart these possibilities and to engage in theoretical worlds.

BR: I love the question, "Can you use *I*?" I feel like it's sort of metonymic for the whole conversation. In design practice, *I* has almost been too present in the past, but it's an *I* that is typically not embodied or contextually situated. I think the exciting shift is toward an *I* that's situated, embodied, contextual, and connected to all of these conditions around it. It's a shift in the subject, and then a much more interconnected communal understanding of how one operates in the world. That has implications for methods and for process, both in design and in theory.

SEE: One last thing about why an *I* that points to overlooked histories and lives is needed – erasure. Over the last few months, I have thought mostly about it from the perspective of "queer erasure" in architectural history. In our field, there is a tendency to say that something does not exist. For example, homosexual relationships will often be referred to as "friendships" or "close relationships." In addition, the nature of what constitutes these relationships, their family life, and the spaces that shelter them – architecture – has often been entirely obfuscated. Sergio Preston, at Cornell, writes about queer families in the 1920s and 1930s in a dissertation called "Authority and Romance: Queer Histories, Modern Homes." Doing a deep dive into histories of modern architecture and queer families – Sergio focuses on modern homes commissioned by queer kin – he rejects the idea of *not knowing*. Not knowing can be something that is actively done by historians or by the popular press – it can be an overt act. Highlighting the existence of longer lineages of spaces for queer kin is thus critical. Sometimes this requires the skill of the historian to read between the lines or, at least, by knowing the context, infer something about the past that may have been consciously obfuscated. So I am excited that there is movement among an emerging generation of architectural historians and architects who are really aware of these histories and the work that has to be done to act against erasures. They have jumped ahead in developing modes of seeing and listening that do that. The expanded idea of *I* marks this type of knowledge.

Bryony Roberts guest edited *Log* 48: Expanding Modes of Practice (2019) and guest edited *Log* 31: New Ancients (2014) with Dora Epstein Jones. She leads the design and research practice Bryony Roberts Studio, cofounded Feminist Spatial Practices and WIP Collaborative, and teaches at Columbia GSAPP.

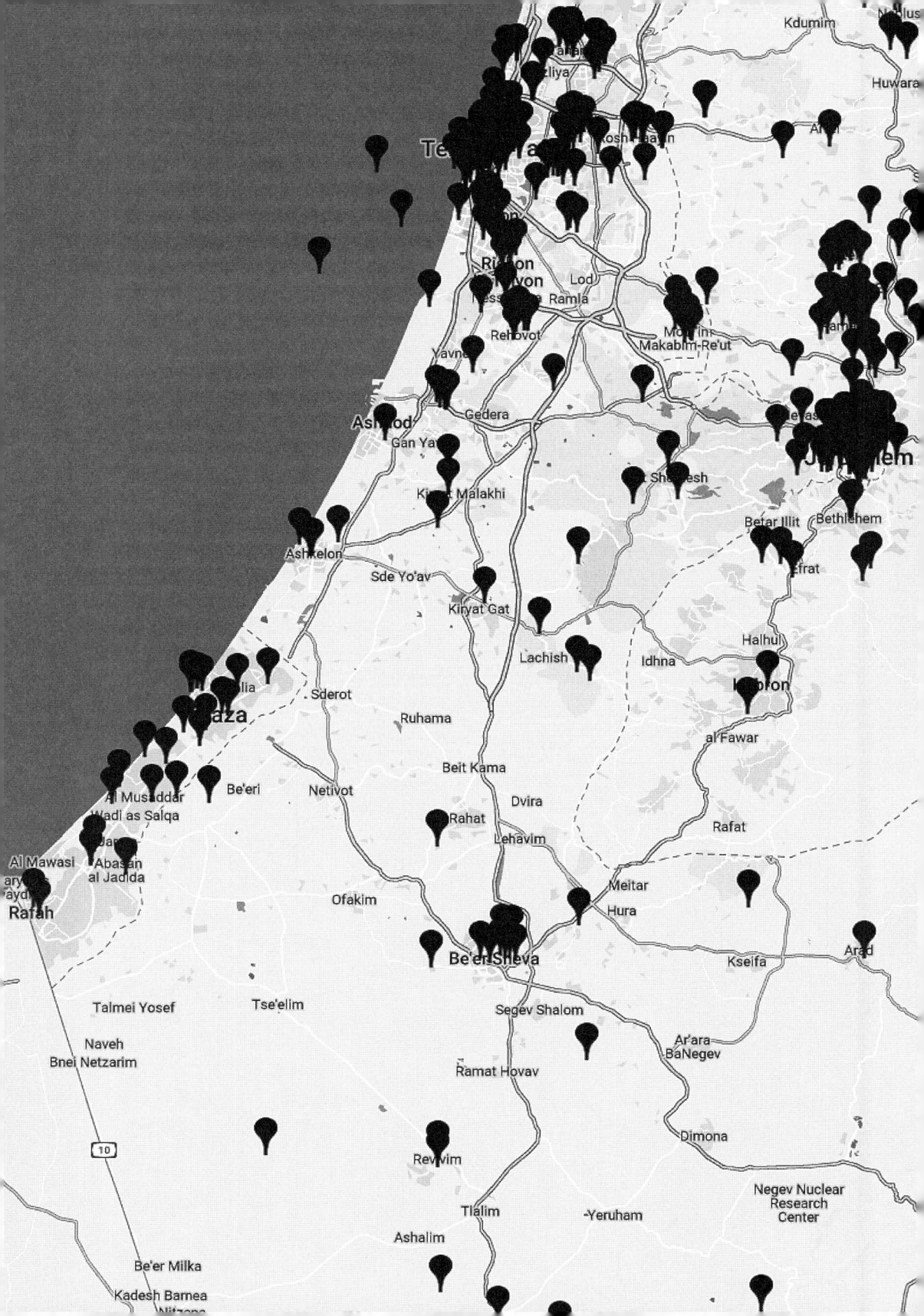

Jaffer Kolb
& Lucas LaRochelle

Something Lost, Something Found

It's been a bit of a struggle revisiting Working Queer, the special section I edited in Log *41 (2017). Like catching a glimpse of yourself in a funhouse mirror, you recognize certain parts — a focus on methods of practice, a reaction to cultural tendencies — but others look off — like a wide face, stretched legs, bulbous knees. Last year, I was on a thesis review for a student who had based their project on* Working Queer. *While intelligent and considered, the work felt disciplined, intellectual, and removed. Where was the liberatory grit? The struggle? The pain and the love? And then years of friendly critiques came back to me; critiques that identified a lack of precarity, urgency, and care in the issue. By pushing against queer space, perhaps I threw the baby out with the bathwater. The issue is on numerous syllabi, fellow teachers continue to send me student responses that I might like, and I still meet people who tell me what that special section meant to them. But those critiques linger.*

In 2021, I was on a panel with Lucas LaRochelle, a designer and researcher who presented the website Queering the Map, *which, according to them, is "a community generated countermapping platform for digitally archiving LGBTQ2IA+ experience in relation to physical space."* Queering the Map *represents a bridge between the act of queering and the vitality of queer space. It has been featured in the* New York Times, Time Magazine, WIRED, Nylon, Vogue, The Nation, *and* Bloomberg CityLab, *among many other publications. The premise is simple, geographically placed anecdotes that speak to the physical immediacy of queer experiences — a digital tool rooted in the material world. Though already a fan of the project, I was led back to Lucas in October 2023, when, suddenly,* Queering the Map *was everywhere as a lens to see another side of the terrible events unfolding in Gaza. It was an anecdotal portrait of a place, a complication in the Western imaginary of Arab Muslim life that helped provide nuance. We caught up on Zoom in early November, to discuss the history of the project and its role in the current cultural moment.* – JK

Screenshot of Southern Israel and Gaza from Queering the Map. The pins, each an anecdote documenting a queer experience in a particular place, are always displayed simultaneously and do not cluster together when zooming out.

JAFFER KOLB: When I was working on *Log* 41, Trump had just been elected president and there was an immediate panic, but I think queer people were still riding the wave of progress that had started in the '90s. It felt like this vector of acceptance was only going up. When Trump happened, it was like a question mark, but it didn't yet feel catastrophic. In the years since, things have started feeling darker and darker, and that moment in history feels less like an exception and more a reorientation of a historical trajectory that's now working against queer bodies.

I have thought a lot about the lack of corporeal urgency in Working Queer, which was more academic, more about method and practice than about personal narratives. So I was really interested when Queering the Map was all over my social media feed with viral posts of queer voices in Gaza proclaiming love and loss in a time of unconscionable violence. It is moving to see, and it's in a format that didn't feel moralizing or heavy-handed. What did it feel like to see those images proliferate and capture this particular imaginary adjacent to the events as they unfolded?

LUCAS LAROCHELLE: The first feeling was deep heartbreak. Reading the stories – some of which were recent and others that had been posted in months and years prior – describing the experiences of living under Israeli occupation, of having loved ones killed by Israeli airstrikes, is distressing and maddening.

Those immediate feelings then gave way to a sense of – and I use this word ambivalently – *power*. Power in the scale at which these stories have circulated across various social media platforms, demanding that we bear witness to the lives taken and destroyed by Israel's attacks on Gaza. Power in the ways they have been used as discursive and affective devices to refute Israel's tactics of pinkwashing – the propagandistic strategy of framing Israel as the only safe haven for LGBTQIA+ people in the Middle East, and using that to legitimize the oppression of Palestinians. The stories function as a kind of evidence that there are in fact queer people in Gaza, in Palestine, who are also among those being murdered and displaced by Israel's siege. They throw a wrench into the narrative that this genocide is somehow in line with queer liberation, recently illustrated by Israel's official Twitter account posting a photo of an IDF soldier standing amid the ruins of a part of Gaza they bombed and holding up a rainbow flag with "In The Name of Love" written on it in marker.

It has been remarkable to see the ways the posts in Palestine on Queering the Map have circulated beyond the site, and even the internet itself. The Dyke Project, an activist group in London, installed posters containing posts in Gaza in over 100 ad spaces in the London transport system. The posts were transcribed onto posters carried during protests in London and Los Angeles. They were read aloud in the Scottish Parliament by Scottish Greens MP Ross Greer, in his speech condemning Israel's pinkwashing and demanding a ceasefire.

On another level, I was also dealing with the technical challenges of keeping the site online, as it was crashing due to the unprecedented amount of traffic it was receiving. There was, and is, a sense of urgency to rework the infrastructure of the site to keep it functioning in order to further the circulation of posts made in Gaza, and in Palestine more broadly.

JK: Following what you were saying about pinkwashing, have you read the postcolonial queer theorist Jasbir Puar?

LL: Yes… *Terrorist Assemblages*.

JK: As well as the essay "Queer Times, Queer Assemblages." She's an important touchstone for thinking about the ways in which the exportation of Western ideology via visibly progressive frameworks – one such example being queerness – have been used as weapons against non-Western cultural systems, under the guise of liberation, but with the spirit of control. Queering the Map represents an assemblage, a collection of interpenetrating perspectives swirling together (I'm paraphrasing Puar, here) to resist a dominant ideology. Have you thought about how or why the map is able to create the space to counteract these cultural narratives?

LL: I'll make a number of guesses. The first would be the map itself. Everyone has an experience of place, of location, so the map as an interface is a very accessible starting point for inviting participation. There is novelty, as well, in the ability to annotate a map – an image that masquerades as objective – with personal experience. This interaction, from a methodological standpoint, is really where the queering of the map occurs – it plays out as a kind of vandalization, a misuse of the tool. It invites multiple perspectives to exist simultaneously on the same plane.

As a result, so many of the stories challenge the mechanics of homonationalism that work to create a binary of "gay-friendly" versus "homophobic" places, which positions certain nation-states, especially the US and Israel, as the former in the interest of framing attacks on the latter as justified under the guise of some sort of civilizing mission of sexual modernity. I think that what many stories on Queering the Map reveal is that love, acceptance, and community still unfold in spite of oppressive governments and social contexts. On the flip side, many stories pinned in regions considered progressive and safe illustrate experiences of exactly the opposite, destabilizing the binary that homonationalism relies on.

My second guess is that the anonymity of Queering the Map is an important factor of its widespread use. There is no user data collected in association with the posts. It's not possible to create a discrete user profile, and so there are no IP addresses, full names, phone numbers, emails, social media handles, etc., associated with the posts on the map. So there is an increased level of safety vis-à-vis anonymity, though it is by no means entirely anonymous. To be totally anonymous on the internet is extremely challenging, but the ability is increased on Queering the Map through an infrastructure that's not rooted in the collection of personally identifiable information. Especially in contexts where there is an increased precarity for queer and trans life, the condition of anonymity is a critical component to why people use the platform in so many differing geopolitical contexts. To be clear, this also includes the US, Canada, and the UK, which position themselves as the safe places for LGBTQIA+ people while simultaneously eroding their rights and protections.

The anonymous nature of the platform is also important because it veers away from the individualism of dominant social media platforms like TikTok, Instagram, Twitter, etc., which are predicated on the discrete user profile. The user of those platforms is incentivized by the accrual of capital in the form of attention. On Queering the Map, there is still the satisfaction of individual catharsis that comes from submitting often deeply personal stories, but its benefit is primarily distributed to the collective readership. The sense of competition for attention stoked by traditional social media platforms is not the primary driver for participation. In this way, Queering the Map becomes a queer map in form rather than simply in content, through its infrastructural *dérive* from the individual toward the assemblage.

JK: It seems like the posts that are most often shared are the ones that speak to a degree of fragility. I don't want to just say tragedy, but the urgency of the situation. Those are the ones that land on my algorithm. It's never the dirtiest ones or even the funniest ones. It's the ones that are tinged with the paradox of their geographical situation – the surprise moment of, Oh, people are queer in Egypt? The ones that gain the most traction seem to deal with the disentanglement, or reentanglement, of geography and feeling. It's a really powerful combination when those stories work against cultural narratives.

I'm fascinated by how the map operates at different scales. When you zoom out, it becomes a data cloud. It reveals density across national boundaries, which promises the idea of a fluid collective. But if you zoom in, the anonymity of the data cloud gives way to individual experiences at the scale of a region, neighborhood, block, or corner. Did you already have a sense when you started how scale would operate in the map? What would be gained or lost if this was an analog project and you didn't have that ability to fluidly go closer and closer?

LL: The aesthetic role of scale and the display of mass on Queering the Map was critical from the beginning, much to the chagrin of myself and developers who have worked on the site. Displaying all of the pins concurrently is a massive technical challenge. The "best practice" when building a map that displays lots of pins is to cluster them. And often those clusters are overlaid with a numerical value. The dilemma with that mode of display is that it pulls outliers into the mean. Thinking with Jack Halberstam's concept of metronormativity, the issue is that to cluster the pins would be to pull data points outside of cities into a collective pool within them, visually furthering the trope that queer life is only present or possible in urban centers.

Maintaining the visual power of mass, at scale, on Queering the Map is important in the same way that it is important the images from protests show their scale. There is an emotional impact to seeing individual pins collected into a mass that a numerical value just can't convey. So it has been an ongoing technical battle to not give in to what is easier in terms of a loading strategy.

JK: What is the actual scale of the zoom that starts to aggregate the data points together? Like, are we talking about a region? Or is it somewhere before that?

LL: It's about the zoom level, which is a numerical scale of one to 22 – one showing the entire world and 22 showing the street level. You can set when clustering occurs, but at any scale, to cluster is to collapse the outlier into the mean.

In 2019, I mounted an exhibition at 4th Space, in Montreal, consisting of 300 posts from Queering the Map assembled into temporary architectural forms. During this process, I thought a lot about what it meant to translate the digital site into something analog and what happens when individual posts are printed out. What does it mean to isolate them, to remove them from their relation to the other stories in their vicinity? An individual story is important, but so too are the surrounding stories – or lack thereof – that contextualize it, complexify it, critique it, respond to it. Printing them out and arranging them in the space of the exhibition ultimately meant building new relationships between geographically distant pins. Rather than attempting to freeze them in place through my own curatorial voice, I opted to make the displays modular and invited visitors to move the story tiles around at will, building new relations between them over time.

The translation of Queering the Map from digital to analog ultimately mediates attention and value. I mentioned The Dyke Project intervention in London, where the switch to analog was beneficial in that it demanded a different level of attention and focus than might occur with the digital map. It also hijacked the authorial nature of physical ad space to confer legitimacy to the stories and the accompanying solidarity statement. A similar augmentation of attention and value occurred in the use of stories in Gaza on protest posters. In these cases, when one story is highlighted from the whole, there are benefits.

JK: You brought up the word *evidence* a few times in your answer to the first question, which connects us to what you're talking about now. Have you read José Esteban Muñoz's "Ephemera as Evidence"?

LL: It was one of the foundational texts that led me to making Queering the Map in the first place. When I use the word *evidence*, that essay is the referent.

JK: Like with Puar, it's apparent these ideas are foundational to your work. I want to touch on this idea of evidence a bit more. In "Ephemera as Evidence," Muñoz talks about things like innuendo, gossip, fleeting moments, or feelings that should count as proof in the production of disciplinary knowledge as much as canonical texts. How do you consider the body of knowledge that you're producing in terms of what it has the capacity to demonstrate or whether it could be used for anything?

LL: One of the key arguments that Muñoz makes is that queerness's vexed relationship to truth is that to become too visible, to leave too much of a trace, often means becoming vulnerable to threat. So the "evidence" of queer and trans life is often fragmentary or opaque, and therefore its ability to function as traditional disciplinary knowledge is diminished. This is very much the case on Queering the Map, as all posts are made anonymously in order to protect the privacy and safety of the authors.

In most cases, the individual texts themselves are not written with the intent to prove anything, or to act as disciplinary knowledge, but rather to mark particular events and describe feelings that emerged from them. I'd argue that the imagined audience for the writing is the author themselves, the people they mention or address directly in the story, and then the broader community of Queering the Map. There isn't an imagined authority to which the author is attempting to prove something as true about their lives.

The site itself is also not set up to be explicitly productive in the process of making sense of the contents. There is no keyword search bar, no demographic data attached to the points, other than what is voluntarily stated or implied in the text. It is not a controlled study set up with the aim to prove or disprove anything specific. The possibilities for using the posts as evidence requires that they be read alongside the contexts in which they are written and to be put in conversation with other sources and modes of knowledge.

The evidentiary nature of the posts has less to do with the question of their truth value as descriptions of events and feelings and more what the text itself does, which is to say, the affects it invokes in its readers. The texts become productive in the ways they circulate and galvanize emotion, producing a sense of affective community, of shared struggle and shared joy.

JK: They are all true depending on how you define truth, right? It doesn't need to be that the activities they described happened or didn't happen. Like the way that you described affect, it remains true, regardless of the precise events themselves. Have you come across *The Sluts*, by Dennis Cooper?

LL: No.

JK: Depending on how strong your stomach is for graphic violence, it is a novel I strongly recommend. It gets pretty disturbing at times, but it's germane to what you're talking about right now. It was written in 2004, but riffs on the 1990s early-internet, rent-boy classified ad culture. It's basically a parafiction about representation through these advertisements. You never quite know what's real and what's fictional, but affect is the important thing, and what it says about gay male desire in the '90s is really what's at stake. It was also ahead of its time in understanding the intersection of digital fantasy and physical space. The novel is constantly slipping into spaces of impossible imagination that are grounded by detailed descriptions of places like bars, boardwalks, and city blocks.

Queering the Map got hacked during Trump's time, right? I want to ask about moderation. What counts as hacking? At what point do you silence or edit something that seems ideologically outside of what you're trying to do? Or maybe another way of asking the question is, Have there been a lot of Israeli or Zionist posts about love and queerness that have received less attention? Are those getting moderated? How do you disentangle your own politics from the stories that you want to see represented in the archive?

LL: The moderation guidelines are no hate speech, no spam, and no breaches of anonymity. It's a moderated platform for a reason, and it has certain ethical commitments that it stands by.

There are certainly posts in Israel about love and queerness, but I wouldn't classify them as Zionist. In fact, many posts in Palestine/Israel by self-defined Israelis are critical of Zionism and of the effects of occupation on Palestinians. Of course, because of the recent circulation of posts in Palestine, there has been a huge influx of vitriolic anti Palestinian or anti queer Palestinian submissions, a few examples being: "Damn all those gay Palestinians? Maybe you guys deserve what Israel is doing to yall keep sucking dick i guess," and "Walked along the shore after a long day of spitting on Palestinians locked in cages…vibes were immaculate." These are quite obviously hate speech.

I have received many emails, recently and over the years since the platform has been online, telling me I should remove posts containing "Free Palestine," of which there are many. Overwhelmingly, the logic given in these emails is that this is not what Queering the Map is for, it is not a political project. I refuse these requests because I believe the liberation of Palestine is intimately connected to the liberation of queer people – given the intertwined histories of antiqueerness, antitransness, and the colonial project. So I would never claim that Queering the Map is a neutral platform.

JK: Have you ever felt conflicted about moderating a post?

LL: I would say 99.9 percent of the time it's quite obvious. More than anything else, we are screening for breaches of anonymity – so full names, phone numbers, emails, social media handles, etc. Hate speech is usually very direct and uncreative attacks on queer people, trans people, people of color, etc. One example of a place where moderation becomes muddier is situations when people are talking about sexual encounters in ways that could be considered fetishistic. There, the content of the story and the way that it's written really matter. Those are slightly more challenging, but even then, in reading them a couple of times, the intent begins to feel pretty obvious. It's certainly not an exact science, especially because it also depends on the particular perspective of the individual moderators who make the decisions.

JK: My critique of how we understand queer space from the '90s and early 2000s is what led me to explore the issues raised in Working Queer. I felt like I was being told something about spaces of sex, desire, and liberation that didn't resonate clearly, but now I want to revisit some of that thinking. One of the brilliant things about Queering the Map is how it occupies this postdigital space of being hyperphysical in a material reality while working as a digital platform. We constantly hear about a nostalgia for lost queer space – digital cruising killed queer space, rent prices killed queer space, something else killed queer space. There's always this sense of loss. Your project occupies an interesting position vis-à-vis that narrative, because it is both a live digital tool that serves as a recording device of memories and is part of that nostalgia machine while also being perpetually new. Is the map a queer space analogous to a queer bar? Is it combating the primacy of digital culture or leaning into it?

LL: I would argue that it functions as a queer space if we define it through George Chauncey's antidefinitional statement, "There is no queer space; there are only spaces used by queers or put to queer use." It is certainly a site of queer use in that it is a map "defaced" with the subjective experience of queer users. Queer relationality is represented in the stories, and then through the dynamics between the pins themselves and the ways they respond, refute, or complexify one another. This does the work of future building in the same way that physical queer spaces provide places for people to meet and generate a sense of ongoing possibility. The circulation of the stories enables readers to be moved by them and, in turn, move through the world differently – trajectories skewed as a result of encountering different perspectives and experiences.

I wouldn't say digital cruising killed physical cruising, but it changed the culture. I don't think they necessarily exist in opposition to one another. Queering the Map is not a replacement for physical queer space.

One of the arguments that Queering the Map makes is for an expanded definition of what constitutes queer space outside of bars, bookstores, bathhouses, etc., by attuning us to the ephemeral or the necessity of the temporal in the construction of queer space – for example, a bench in a park where people shared a kiss. The pins mark space-times that become queer spaces, not necessarily in an ongoing way or in a way that is sensible to others, but that come into existence through the relation of queer people in a particular space and time. In many cases, they illuminate something about the sociopolitical contexts of a place and the infrastructure or architectures that enable the meeting (or not meeting) of people in particular ways.

JK: Has anyone ever tried to go on a little queer mission to find these spaces in real life? Like a road trip to stop at the pins? Because so many of them represent something so specific in terms of place, time, and relationality, and so much of the queer imaginary is the way that affect produces a material value. That bench means something so powerful and spatial and physical at that moment, but then someone else sees just some dumb bench.

LL: A number of years ago, I led a workshop for the graphic design summer school, "A School, A Park," in which we went around and took rubbings of locations of pins in Montreal. One of the important outcomes of that workshop was that in most cases you can't reliably find the place that is being described. The mapping on Queering the Map is both intentionally and unintentionally imprecise. And so we don't know if someone is talking about this side of the street or the other side of the street. Is it that building or the other building? In trying to encounter the actual locations, one is always left slightly askew or unsure. A sense of indeterminate possibility, of the "might have happened here" or "might happen here in the future," emerges through the process of trying to touch the physical locations that Queering the Map archives digitally.

JK: It's the embodiment of the queer utopia. You can never get there, all you can do is get a little closer. I want to talk about the lineage of mapping. Earlier you said that Queering the Map willfully misappropriates or misuses mapmaking and map reading. The map is a map until it's no longer precise. And that imprecision is the most interesting space to occupy. Is there a particular kind of post that really annoys you?

LL: I guess sometimes I get annoyed by overly cringey stories. To be fair, my annoyance has almost nothing to do with the stories themselves, but with the experience of moderating. I will read a beautiful account of someone falling in love, then a story of someone being disowned by their family, and then something quite cringe, all in succession. The discordance in affect from one submission to another is bewildering, to say the least.

Moderating has done wild things to my brain. For the past couple of years, I've been working on a project called QT.bot, an AI that's trained on all of the posts on Queering the Map, which in turn can create speculative narratives of queer and trans life. One of the aims of the project is to think through the limitations of the confessional mode of writing as it emerges on Queering the Map, or of sentimentality as a political strategy. This AI model can produce stories that unlock queer affects in ways that are, let's say, methodologically queerer than the source text in terms of how subjectivity, time, space, and affect begin to explode and recombine. My interest in these texts is very much informed by the emotional whiplash of moderating, in that the stories QT.bot creates feel like the most articulate expression of the contents of the site all at once.

This project has been in resistance to that deductive mode of sense making. It uses machine learning models that are designed to distill conclusions from a given dataset, but manipulates them to do exactly the opposite. I am particularly fascinated by the QT.bot narratives that fail to make sense. In their failure, they open up new kinds of possibilities for language and for thinking about queerness as a form of relationality that breaks or finds new forms in and through its actions. Rather than working with an output that passes as a real story, I am interested in what happens in the break, what happens in the collapse of combining all these voices into a discordant choir.

I've been working on a platform version so that people can communicate and coproduce stories with QT.bot. The dilemma with creating a publicly accessible version is that it occasionally produces really fucked up stories, simply based on how the words are arranged in the sentence. So the question of moderation again becomes central.

JK: That seems to be the direction of all these chatbots. They just reveal themselves, very quickly, as monsters.

LL: Yeah, they have no ethical commitment to anything.

Jaffer Kolb guest edited Working Queer, a special section in *Log* 41 (2017). He teaches architecture at MIT and is cofounder and principal of the New York–based architecture office New Affiliates.

Dora Epstein Jones & Katharine Hayhoe

Hope Begins In a Dark Place

Dr. Katharine Hayhoe is a Paul Whitfield Horn Distinguished Professor and an Endowed Chair in Public Policy and Public Law at the Texas Tech University Department of Political Science. She is also chief scientist for the Nature Conservancy and a leading voice on climate change. Her latest books, Saving Us: A Climate Scientist's Case for Hope and Healing in a Divided World *(2021) and* Downscaling Techniques for High-Resolution Climate Projections: From Global Change to Local Impacts *(2021) make the case for mitigation efforts at every scale and from every value system. Her dual role as a climate scientist and as a public figure allows her to understand and use climate observations, scenarios, and models to effectively translate and communicate the latest scientific findings to many sectors of society and production, from agriculture to public health. I believe that we, in architecture, need to hear her message too; and so, on a blistering and brutally hot October day in Texas, she and I met in the tiny carbon footprint of Zoom. – DEJ*

DORA EPSTEIN JONES: What is your most urgent message to people in architecture and in the design of the built environment today?

KATHARINE HAYHOE: We need to know that climate change is an *everything* issue. It is already affecting every aspect of our lives, including the built environment, and its impacts are increasing. This means that today we need to be building for the future, not the past.

    The way I look at it is like this. For thousands of years, we humans have been driving down the road looking in the rearview mirror. All of our building standards, our building codes, and our building designs are based on the conditions of the past. That's effective if the road is relatively straight – in other words, if the climate isn't changing. Today, however, we've already hit an unprecedented curve in the road. The climate is changing faster than at any time in human history. That's why it's essential that we change the paradigm of our buildings so that we're looking down the road, toward where we are headed, preparing for a very different future.

I think of a Bangladeshi architecture student who took one of my classes at Texas Tech. Much of Bangladesh is low-lying and will be overwhelmed by sea level rise. There's also a tremendous flooding issue in Bangladesh with monsoons dumping more water in a warmer world. So for his final project, this student chose to create a series of evocative drawings of what a Bangladeshi town could look like if they lived *with* the water instead of against it. In doing so, he created a beautiful and compelling vision of what a better future could look like if we start planning for it today.

Understanding and preparing for the risks of climate change, the need to build resilience, and the potential to create a better future, even in a warmer world, must be part of our perspective today. But we also need to understand that the built environment is a huge source of the problem as well. Depending on how you allocate the responsibility, up to 40 percent of global greenhouse gas emissions are associated with the built environment. Emissions are generated when new materials are created for construction (concrete alone is responsible for up to eight percent of global carbon emissions), when we use fossil fuels to heat and cool our homes, and by the electricity we use to power our buildings.

That means there's tremendous potential for the built environment to be part of the solution, both in building resilience to climate impacts and in reducing the emissions that are driving the crisis. It's not just about reaching net zero. Sustainable and climate-smart building practices even have the potential to turn the built environment into a net sink of heat-trapping gas emissions rather than a source. From the sustainable use of mass timber to carbon-negative concrete, many building materials can sequester carbon rather than release it.

We're also just starting to understand how the building materials we use affect our health. I'm not only talking about urban planning and walkable cities – the "15-minute city" concept is really interesting and it's certainly gaining a lot of momentum. But what shocks me as an atmospheric scientist is that I did not even know how harmful gas stoves are for our health until just a few years ago. I wasn't aware that gas stoves were linked to six times higher rates of childhood asthma, or that, even when they're off, they still leak dangerous pollutants into our home. And it turns out that part of the reason we didn't know is because gas companies were using the same disinformation techniques to keep us in the dark as fossil fuel companies have been using to muddy the waters on climate change over the last 30 years.

DEJ: Wait until you hear about plywood!

KH: Exactly. The health connection offers a tremendous opportunity to educate, because who doesn't care about their health and that of their family?

For example, we moved into a new townhome recently. We were able to choose a few of the options, so I asked, What stove are we getting? They said, Oh, you're getting a top-of-the-line gas range. And I said, Don't you know that they're massive sources of air pollution? Not a single soul in that room, neither the architect nor the builders, had ever heard that before. So I told them, This is something you really need to be aware of. It's your customer's health you're putting at risk. You should at least inform them, and give them the option of an electric range.

This is just one example of how architects have tremendous responsibility and tremendous potential to make a huge difference, from positively impacting the lives of the people who live and work in the buildings that they construct, maintain, and renovate, all the way up to the global scale, where they play a significant role in altering the future trajectory of human society on this planet.

DEJ: I can see how we can make impacts with our choices and specifications, but the question for me also comes down to a strategy of collective energy. How do we come together as a group of people to create lasting change, working into the future, when there's always someone who is willing to keep putting in the gas stoves? Do you have any recommendations for that? Can architecture do this without causing the need for huge policy changes, which are slow?

KH: Can architecture take these actions? Yes. Can they implement them at scale without policy changes? No. Right now, we do not live in a free market. We live in a market that is heavily skewed toward maintaining people's dependence on fossil fuels. And we know that the status quo is always easier and cheaper.

We need social change, but we know that for social change to occur, we have to have the *ability* to change. In other words, you can't replace carbon-emitting concrete or a gas furnace if there's nothing to replace it with. These days, however, we have plenty of options for replacing high-emitting products. Heat pumps are gaining in popularity. Green concrete is available. Rooftop solar is becoming cheaper every year.

We also need early adopters. Some architects are able to work with people who have the financial resources and the education to desire and be able to be early adopters. Once the cost curve and the knowledge curve start to come down, the next wave of people will be willing to spend perhaps a little bit more money than the status quo.

That's how we can start to build the political will we need to advocate for policy change. And there, it's important to recognize that it doesn't have to begin at the federal level. Effective policy change can happen in a city, a county, a neighborhood, or even a company.

Don't wait for policy, though, because it's often the last thing to change. Bring new options to the table and get the early adopters, the pioneers, and the larger organizations to buy into these options, making them the standard in the buildings they build or renovate. In Germany, for example, they've created panels that you can snap onto an old building to create an envelope around it, massively reducing its energy load without changing a single thing inside what might be a centuries-old structure. In Canada, for example, the founder of Mattamy Homes recently made himself the chief sustainability ambassador for the organization. He's deeply committed to cocreating the new, climate-friendly options we need and implementing them in homes across the country.

Change can happen without policy, and then it starts to snowball. The more it snowballs, the more impetus there is for policy changes. And if the solutions we create have the potential to be produced at scale, with financial savings, they can even take off with or without policy. So, do we need policy? Yes. But is policy sufficient? No. We need action at every level.

DEJ: That's not outlandish, given there are professional associations and professional licensures and codes that regulate our existence, that doesn't seem like a crazy thing to ask for. I wish we could just get architects to take a hard line and say, We're not going to participate in anything that doesn't contribute to mitigating the climate emergency. But when it comes to talking about ethics in architecture, we're usually talking about more local actions like don't screw over the client or don't do anything bad to the environment, meaning don't dump waste or anything like that. But other than that, it's a pretty loose thing. Do you think that we need to get a little firmer in light of the climate emergency?

KH: Yes, I do. The built environment is a big piece of the pie in terms of what's contributing to our triple crises of pollution, biodiversity loss, and climate change. Not only that, but climate change is a threat multiplier. It's accelerating many of the social problems we already have, including increasing socioeconomic inequity and magnifying the historic discriminatory practices that affect people's homes and neighborhoods. For example, decades of racist practices like redlining have also put low-income neighborhoods at much greater risk during heat waves, flooding, or hurricanes. This is also the responsibility of the building sector, which means it has the ability to contribute to change. It is possible to address many of these inequities by working on climate-resilient housing in low-income neighborhoods – helping homes prepare for heat, flooding, and storms, installing green infrastructure that cools the area during heatwaves and soaks up water during floods, and facilitating the services that allow people to access emergency assistance and recovery programs.

What I would say is that with power comes responsibility. And this sector has tremendous power to change the world for good in so many ways. At Texas Tech, we were just awarded a large Housing and Urban Development grant to build a center that focuses on best practices for climate-resilient housing in low-income neighborhoods. I'm very excited to start working on that, along with my colleague Ali Nejat.

DEJ: Oh, wow, congratulations! One of the things that I really admire in your work, as a person and as a writer, author, scientist, is that you have a compassionate and caring approach to the scales of responsibility. What does it mean to work in the ways that you talk about?

KH: We live in a world where people feel increasingly powerless in the face of rising threats to our health, our well-being, the safety and stability of our world, and the future that we're leaving our children. As we see disasters mounting – for example, with this past summer's wildfires, heat waves, floods, and droughts – people's awareness and worry have increased, but their levels of helplessness have also increased.

To put it another way, people's sense of agency plummets as we ask ourselves, How could I end the wildfires in Canada? How could I stop the weeks of 100-degree temperatures that we've experienced in Texas? How could I prevent the waters off the coast of Florida from reaching hot-tub temperatures, killing the corals that people just spent the last decade carefully planting to rejuvenate the reefs? What could I do to make a difference?

And at the same time, given the urgency of this issue, many people are also fearful of the speed at which solutions are being implemented. They might feel like, I've always lived my life this way, and now they're talking about all these different things that I'm not used to, like heat pumps – I don't even know what those are! And electric cars that don't run on gas so if I run out of battery, I have to get towed. I don't know how these changes will affect me and my family. Some people genuinely fear that the cure is worse than the disease, that climate solutions will decrease their quality of life far more than climate impacts will.

Now, let's be clear. Anyone who believes that has absolutely no idea of the magnitude of the impacts that are coming. But it's hard for people to wrap their minds around what's happening. We're confronting changes at a scale we've never seen before. We have no analogue for what human society will look like if it's confronted with this scale of change this quickly.

So how do we move forward? While we need to be worried about what's happening, fear alone is not the answer. Neuroscientists tell us that our human brains are not wired to respond in a positive, constructive way to fear. In the long term, fear paralyzes us, and that's exactly what I'm seeing today. People are being paralyzed by fear.

So what's the antidote to fear, to despair? The antidote is action-based hope. I'm not referring to a false hope – that if I just bury my head in the sand, everything will work out. It won't! Neither am I referring to positive thinking, because we can think positively all we want but that won't change the outcome.

By definition, hope begins in a dark place. You don't need hope if everything is fine. You only need hope when things are not fine, and that's exactly where we are today. Hope begins with recognizing that it's bad and is getting worse. That's the first step.

The second step, however, is recognizing that a better future is possible – not guaranteed, but possible. We need a vision of what that better future could look like. For example, livable, walkable, green cities with blue sky and clean water, ample and abundant food, and interactive communities. Architects are very good at imagining what the future looks like in the images they draw and the visuals they share with people, so I believe they're ideally suited to provide us with that next ingredient of hope.

Step three is that we have to lay out and describe a realistic path for us to get from where we are today to where we want to be in that better future. There's no point envisioning a future that can never be achieved, no matter what we do. That's not a future, it's a fantasy.

The final step is that each of us has to know what we can do to help the collective "we" progress along that path. Our personal sense of hope is directly tied to our sense of efficacy. If I do something, how will it make a difference? Each of us needs to know what we can do to accelerate us along that pathway and increase the probability of reaching that future. We can't do it alone, but I'm convinced we can do it together.

DEJ: So, if we did declare a discipline-wide climate emergency, it sounds like there's going to be some discomfort for a while, but we'd be on our way to the greatest possible comfort given the climate circumstances.

KH: To overcome our discomfort with rapid change, we need a vision of a better future. There must be something that we are moving toward that is so positive, and so worthwhile, that it overcomes our fear of the speed at which our lives are changing. Take the telephone as an example. When I was a child, our telephone was a party line that we shared with our neighbors. You could only answer the phone when it was your ring (ours was long-short!), and you never knew who might be listening to your call.

Fast forward to today, and we hold something in our hands more powerful than scientists at the world's biggest supercomputer labs had access to when I was born. How did that change? It didn't happen by telling people they really ought to buy a smartphone out of moral responsibility, that they had to give up the party line telephone because we all need to do this. No. If you go to the mall when the latest iPhone is coming out, people are lined up to get it. They are excited about making the change. They have a vision of how much better their life is going to be if they do.

Now, I'm not saying consumerism is the answer, don't get me wrong! What I'm saying is that Apple understood the power of a positive vision of the future. Their marketing scheme was based on how much more organized you would be, or how much fitter you would be, or how many better recipes you'd have access to, or how you could connect with your distant family members more often. They created a vision of a better life, and that's what drives people to make radically different changes at speed. That is how our brains are wired. As humans, we want to move toward something better.

DEJ: Yes! I think a lot about the national emergency during World War II. We can look at how rapidly modern architecture went from being a vision to being implemented, particularly in the immediate postwar period, nearly everywhere, in what, 30 to 40 years! That seems quick. I hope that the response to the climate emergency can do the same thing. But do we have 30 to 40 years?

KH: The good news is that we're not at the starting line. Consider how we already have windows that can collect energy from the sun, we have heat pumps, we have net-zero homes and carbon-negative building materials. We already know how greening our cities can make us more resilient to heat and flooding, as well as cleaning up our air and providing habitat for biodiversity. We're well along that path, we just have to speed it up.

DEJ: How fast?

KH: Here's what the science says. The faster we go, the better off we'll be. There's no magic number of cigarettes you can smoke until you get lung cancer, but you know that the less you smoke, or the sooner you stop smoking, the healthier you'll be. It's the same concept with the heat-trapping gas emissions that are driving climate change. The more we produce, the greater the risks. On the other hand, the faster we can transition off fossil fuels and the faster we can make our built environment resilient to these changes, the better off and the safer we'll all be.

The United Nations' Intergovernmental Panel on Climate Change issues a set of comprehensive assessment reports every few years, synthesizing the latest science in thousands of pages of excruciating detail. However, they're also clear that all of these scientific conclusions can be summarized by one simple statement: "Every bit of warming matters. Every action matters. Every choice matters." I see that as a very empowering message, that everything we do truly does make a difference. Because if that's the case, then what are we waiting for? It's past time to hurry this transition up.

Dora Epstein Jones guest edited, with Bryony Roberts, *Log* 31: New Ancients (2014). She is a professor of practice in the School of Architecture at The University of Texas at Austin.

*Savinien Caracostea
& Anders Frederik Steen*

Eat the World We Want to Live In

Since the publication of Log 34: The Food Issue, *in 2015, there has been an increased urgency to rethink our food systems and the way we eat to address the major environmental, social, and economic concerns facing us. Eleven Madison Park, one of the most highly acclaimed fine dining restaurants, transitioned to plant-based menus following the pandemic and partnered with a nonprofit to provide meals to food-insecure districts in the Bronx, Brooklyn, and Queens. A new generation of younger, highly conscious chefs also displays a radical awareness of their role in stewarding a better tomorrow by providing healthy, simple, creative, and locally sourced fares. Their impact on their communities and on the planet are the only stars they are after.*

Underpinning this new wave is another movement that has been steadily growing over the past decade: natural wines. Natural wines are typically made using only native yeasts and grapes grown without the use of pesticides or other additives. Anders Frederik Steen started his journey as a winemaker in 2013 and has since become a cult figure in the field. Transcending the concept of vintages, each of his wines has its own arresting name printed on the bottle's iconic plain white labels in Times New Roman, bold. "When a piece of rice paper hits the glow of a cigarette." "Don't throw plastic in the Oceans, Please." In 2022, he published Poetry Is Growing in Our Garden, *his field notes between 2013 and 2020. Steen lives in the Ardèche region of France where he and his wife, Anne Bruun Blauert, produce some of the most unique and delightful wines I've ever tasted. We spoke over a video call in mid-July, as he was readying the pressoir for the upcoming harvest. – SC*

SAVINIEN CARACOSTEA: How did you get into making natural wines?

ANDERS FREDERIK STEEN: I'm educated as a chef originally, and for many years I worked as a chef. Later on, I got an education in London as a sommelier. What made me go into being a sommelier was basically curiosity. I wanted to know the wine better to be able to cook better. I became a sommelier at that point. Ten years later, when I started making wine, my idea was simply to make a few vintages. Again,

I was driven by curiosity about how wine is actually made. When you work with wine, whether as a sommelier, importer, or whatever, you taste finished wines, fermenting wines in barrels, and wines that are in barrels but meant to age. So you're often very distant from the raw material part of the wine-making process. I was curious about when you pick the grapes. If we pick them at a certain point, it produces one kind of wine, but if we pick them at another, what wine will it be then? Later on, I became curious about all the technical stuff. What if we de-stem? If we don't de-stem? If we do direct press? What does this mean to the finished wine? And then, just like everything else, you get grabbed by the thing and your curiosity becomes more than you can control. So I ended up making wine full-time.

SC: In reading your field notes, I found it fascinating that you can actually guide or not guide the wine, and how that is an essential part of the creative process. You describe it as being more intuitive than the more market-driven wines, which you say are tailored to specific markets.

AFS: First of all, I have nothing against wines that are tailored to a certain market. It's just that I think you feel a little less of the winemaker, the grapes, and this love for the wine. Once you start to produce wine for a market that you think needs a certain kind of wine, you lose a big part of yourself. Anne and I make the wines that we would want to drink. But one thing I quickly learned during the first years of making wines is that it's not possible to make them just the way you want them. What is important is that you are able to adapt constantly. The grapes have different kinds of expressions that you cannot change. All you can do is adapt. It's like colors in a painting or notes in music. You have a certain tool set, and within that you can play around. For example, a grape berry has different kinds of qualities. If we press it, it's one thing, only the juice. If we press it slowly for a couple of days, it's a different kind of juice. If we de-stem it and let it macerate for two or three days, it's another kind of juice again. And if we let it macerate for a month, it will, again, be something else.

The process is very simple. I say that it is by intuition, but intuition is never without knowledge – intuition alone is not worth anything. The experience of tasting grapes and tasting wine helps us to know if a grape can produce wine if we do this or that, or if these grapes can be combined with those grapes, or the juice we have in this other tank can be used to make the wine we want. It's blending raw materials. I say it's intuition because I'm not exactly sure what I'm doing.

SC: It's interesting to hear you compare it to other art forms, like painting or classical music versus improvisational jazz, which has a bit more play. In a way, you are playing with the grapes, playing with the weather, conducting them as an orchestra of sorts.

AFS: Exactly. We can argue that jazz is the most free-form music, but I think the talents of jazz musicians and of classical musicians are actually very close to each other. It's the way they express themselves that's different. That's also what I feel more and more in the natural wine scene. The movement has been going on for 25 years now, but in the last 10 years, it's really evolved. Often, natural winemakers are known as free-spirit, crazy, creative people, but I think we have more semblance with classical wine production than we want to admit because, while our wines express themselves differently, the knowledge that is behind them is equally profound.

SC: You speak about natural wine making as a movement of free-spirited people, but also as struggling with issues of regulation, with the industry trying to pin down exactly what it means. Can you talk more about that dynamic?

AFS: Well, in France we say it's a double-edged sword. The regulations are quite helpful because they make the process easier for consumers to understand. They also make sure that fewer people will cheat with the product because there's more control. But on the other side, we lose the freedom to express exactly what we want without having anybody looking over our shoulders. I think we lose some of the very spirit of natural wine because natural wine was meant as a revolution. It was against not only classical wines but also the way these wines are being grown and made. I mean in terms of the use of chemicals, etc. So we need to continue.

SC: Having an architecture background, I see a lot of similar concerns in the architecture world, from sustainability regulations that push toward standardization to real estate developers driving the discipline toward construction that will make them the most money, such as luxury condominiums. As a result, most new buildings signal wealth, they signal sustainability, they signal creativity, but they are often completely inappropriate for what most people need because they're basically speculative investments. Are you feeling similar dynamics between the wine creators and the market-driven products?

AFS: I see it very much. It's funny, because I just came back from Barcelona. Anne and I went to see Park Güell, Gaudí's magnificent park with buildings that are completely beyond what you can imagine. We spoke exactly about this. When did we stop allowing artists, or fantastic, crazy people, to build these things? When did we decide that buildings had to be square, made with a purpose, and so on? And the conversation went to wine and food and many other products that are, of course, created to be consumed. It's a clash that we see in many fields now. What is the best piece of music? Is it the song on Spotify with the most listens or the one with the most likes on YouTube? Or simply a piece of music you like the best? I'm not sure. Well, I know what I think myself, but measuring this is impossible. Likewise, with wine, if the purpose is to sell millions of bottles, even though it is under the category of natural wine, I think you've lost it, actually, because it's not possible to do what we do. I mean, we need to create a distinct distance between what we consider an artistic expression and a product in the same category. In a couple of years, I think you will see natural wine more as a way to categorize a production method than as a style of wine. Right now, classical wines can be something from Grand Cru, Burgundy, Champagne, standard wines from the Rhône Valley, all the way down to supermarket wholesale rosé from Provence. We will see great wines of the highest quality and some that are the most experimental, but we'll also see the wholesale from Provence, made correctly, but just as boring.

SC: Can you talk more about your creative process and what makes a great wine for you? How do you balance the natural expression of the wines with your own knowledge and taste?

AFS: Balance is a very complicated thing to explain because it's something that happens naturally. Like in architecture, if something isn't in balance it falls apart. But when something is in balance, it's very difficult to say why it's so beautiful or harmonious. Wine is the same. When we make the wines, it's by tasting the wine. Sometimes we feel they're unbalanced. Sometimes the acidity is too much. The oxidation is not right, or the fruit is too much, or whatever. There can be many flavors, so it's not worth mentioning all of them, but the balance between all of them needs to be there. There's no formula that says, okay, when it's a linear structure, it's good.

In my book I talk about this pyramidal structure, which is something I have in my head all the time. If I can create a structure with three components – acidity, saltiness, oxidation, tannins, or fruit – I can balance them to make a solid triangle, a pyramid. Then I can add on anything. The structure in the wine is like the foundation of a house. At the moment, we're building a cellar. We are digging out a cellar under an 800-year-old house, 100 meters from where we live, and we are remaking the walls, the staircases. Everything was built in stone, and we continue the same way. If the foundation stones are well situated, then you can build as high as you want.

What *balanced* means changes constantly, from vintage to vintage. Some vintages allow us to make certain kinds of wine because it's a warmer vintage or a colder vintage, or more humid or whatever. There can be so many factors in weather and in the structure of grapes. So some years a balanced wine is one thing, and the year after, well, the balanced wine is something completely different.

SC: What's interesting about eating or drinking things that are a bit unpredictable, especially when in good company, is that it breaks habitual patterns and opens our minds to discovery, to collectively understand what is going on, and to posture ourselves toward this novelty. Do we like it? What can we learn from this? Drinking your wines encourages us to get into this open mindset, which you then use to introduce poetic or political statements. One of your bottles, for instance, is labeled "Let's Eat the World We Want to Live In." Can you give us a bit more context about how you see your project fitting into an activist role in the agriculture world specifically?

AFS: Wine is different from strong spirits or beer. Wine is a social liquid. To drink a bottle of wine, it's better to be at least two or three people, whereas beer and spirits can be, and often are, drunk alone, without company. Wine can be drunk with the purpose of being together, and can be the key that opens the door to conversations. For me, this is one of the cornerstones of what we make. In a way, I see Anne and myself less as winemakers and more as politicians. We provide a few words on our labels to put on the table, and from there the dream is to have people talk about it and think about it themselves.

In a couple of weeks, we will bottle another wine that will be called, "Call You Later, Bad Lighting." It seems like a silly sentence, but for me it's very political. It's very much about the way we use social media and present everything in our lives as if it were perfect.

I believe very strongly that the biggest change we can make is made by the people who vote, not those who are elected or in governments. When we want to change the structure of society, we can propose ideas, but it takes a long time before an idea gets to the government. And after that, if it goes through, it also needs to be implemented. Changes can take decades, but what is very, very efficient is the money, the consumers and how they use their money. We see it in fashion. Last spring, everybody bought yellow. And this year, everybody bought green. So last year the fashion industry produced only yellow. This year they produced only green because the money is the power.

When Anne and I write "Let's Eat the World We Want to Live In," it's because we want people to go down to the supermarket and buy organic stuff, buy products from people who are treating their employees correctly, and to stop supporting people who are racist, culturally ignorant, and so on. What is important is that when the money is talking, we will see the changes right away.

SC: The difficult part is what Henry Ford said when he started making cars – "If I asked my consumers what they wanted, they would've said, 'A faster horse.'" So it's also showing people what they could want, what an alternative could be, and then seeing how they respond to it. I don't think the general population imagines what they want before it's presented to them.

AFS: Ford is considered one of the most important figures in the new modern and industrial world. But it's a fact that with him and his systematic mass production, respect for craftsmanship disappeared. Before Ford, a mason, a blacksmith, or a carpenter was a very important person in society, their work was creative and often of very high quality. The better a craftsman was, the more he or she was respected. After Ford, craftsmen became factory workers and it was the speed of their work that was valued, not necessarily the quality. Before there was equal respect for academics and craftsmanship. That got lost. Natural wine represents a departure from this mass production of monoculture that represents the old, classic wine world, the wine world that is dominated by elder men and their habits of drinking certain kinds of wines. Natural wine offers a more conscious way of living in terms of organic farming, sustainable production, and labor politics. It's not that I want to be this organic farmer who works in a medieval way with a donkey and a straw hat. I just think that instead of constantly coming up with new things, we should go back and think about what were the things that made wine great to begin with. The answers to today's problems are, in my opinion, to be found in yesterday, not tomorrow.

I live with Anne and our kids in a house that is 1,100 years old. It was built with stone and very old wood. The climate inside the house – the humidity, the freshness of the air – is very high quality. Today it was 44 degrees [111 Fahrenheit] where I live, but in the house, I think it was maybe 25 [77 Fahrenheit]. So something is working. There are many things that allow us to have a house that is comfortable, such as walls that are very thick. But why do we build concrete houses with air-conditioning systems? Concrete is not very good for the environment. It doesn't work without air conditioning. So why do we continue doing this? The Industrial Revolution gave us speed, but we have never built as badly as we did in the '60s, '70s, and '80s. Everything had to go so quickly that craftsmanship was forgotten. When we are rebuilding our cellar today, we are paying the price for mistakes made 50 years ago. However, I have a feeling that this is a trend that is about to change. The respect for old houses, old ways of building, and craftsmanship is increasing.

SC: It's true. Investing in a market-driven monoculture depletes our collective soil entirely, and there are people and practices being weeded out in the process that probably really need to be there, and a lot of resources put into initiatives that are hurting the ecosystem. Just look at New York City and the gentrification here, where neighborhoods once filled with artists, creatives, musicians are suddenly taken over by luxury condominiums and fancy hotels. That's basically the architectural equivalent of an agricultural spray that kills everything except for the one crop developers are after, which is the money crop.

AFS: As you say, people are getting weeded out. That's the problem. The poetry in a community, in any city, is its diversity. Once we start to standardize this and make it purely about the economy, people get weeded out and the poetry disappears. Embracing diversity in New York City or in a vineyard is very much the key to solving all the problems you have. The more plants we have of different sorts, the more insects, the more birds, the more animals we have in the vineyard, the better, the healthier the soil, and with that, healthier vines. It's a circle. And I think it's very much the same in a city. When prices rise, artists, musicians, and single-parent families can't afford to live in those neighborhoods. So it's also a political question. Just as big cities need subsidized apartments, we need to be able to say, okay, growing organically is very expensive because you grow fewer grapes. You do wine in a certain way. The risk is higher, and so on. But instead of helping the big-ag industry, we should support this kind of production. Could a solution in architecture and urban planning be to think of social housing complexes more like small households or villages? Instead of building tall, depressing buildings made of concrete, we could imagine areas with space for a natural diversity, business owners, bakers, butchers, private or collective gardens for vegetable production, chickens – basically as a village.

SC: The pandemic has stimulated a resurgence in community-driven urban projects, but especially in big cities like New York, the high cost of realty is stifling initiatives that are not already well-funded. The politics and thinking about cities and urban design have been historically about applying theory. But one line I like in your book is, "What's good in theory doesn't often work, whereas intuition is pretty much always a winner." We need to develop a more fertile soil for cities as well, which would encourage a certain amount of experimentation.

    The historian Carlo Ginzburg alludes to the idea that our civilization is not evolving but rather fermenting. Things aren't becoming clearer and simpler. Instead, complexity is becoming more rhizomatic and apparent. What does the concept of fermentation mean to your work? Maybe it's just the wine talking, but perhaps very complex issues can become clearer when we start thinking about them through the lens of natural wine. How has embracing the unpredictable side of the fermentation process informed your perspective?

AFS: The romantic picture of a winemaker is this great god of what happens in the cellar, but it's not true. Fermentation is a very wild mechanism. Much like urbanism, it's a machine nobody can control. Once you get it started, you need to accept that you're no longer in charge. It's the wine expressing itself. I think that is maybe one of the keys to what we said before about trying to standardize everything so it's easier for consumers to understand. Anne and I are not winemakers. We see ourselves as wine followers. We just put the grapes in a tank and then we follow it from there. We accompany it. We're keeping the wine company. We're tasting it, we do things, but we're not really making it. Curators of wine, more than makers. If we take that perspective to a larger scale, we can maybe see ourselves less as the people creating stuff in the world and more as people who are following things and keeping the solutions company to enable them to be what we want them to be, but also to accept them. The parts of it that we can't control become what's interesting.

Savinien Caracostea was guest editor, with Jan Åman, of *Log* 34: The Food Issue (2015). He is a baker, designer, and strategist based in New York City, working at the intersection of design, culture, and technology.

Phyllis Lambert

Remembering Jean-Louis Cohen

On August 7, 2023, while he was preparing to make jam from the fruit on the great fig tree at his home in the Ardèche, Jean-Louis Cohen was stung by a bee, and died. The tragedy: So much was given, and so much was to come.

What Jean-Louis accomplished in a day, a week, a month, a year was incredible. And yet, when you were with him, he was totally with you, without any sign that anything else engaged him. Clearly everyone who knew him felt this way. When word of his sudden death spread, tributes filled both digital and print media on multiple continents. In his lifetime, Jean-Louis was chair in architecture and urban form at the Collège de France; the Sheldon H. Solow Professor in the History of Architecture at the Institute of Fine Arts (IFA), New York University; a visiting professor at Princeton University, a member of the visiting committees at Harvard's GSD and the American University, Beirut; the scientific committee of the Centro Palladio, Vicenza; chair of the scientific committee for the conservation of the Constantin Melnikov House, Moscow, and the scientific committee of the Cap Moderne Association, Roquebrune-Cap-Martin; a member of the Fondation Le Corbusier committee of experts on built work, in Paris; and a member of the Architecture and Design Acquisitions Committee at the Museum of Modern Art, New York. The students working with him now wonder how they will carry on. One former IFA student recalled a field trip to Los Angeles, with "Jean-Louis gesturing wildly out of his [car] window at some building or landscape he couldn't wait to share." Similarly, when leading a tour of an exhibition he curated, Jean-Louis would expand on the selection of objects and images with an enthusiasm that was contagious.

Jean-Louis explained his universal generosity: "I like to share knowledge and I do not keep it for myself, for my books. I'm curious about other people." Over the years, the development of his research is recorded in his growing bibliographies and CVs. By my preliminary count, and according to these documents, from 1974 to 2019, Jean-Louis authored some 57 publications, contributed some 270 pieces to collected works and exhibition catalogs, and published roughly 440 essays and

Jean-Louis Cohen (1949–2023), photographed in 2009.

articles in periodicals (including *Log*). To this, we can add reports on research and commissions, as well as audiovisual and radio programs. He just missed seeing the publication, in September, of *Detroit-Moscow-Detroit: An Architecture for Industrialization, 1917–1945*, which he coedited with Christina E. Crawford and Claire Zimmerman.

Some of Jean-Louis's deep research resulted in exhibitions and their catalogs, which include *Scenes of the World to Come: European Architecture and the American Challenge, 1893–1960* (1995); *Architecture in Uniform: Designing and Building for the Second World War* (2011), and *Building a New World: Amerikanizm in Russian Architecture* (2019–2020), all produced with the CCA. Among other shows, he also curated "Casablanca, naissance d'une ville moderne sur le sol africain" at Fondation Electra in Paris (1999); "Lost Vanguard: Soviet Modernist Architecture, 1922–32," with Barry Bergdoll, at MoMA (2007); "Interférances/Interferenze: Architecture Allemagne-France 1800–2000," with Harmut Frank, for an exhibition in Strasbourg and in Frankfurt (2013–2014). When he died, Jean-Louis was deep into his work on a planned eight-volume catalogue raisonné of Frank Gehry's drawings. The first volume, on the years 1954–1978, was published by Cahiers d'Art in 2020, is but a fragment of the work. How many other articles, reports, and publications are now orphaned, as well as those Jean-Louis planned to research, including an exhibition with the CCA on North Africa?

In a sense, Jean-Louis built his own culture of architecture. He was born, in 1949, into a Parisian family that, he said, had two passions: science and politics. His grandfather Marcel was a celebrated linguist of Afro-Asiatic languages. His father, Francis, was a leading intellectual in the French Communist Party, where he pursued a policy of cultural openness, and his mother, Marie-Élisa Nordmann, was an Auschwitz survivor who became a chemistry professor. All three were prominent members of the French Resistance. Their activism was part of Jean-Louis's persona, as was mastering languages. In addition to his native French, Jean-Louis was fluent in Russian, English, German, and Italian, and could read Spanish and Dutch. This facility gave him the ability to conduct research into primary sources without mediation and allowed him to move in depth across interweaving cultures.

As a teenager Jean-Louis became immersed in the cinema, and moved away from his early interest in engineering to architecture. He attended l'École Spéciale d'Architecture in Paris, the only private school in the discipline in France.

The school had been created in 1865 to counter the conservative teachings of the École des Beaux-Arts. Ironically, after the student uprisings of 1968, everything changed in French education, and Jean-Louis joined one of the new schools of architecture that he had a part in creating, and immediately after graduating, in 1973, he began to teach architecture and to publish.

Of the first four books in which Jean-Louis published essays in the 1970s, three engaged with subjects he would continue to pursue: Le Corbusier, the Soviet Union, and the city. *URSS, 1917–1978: la ville, l'architecture*, published in 1979, with coauthors Marco de Michelis and Manfredo Tafuri, was an indication that preeminent scholars were interested in his work. The 2013 exhibition Jean-Louis curated at MoMA, "Le Corbusier: An Atlas of Modern Landscapes," was an example of his process of continuous return, as he developed strands from his almost yearly participation in conferences, lectures, publications, or exhibitions on Le Corbusier to present varying aspects of the work of the architect.

Jean-Louis's many teaching appointments began with problematics in urbanism and his interest in contemporary architects, among them James Stirling and, of his own generation, Paul Chemetov. But his love of history drew him to research. In 1981, to enrich the breadth and depth of his research, and thus assure his ability to advance academically, he enrolled in the great École des Hautes Études en Sciences Sociales (EHESS) in Paris. After earning a PhD in art history, in 1985, he then qualified for the *Habilitation*, a prerequisite to supervising PhD students and to obtaining tenure at a university in France, which, Jean-Louis noted, "Very few people trained in architecture have passed this rigorous process." From 1991 to 2005, Jean-Louis was director of a joint postgraduate program between architectural schools and universities in Paris and the EHESS and l'Institut Français d'Urbanisme that led to the first PhD program in architecture in France, which he inspired and cofounded. He also began teaching regularly in the United States in the schools of architecture at the University of Pennsylvania, Princeton, Harvard, Columbia, and others. In 1994, he was offered the Sheldon H. Solow professorship at the IFA.

A natural at public interaction and persuasion, Jean-Louis gained wide-ranging influence through architectural institutions and curatorial projects. It was in this context that my relationship with him grew. Although we had different memories of each other during the 1980s, our long-term relationship and friendship began in 1989, the year the CCA opened. Jean-Louis discovered the collection, and soon, with the CCA head curator, began developing the exhibition "Scenes of the World to Come," which opened in 1995. In 1997, he became a member of the CCA selection committee for scholars in residence and chair of the Collection Research Program committee. Jean-Louis joined the CCA board in 1998, the same year the French Minister of Culture appointed him to create a center for architecture and built heritage, the Cité de l'architecture et du patrimoine, in Paris. Although the CCA was on a considerably smaller scale, Jean-Louis found that being in the world of the CCA, he learned how an institution operated. Being involved mostly in academic organizations, he had not managed or supervised an institution. As he said to me, "I learned a lot about what it meant to have a budget, to plan expenses, income, to deal with the stuff I had to deal with." He was a remarkable collaborator with the CCA for some 30 years.

Today, the CCA is home to the vast Jean-Louis Cohen Fonds, the archive he donated in 2019 and continued to add to. The Fonds consists of his records as a professor, researcher, author, and curator since 1969, including material related to numerous major projects and a large collection of photographic documents – his own slides and his collection of Mallet-Stevens photographs. Archival processing of the Fonds is ongoing at the CCA and will be accessible to researchers in the spring of 2024.

The archives of Jean-Louis Cohen are a gift to polylingual researchers, an offering of delight, discoveries, and communion with a great inquiring mind. Jean-Louis hoped that his archives would be used to further advance and challenge the theories he developed and the conclusions he reached through his work. And so the work lives on.

Phyllis Lambert is the founding director emerita of the Canadian Centre for Architecture in Montreal.

Cynthia Davidson
with K. Michael Hays,
Andrew Holder
& Anna Neimark

Toward a Theory Of Inscription

In 2017, K. Michael Hays, Eliot Noyes Professor of Architectural Theory at Harvard's Graduate School of Design, and Andrew Holder, a principal of The Los Angeles Design Group and an associate professor of architecture at the GSD, curated "Inscriptions: Architecture Before Speech," which was on view at the GSD January 22–March 11, 2018. A weighty catalog of the same name was published in 2021. Here, Hays and Holder discuss their concept of inscriptions along with Anna Neimark, a teacher at SCI-Arc and a founding principal of First Office, in Los Angeles, whose work was included in the show. The following conversation, which took place in October 2023 via Zoom, begins with Michael laying out a brief history for a theory of inscription. – CD

K. MICHAEL HAYS: The *Inscriptions* project recognizes a new architectural ethos, emergent since the mid-1990s, in which the symbolic authority needed to ground the meaningfulness of architecture's collective community has been steadily challenged, if not simply ignored. Since the linguistic turn in the 1960s, architecture theory had embedded itself in the regime of the signifier – a model of architectural signification based on the historical disciplinary confidence that certain visible architectural types and tropes would find their empirical referents in the "real world" of nature and society, making an architecture that seemed authentic and accepted, realist and populist, because it was based on referential appearances and consensual meaning. The construction of signifiers with the assurance of finding their signifieds has been our primary way to theorize and interpret architecture for nearly 50 years.

The regime of the signifier unfolded first as a kind of appropriation of the imageability of the technical and "vernacular" landscapes by the various semiotic factions until the 1990s, when, at least among most academics, the foundational myth of universality woven into that regime came to be seen as an ideology now widely regarded as too Western, too White, and too male. The master signifiers, the canon, the precedents and referents, which is to say, Architecture's Symbolic, had betrayed architectural theory and its critical project.

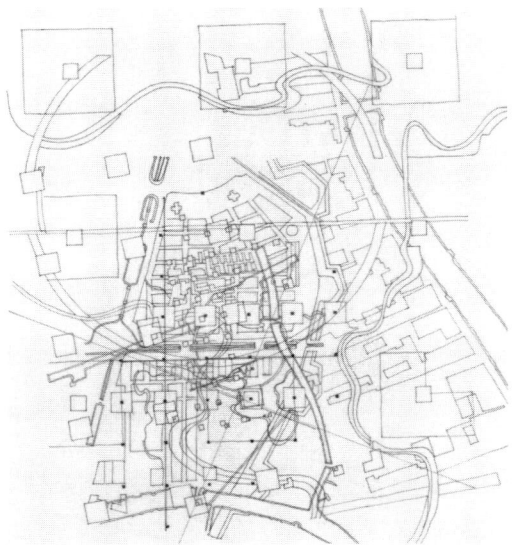

Eisenman/Robertson Architects, Project for a Garden, Parc de La Villette, Paris (Chora L Works), 1986. Site plan sketch showing superposition of Cannaregio and La Villette sites at different scales.

Given this historical context, I want to make a two-part claim. First, the recent demise of the symbolic authority of architecture has produced a material remainder or residue – including indexical marks and figural glyphs – in the form of what, following Paul de Man, I call "material inscription." Second, the evolution of Jacques Lacan's thinking in the 1970s, which was a deconstruction of the regime of the signifier and a refolding of the symptom into a neo-subject, precisely scans the disinvestment in the architecture theoretical discourse and the rupture of the Symbolic in the architecture around at that same time. We can use certain developments of poststructuralism, especially Lacan's "Borromean clinic," to extend our own line of inquiry into the practices exhibited in "Inscriptions." Choosing the theory of inscription as the defining rubric of our project is anything but arbitrary.

I am also interested in Lacan because he credits architecture with an unusual primacy as the original art, the art that designates the site of what he calls the Thing – that is, a kind of absolute Other and impossible object of desire. He writes, "We see the link forged between the temple, as a construction around emptiness that designates the place of the Thing, to the figuration of emptiness on the walls of this emptiness itself" [*The Ethics of Psychoanalysis*, 140]. There is an ontological apparatus that generates architecture from nothing, leaving as residue ontic remnants in the form of glyphs and figures on the walls of the architecture itself. So Lacan, like Hegel, sees architecture as a combination of an image and a materialization – of signification and matter – the one necessarily unfolding from the other. This archaic architectural dialectic is the first attempt to organize meaning in a way that comes out of the material and the procedures of construction itself, but without the sanction of any kind of paternal, symbolic authority. Instead, a new subject (or *agencement*) organizes the leftover marks of the Other with newfound agency. It is the symptom, rather than the signifier, which becomes the subject's elective and singular mode of inscription. This working out from the symptom is the source of new styles and manners. So that's the claim of the *Inscriptions* project, and that's where the consequences and attributes of the notion of inscription come to life and achieve detail.

CYNTHIA DAVIDSON: Andrew, I think the ball now goes to you.

ANDREW HOLDER: It's useful for me to begin by delineating the similarities and differences in the ways Michael and I understand the project. I find it interesting that Michael lodges the project in the longer history of models of language and how they make their way into architecture. I suppose the way in which I can accept that is to understand models of language as having two axes. There's the axis of horizontal progression through time that Michael beautifully articulated, but there's also the vertical axis, which asks, What are the rules of the game now? What's thinkable? What's allowable? What positions can architects take? Most of my interest resides on the vertical axis.

I survey the landscape of contemporary work and try to articulate what I understand to be the implicit rules of operation, and therefore the commonalities of work these rules produce. First, I believe there has been a turn, in the past 10 to 15 years, toward architecture that wishes to be read or registered in physical terms, as though it were self-evidently the result of a construction process or even a process of assembly that is still in progress.

As a corollary to that, construction presumes a preexisting field of equipment or parts and a set of techniques for putting them in play. It seems to me that some of the parts that contemporary architects are playing with are fragments or residues of the history that Michael outlined. Contemporary designers are taking up the residues of architecture's old interests in signification, like, for instance, the superposition drawings that were been used in the 1970s and '80s by practitioners like Tschumi and Eisenman – in their respective schemes for Parc de la Villette – to make present architecture's systems of notation.

The superimposed orthographic drawing is present again, but now as a part that is available for physical construction, as in Sean Canty's studies for facades or Michelle Chang's "Scoring, Building" pavilion. The way the drawing is used now is not at all what was intended during the first go-round. The drawing as a system of representation is now being taken as an element and procedure for assembly.

This stress on construction is neither arbitrary nor solely formal. Architects are making analogies between the construction or assembly of architecture's appearance with the construction or assembly of a social order.

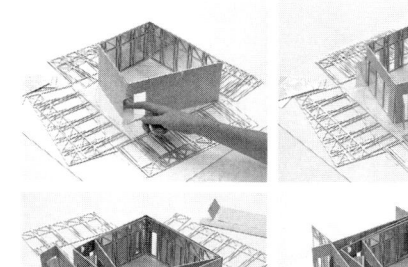

Michelle JaJa Chang, model for "Scoring, Building," Mackey Apartments, The MAK Center for Art and Architecture, Los Angeles, 2020. Photos courtesy the architect.

A connection is being drawn between form as an assembly and the kinds of *gatherings* that might happen around it.

All of this puts Michael and me on different sides of the same coin. If Michael is interested in a continuing historical line, I'm interested in cutting sectionally through that line to evaluate the present. If Michael's interested in models of psychoanalysis that form the individual subject, I'm interested in group phenomena, particularly in how architecture initiates groups or allows us to imagine that the audience is a collective as opposed to a mass of individually observing subjects.

KMH: The new model we're looking for organizes signification through the image, but, equally important, it achieves imageability through its construction or assembly and the managing of material. Both components are imbricated equally, whereas the previous regime of the signifier was not able to bring those two dimensions of the object fully together. Further contrasts between signifier and inscription include the historicization of the distinction between art and craft, or high and low, distinctions that are blurred in the inscription, and a crossing of boundaries in terms of the scale of the object. An inscriptive architecture can be quite small or quite large, from nano-object to the planet. I think Andrew's examples of analogies could be expanded, too, between the constellations of inscriptive patterns and the appearance of new social forms.

AH: I think that's well put. I should specify a bit more what I mean by the word *construction*. I use it reluctantly. Maybe a better word is *assembly* because it's easier to think of as having two separate aspects. There is a "real" register to assembly, as in architects specifying how 2x4s go together with nails or screws. There is also an imaginary register to assembly that is not working in the realm of "real parts" but rather depends on readership in order to isolate parts and imagine using them. Exhibit *A* for this kind of double sense of assembly would be Andrew Atwood and Anna's Dolmen proposal for MoMA PS1.

Large sections of that project had to do with construction specifications and "real" parts – the way stain is specified, 4x8 sheets of plywood are panelized, 2x4s are framed up in hollow walls, how deck screws are specified. There is also, though, the gigantic order of assembly that reads as maybe seven legs with a capstone stacked precariously on top, stabilized with the aid of little shims. Those rock-like boxes are an artifact of reading the Dolmen as a stack of rocks. It's not "made" of them in the same way it is made of 2x4s. It's interesting to me that Andrew and Anna play in both of those registers of assembly. There's no insistence that literal construction is somehow more real or more natural than the imaginary order. These things are imbricated. One cannot pull them apart in that work.

CD: Anna, I want to hear from you, but first I have a question for Andrew. In the catalog you use the word *gathering*, you say *Inscriptions* gathers things, and just now you mentioned gatherings around assembly. For me, the idea of inscription means a cultural project of writing. How did you decide to call this gathering of work *Inscriptions*?

AH: I'm sure both Michael and I will want to respond, and we'll probably have different inflections that are nonetheless complementary. *Inscriptions*, for me, was a found object, not something I invented or actively chose. The occasion for the show and the book was an opportunity that Michael had to curate something while he was interim chair of architecture at the GSD. He was interested in the notion of inscription for several years before I arrived at the school and already knew it would be the conceptual focus of his work in the show. When I arrived on the scene, I had an interest in finding an umbrella term that would capture what I thought to be a widely shared design procedure across many practices over the span of a decade. When Michael said, "We're going to call the show 'Inscriptions,'" I thought, that'll work.

One of our favorite habits in contemporary architecture is to describe our field as diverse, not only in terms of its practitioners, but also, and *therefore*, in terms of the optical register of our products. Like, *Look how different things are from one another* is said with self-satisfaction, as though a diversity of laborers and diversity in production were causally linked to one another. I am all in favor of the diversification of our ranks, and also of the diversification of our products, but it seems to me that what's being produced is far more similar than it is different, no matter who's producing it. And the nature of its similarity has to do with a design procedure that is shared – probably unconsciously in many cases, but it is still a useful way to start reading the work back to the people who are making it.

We've already begun making a list of commonalities. It's sourced from different places, but they've all been hypostasized as parts. Form is present and not present in all

First Office, Dolmen proposal for MoMA PS1, 2016. Drawing courtesy the architects.

of the work. Here, I appreciate Michael citing Lacan on the temple "as a construction around emptiness," which is the perfect allegory for the status of form in contemporary projects. Again, to invoke Andrew and Anna's project, not only is the Dolmen literally hollow, as it's Type V construction, but its form went missing, or it was a kind of falsework that was removed after the fact. There's no actual dolmen there, no trabeated stack of unitary material working in compression to house a sacred rite. Theirs is an approximation of an original form, a contemporary project built around a semantically and materially hollow center.

If you have the stuff that it takes to make something and a form as target or task, then a good word to describe the interaction between those two halves is *inscription*. Form gets built from parts that were not necessarily intended for that purpose, and in the process, it suffers the marks of its own coming into being, with all its abrasions. So while I certainly can't claim to be the one to put the word *inscriptions* on the table, I enjoyed arriving kind of late, grabbing it as-found, and saying, I can use this, too. You may have had different intentions, Michael, but I find the word useful as a way to name a common procedure that seems obvious.

KMH: For me, the word *inscriptions* enters the issue of signification at the conjuncture of seemingly purely indexical operations like cutting, stacking, folding, casting, and scattering with contemporary reflections on the performative marks of material extraction, labor, and territorialization. We have all these indexical operations and social conditions, but what about form? In this regard, de Man helpfully asked of inscription's materiality, "how this materiality is then to be understood in linguistic terms." He answers with what he, following Lacan, calls the form of the *letter*, Lacan's generative signifier-in-isolation: "The play of the letter and the syllable, the way of saying . . . as opposed to what is being said . . . as meaning-producing tropes are replaced by the fragmentation of sentences and propositions into discrete words, or the fragmentation of words into syllables and finally letters." It's important that the letter alone is meaningless yet necessary. It holds a space, it is a spacing. De Man calls the consequence of this rarefaction of the material support of writing many things, but his most powerful expression is "the undoing of cognition and its replacement by the uncontrollable power of the letter as inscription" ["Phenomenality and Materiality in Kant," 82, 89].

So to me, inscription is the writing of architecture into a particular kind of generative diagram – a dynamic operator populated with traces and glyphs, condensed particles, and tracks of forces, all sedimented out from diverse histories, all irreducible forms of architectural knowledge ready to shape specific projects.

CD: Anna, there's a lot on the table now that you can choose to respond to, but I'm interested in the text of your catalog entry, your idea of the blank and filling in the blank. To me, the blank resonates with this idea of emptiness, but at the same time you're filling in the blank by writing. So where does your work fit in this idea of inscription? How do you read it as an architect making things, specifying things, and attempting to fill in the blanks?

ANNA NEIMARK: Thank you, Cynthia. You have well positioned my entry into this conversation. I especially liked Andrew's suggestion that there is a metaphor of time that operates in the background of the *Inscriptions* project – a horizontal time of the historical trajectory as well as a vertical time of the contemporary moment. What I can add to this observation is the possibility of a collapse of time altogether, directing the horizontal and vertical axes inward on their origin. To illustrate this junction with a dolmen might be fitting. This prehistoric monument reaches us from a time before history. It precedes writing or other forms of inscription. It has a blank character that can be filled in with new modes of work, and so it invites us to dwell on our contemporary moment through an anachronic encounter.

In the entry that Andrew Atwood and I contributed to the *Inscriptions* catalog, we describe a dolmen as a kind of *formulaire*, what in English we refer to as "a blank form." Of course, a blank is never empty. It prompts us to fill out a series of boxes or gridded lines with specific information. The blank predetermines our entry by offering formats within which we can operate. And as we take account of other formulaires out there in the world, we recognize the conventions of drawing, of building, of writing, of publishing. Such conventions or agreements move through different media surrounding the discourse of building. And we conform to certain rules of engagement that are strategic, tactical, structural, and – here I return to the '70s – even structuralist.

So, we can position First Office within the vertical network of contemporary practices that Andrew is describing, as well as along the horizontal lineage that Michael has outlined. I know that Michael has worked hard to produce a caesura between the project of the '70s and the work presented in the *Inscriptions* catalog. However, I think we tend to inflect that project rather than produce a rift with it.

For example, we see the article "Notes on Conceptual Architecture" by Peter Eisenman – the publication in which he redacted the text, leaving us only with footnotes [*Design Quarterly*, 1970] – as a form of inscription. Erasure is as much on the table as writing. It is a conceptual mechanism for emptying out one content to make room for another. The new content can reflect a contemporary approach to materiality, fabrication, and all the machines that make our design processes explicit.

Now, I use Bruno Latour's expression "to make things explicit" strategically, to put another question on the table, which has to do with a break between the architects of the 1970s reading theory or psychoanalysis and the architects of the 2020s reading history or sociology. I asked Michael to introduce today's conversation because, as it turns out, not very many of us in the contemporary scene are familiar with de Man's writing or Lacan's diagramming. In my education, the word *inscription* came from reading Latour. I am thinking, in particular, of the 1986 essay, "Visualization and Cognition," where he describes a theory of deflation through simple and durable modes of representation. It is curious, and perhaps not coincidental, that the same word is used in a different context, this time in the context of the history of science and technology. What Latour denotes as *inscription* includes the mundane forms of "paperwork," such as charts, graphs, and logs, in the context of scientific production.

So, we can recognize how humble paperwork, delineation, packaging of information, and coding can travel to produce large-scale effects for architectural production as well as to make collaborative conditions for work possible. Perhaps Andrew's point about gathering resonates also with this description, in which inscriptions facilitate communication with one another across historical time as well as across collaborations happening in the present.

CD: In the catalog, Marrikka Trotter asks, "What do you do at the end of history?" She replies, "It's not a bad idea to mockup space for another history to begin." Andrew, Anna, do you think *Inscriptions* is an attempt to mockup a space for another history to begin? I mean, Anna, you just invoked Latour rather than Lacan. Michael and I are the same age. You, Andrew and Anna, are probably similar in age. What's really happened over the years? Is it a good idea to mockup space for another history to begin?

AH: I appreciate Anna's identification of two different kinds of text that are informing these discussions. I think she's exactly right. Theory comes to us in 2023 really via the way Cynthia and Michael's generation was reading the transition from structuralism to poststructuralism in France, first through Saussure and Lévi-Strauss, then Foucault, Derrida, Lacan, and so on. More recently our generation has been reading Kittler, Latour, Daston, and Galison, then in our own field Eigen, Allais, and Çelik Alexander. I think Anna used the word *historical* to characterize this group. I might use the word *materialist*, as in they've underscored the importance of tracing architecture's charts of accounts. What moved where? Who did it? What were the informational mechanisms that connect those two, the what and the who?

So now it's my turn to have it both ways. I think *Inscriptions* welds back together a utopian function of architecture, putting on the table imaginations of what could be, with a materialist logic, being faithful to architecture's charts of accounts, who's doing what and with what material. I know that the utopian function of architecture is not the same thing as theory. I'm not trying to blur those two concepts. But I would say that the imagination of what could be or what we wish to do is separate from the literal accounting of stuff, like when we're looking at a construction site. *Inscriptions* derives its energy from pulling apart the imaginative impulse of what we wish to do from the material of its making and then fusing the two back together.

Form's first role in our contemporary moment is the former. It furnishes a collective understanding of what the job of architecture is. It shows up on site as an emptiness that answers the question, What is the task at hand? Building a collective understanding in the present moment is no small feat, and this is why we're seeing not just ancient forms but more broadly anachronistic forms that are out-of-time and have the quality of being always already in place. Anachronisms run the whole gamut of *Inscriptions*' reach, from pyramids to giant creatures. Giant creatures maybe carry a whiff of a sort of sci-fi futurism, but they're always already known in advance in the same way pyramids and ziggurats are.

If form arrives to initiate a collective undertaking that is broadly understood, then the materialist side of the equation is rooted in the equipment and procedures of

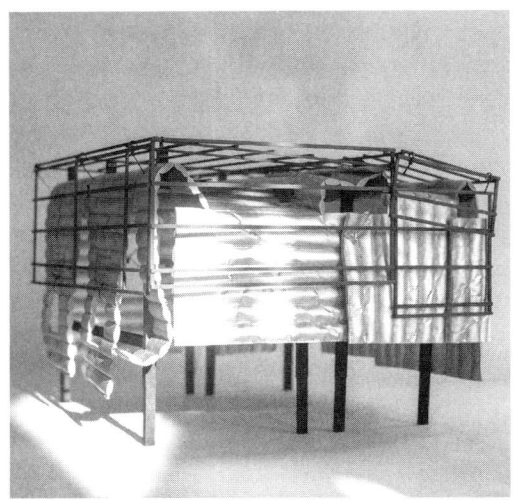

Current Interests, model of SilverHouse Studio, 2021. Image courtesy the architects.

construction. We see the literal constructive parts arriving on the scene and being disposed toward this formal end. This is how I understand Current Interests' experiments with the SilverHouse Studio. The form of the studio is the task at hand, then they show us the batt insulation, the light steel framing, the tar-paper roof, which sort of sequentially prop and drape the form. The mapping of form/materialism onto collective task/construction is a little too neat because the imagination of form is present even on the side of construction where parts are both "real" and the product of readership, like the two registers of the Dolmen. The point here is that two halves are constantly being separated and combined.

Something similar is at play in Xavi Aguirre's work with stock-a-studio. The forms are simple boxes but they initiate a collective understanding of what is to be done. The material means to accomplish these tasks are interesting for their super-accountability, down to the level of receipts. If I understand the process correctly, in some projects Xavi goes shopping at Home Depot for metal struts, rachet straps, and sandbags, keeping the receipts so the material can later be exchanged for things they need in other projects. The process of shopping and exchanging is a way to demonstrate their mobilization of supply chains toward a formal end that is already understood from the get-go. All of this is to underscore the energy and potential in hybridizing these two tranches of text that function in different ways but can be usefully combined in architecture.

KMH: I think the most important thing, and we keep saying it, is our effort to make a materialist model rather than an idealist model of this mythical origin of architecture. And there are discursive forces that are as equally determinate as visible, mechanical, material forces. Both should be counted as within the domain of *Inscriptions*. Architecture is, above all, the art of marking, orientation, and the processes of making. In a Marxist reading, all this would be counted as materialist. But we're also trying to find new modes of materialism – a diversity and plasticity of operation also count. And this is where, for me, architecture can lay claim to the question of medium as being central. But architecture takes its relation to other media as just part of its relation to the world. Architecture is already the primary mediator between matter and signification.

CD: Anna, do you agree with that?

AN: Yes, perhaps. Since Michael is calling architecture a mediator, I would like to recall an image that could help mediate some of these thoughts. I think we are all familiar with Pieter Bruegel's 1563 painting of *The (Great) Tower of Babel*. I would like to zoom in on this tower in distress and recall its mythical origin story in relation to the materialism of its painted figure. The story begins with a people without a name who come together after the great flood to build a tower in order to make a name for themselves. God, of course, gets very angry, and says, "I will confuse, or *levalbel*, their language," a word still used in the Hebrew today.

This kind of confusion is perhaps part of the project of inscription, which is to say, it does not necessarily point to language that has definite meaning, but it can also hold the meaning of confusion in focus, and maybe it is a very productive confusion at that. In this painting, we encounter the overlay of the narrative from the Bible with its image by Bruegel. If we traveled to the base of the painted tower, we would notice the laborers. We would see how, in the Port of Antwerp, the stone was being brought and assembled. We would see the pulleys and the machines. We would see references to structures like the Roman Colosseum or even the fortifications that are of Bruegel's time. Here, too, time is collapsed or confused. Inscriptions are being chiseled into these stones before they are assembled. Could this be the utopian project that Andrew is alluding to, under construction? Its labor and materialism are on display, and so is the threat of the disillusion of its idealism.

Let's come back to Cynthia's question about the possibility of a new moment for history. Because if we have constructed this tower of meaning, which now appears to have collapsed, leaving us with "levalbel" – the stones for construction have different inscriptions on them that we can no longer decipher or agree upon, as we would have in the past – what is this moment, historically speaking?

If before, we could agree on the imageability of architecture through its monumentality, its iconicity, through the construction of an avant-garde practice, through the construction of Babel, perhaps now we have come into a moment when we have fractured those grandiose plans. Then we begin to occupy the position of the rear-guard. We are not at the front lines of some sort of construction, but are laboring in the background, building up the center again by slowing

Pieter Bruegel the Elder, detail of *The (Great) Tower of Babel*, with workers and materials, 1563. Courtesy Kunsthistorisches Museum Wien, Gemäldegalerie.

things down, slowing things down so much that it takes time to decipher, time to read, and time to reconstruct the arguments that hold everything together in order to produce meaning again.

CD: Andrew, is that what you set out to do?

AH: No and yes. As usual, Anna is a few steps ahead of me. I would state it slightly differently. We are experiencing a historical lurch, but because time only flows in one direction, it's a lurch forward from one characterization of the field to another. By "field," I mean architecture's relational structure, how one building relates to another, how that sets up frameworks for judgment and criteria for success.

I think we could say, 20 or 30 years ago, that form had a very particular function in the field, which was to specify positionality. Ideally, form would specify positionality so acutely that a particular station in the field would only be occupied by one person. Although both Graves and Eisenman used the same design procedure of a manipulated cubic volume to produce many of their early houses, for instance, it's exactly the distinction in the results that would immediately indicate that a Graves house is not an Eisenman house.

Because form had to do that work in architecture's relational structure of that moment, we saw an explosion of formal differentiation that was direct and comparative. We're now lurching toward a configuration of a field with different rules. Form is no longer expected to individuate. Rather, form is now a stake in the ground that permits various architects, and maybe even various publics, to gather around it. My even saying that indicates another set of differences between the field now and the field the way it used to be.

This shift entails a whole set of differences in the relational structure of the field. For instance, I'm not so certain that there are now definite lines between architectural producers and architectural consumers. The work we collected in *Inscriptions* is meant to be broadly legible to an architectural audience of experts, but it also takes pains to make itself legible to a much broader segment of the population, and the design procedure of inscription is starting to nudge those two groups together.

Additionally, I don't know if there's such a clear distinction between the "before" time of design and the "after" time of reception anymore. That distinction would've been critical in the prior configuration of the field. People had to go away to the private space of the studio through shared design models to produce fully individuated form. Now, if anything, the constructional aspect of buildings signals a working-out in public. *I am in progress. I am potentially susceptible to rearrangement. All of my parts are not put together as ineffable, perfect wholes, but could be placed otherwise.* For me, to borrow a phrase from Anna, that is a deeply confused way of handling time, but it is also deeply optimistic in the sense that it does not seem as though

architecture is interested in protecting its secret procedures.

Rather, it's in the business of opening up *technologies of apprehension*, to coin a phrase. Buildings show people how to grasp their parts, borrow their procedures, and use them to other ends. This is like my own House 1, where a system of freestanding walls and roofs is arranged around the form of a ranch house. The separateness of those elements allows them to be understood as available for use, and the system of props and supports allows observers to imagine how they were assembled. Admittedly this is a primitive technology, but the point is not the novelty of assembly methods, but rather the sophistication of how assembly is made visible for anyone who wishes to trace the imaginative order of construction and reapprehend it for other ends. For me, that's both a shift forward and a very hopeful take on what form is doing now. I think the system of rewards and the system of judgment are totally different than they were 30 years ago.

AN: Andrew, by making assembly visible, you inscribe a pedagogical intention into the field. It is not by chance that you and I will go teach studio on our respective coasts right after this conversation. This makes me think that the producer and the consumer are not necessarily the architect and the client but the pedagogue and the student, at least within the group of projects that we are looking at and among the group of people gathered here. Let's remember that we are all teachers. We are all thinking through pedagogy. And the work that we are discussing comes from an academic practice more so than, let's say, professional or corporate practice. I am not saying we are not professionals. I'm just saying that we approach building from a different place. And so, to this audience, in the act of gathering for studio, evaluation and reward are based on educational models.

The Los Angeles Design Group, House 1, Los Angeles, 2016. Photo: Saam Gabbay. Courtesy the architects.

CD: That's a really important point, Anna.

AN: We are operating in a particularly closed context. We are not out in the world, producing the Tower of Babel, which is a tour-de-force monument. We are not in the cavalry of the avant-garde, holding a flag while riding a horse. We are at our desks, doing something with our hands, and we are showing, by repetition and by example, a way of practicing to become an architect as we operate through critique, which is still the dominant mode of pedagogy.

This summer, while working with my thesis students at SCI-Arc, I came across the first episode of Julia Child's cooking show on GBH, in which she demonstrates how to make an omelette. She just shakes the pan. There is nothing in it. There is no egg, no butter, no flame. She stands in front of the camera and simply shakes an empty pan to show us how to handle it. She calls it a *tour de main*. A tour de main – the turning of the hand – is, I would argue, the antidote to the tour de force. It is a quick way to make an omelette. It is also a helpful metaphor for describing studio practice. I just want to, again, deflate our ambitions and remind us of our role in the production of architecture in this pedagogical context.

AH: I do want to credit Anna with performing a very inscriptions-like rhetorical move just now, with her radical deflation and bringing-down-to-earth. I hear it as, What do you need? A pile of blocks. That's all you need. I would say monumental humility describes a lot of the work in the book. Niraj Bhatia's playground equipment made in the form of ziggurats is an example. That's a similar bringing-down-to-earth of the sacral pretensions that the ziggurat might carry. Deflating pretension doesn't make the work potentially less profound in terms of its effects, but it does tend to miniaturize – maybe my preferred word would be to *anthropomorphize* – the space of design operation. The project can be as small as a studio or a playground. It can be just joining 2x4s. But neither of these shrink the circle of its possible effects. If anything, the circle gets bigger because it is now open to more comers.

CD: Andrew, you said that judgment and rewards have changed. Are you referring to the judgment an architect makes in the design or construction process? Or were you talking about a curatorial judgment? And what do you mean by rewards? I'm assuming the rewards are design rewards.

AH: Part of what I'm sensing is an alignment between the varieties of judgment that you just mentioned – curatorial judgment and an architect's internal judgment of the design process – perhaps *discrimination* is a better word for the latter. In both, there is now a habit of taking architecture's forms as a given, as though the form itself is not what's under interrogation when we ask, What categories does this building belong to? – a question of curation – and, Is it good? – internal judgment. In both spheres, we instead speak in the language of social goods to describe a set of effects that could have to do with the building's participation in an energy economy or a social economy or a political economy. But there's a funny taking-for-granted of form as something given or automatic, which is aligned with the way that *Inscriptions* thinks about forms appearing as if they had been imposed on the architect, drawn from a prepared catalog – albeit one visible only after the fact, a document of future possibilities encountered from the anterior.

Alongside this, we can see the collapse of a whole set of institutionalized rewards that just 10 or 15 years ago would have been both powerful and aligned with each other. A case in point would be the MoMA PS1 Young Architects Program, which is no longer a going concern. While it was operating, there was a period of alignment between that program, the exhibition program at spaces like Storefront for Art and Architecture, and fellowships for young architects like those at the University of Michigan and Ohio State. Beginning in the late aughts, there was a lot of overlap in the lists of people who participated in these. Then YAP went away, and the Storefront exhibition series and the fellowship programs no longer have much in common. Perhaps that's a good and healthy thing, but it's only possible because the more diverse concerns are downstream effects that presume form is already in play.

KMH: May I add that the new status of form in the *Inscriptions* model also entails a new form of agency, where some "author-function," in effect, assembles from the discourse certain part-forms, or proto-forms, not at the level of a building type or a referent, but as diagrammatic pieces of architecture analogous to Lacan's letters in a sentence, and then completely distorts them, processes them, combines them, and further strips or elaborates them. There is agency, even as the discourse pushes and pulls at the generative power of the inscriptive infrastructure. But these forms of inscription perhaps become intelligible only in a context that is still attached and beholden to the discourse. The inscription is what is irreducible in the architectural signifier – I take that to be what Andrew means by "picked from a catalog." It's a kernel torn from the Architecture Thing. It becomes political – and historically here and now – only when it is given performative force, and that comes from some kind of agency.

Take the Ionic scroll as an inscription. The irreducible, material glyph of the column-signifier that determines the entire order of the classical temple is a material inscription in isolation, abstracted from relations of sense. But, where the signifier derives its "meaning" from the highly controlling

Symbolic as a place of collective signification – here, the classical system – the inscription is self-isolated yet highly generative and connectible. Think of what Borromini or Guarini did to the scroll – *le Pli*! And the scroll consorts with the unconscious and the Real.

At other times, Lacan instructs that "the letter designates an assemblage . . . letters make up assemblages . . . they are assemblages," and then, "the unconscious is structured like the assemblages in question in set theory, which are like letters" [*The Seminar of Jacques Lacan*, Book XX]. The letter as assemblage – *agencement* is Lacan's word, agent of the unconscious and the surreal, inaugurator of social complexity through its fluidity, connectivity, and iterability – is close to Lyotard's use of the term *figure* in his *Discourse, Figure*. Like the figure, the letter – and likewise, the inscription – is a socially inscribed mark that raises the object to the dignity of the Thing. Yes, I think that feels right.

AH: That's very helpful, Michael. What I just said about judgment and reward and the shifting nature of the field may sound like a tragedy, but I don't think it's a tragedy. It's just a reconfiguration of attention. I don't feel sad about it. As attention has shifted away from form and toward other concerns, form becomes acutely present and specific to the point where we could enumerate, in *Inscriptions*, a fairly comprehensive list that would cover the majority of forms one is likely to see in contemporary practice. The pitched-roof house is foremost among these, but everyone's also doing stacks and so on. The catalog of possibilities is clear, which allows practitioners to conduct designerly activity on, against, and around form. It's a legitimating opener that allows all kinds of other concerns to come to the fore.

CD: Anna, do you agree with Andrew? What is a position in your practice, First Office?

AN: Andrew describes some important factors of the contemporary scene and perhaps we can add to those interests of representation, politics, and identity other discourses that have also dominated the field over the last 30 years and are not part of this catalog. Some work that this collection is a reaction to are practices that engage in digital parametrics, projects that embrace object-oriented ontology [OOO], images that are constructed, multiplied, and manipulated by AI. Together, this group of things dominates the discourse of imageability. It seems to me that certain techniques of image making fall outside of the logic of *Inscriptions*. There are categories in the book and the exhibit that necessarily include some things while excluding others.

KMH: To think about the basic signifying unit of architecture as inscription, rather than as a signifier and referent, produces a deeper, more infrastructural articulation of the discipline – like Andrew's vertical cut through the discipline. The inscription is certainly imageable, as is a signifier, but it's not in itself an image. The inscription produces a mark and a surface schema, a trace pressed into a trait, demonstrating the necessity of that assemblage for signification.

CD: I think what you've just said, Michael, also leads – and I hope Andrew and Anna agree – to why you use Greimas's semiotic square as a way of organizing this imageability.

AH: If we were going to be strict structuralists, then Michael and I would claim that there has been a shift in the order of thought that is inescapable. I don't know that I'm totally willing to go there.

CD: You're not willing to say what that shift is, or to make that shift yourself?

AH: To make that shift global and inescapable.

I'd rather acknowledge limits to the claim. Anna's provocations are useful. What about parametricism and what about AI – leaving OOO aside because it didn't produce much?

The parametric is interesting because it's a clear design procedure that now seems a bit stranded historically in a way that *Inscriptions* can help diagnose. As I understood it, in the early 2000s, much of that work was trying to identify a set of parameters as inputs to the generation of buildings, which would then produce always renewed forms. Never quite being able to pin down and name its formal products was a sign of success. Parametricism continually produced a new kind of spacing that would accept strong qualifications of beauty, like elegance, intricacy, or voluptuousness, but only weak nouns, like blobs or tubes. There was a moment when those qualities went from being signs of a profit-able enterprise to one of parody. I would date the end of that turn to the first renderings of Zaha Hadid's Al Janoub Stadium in Qatar. Its vagueness as a noun was not a virtue but a vacuum to be filled with the lowest common denominator. It went from being a kind of unnamable, ineffable form to merely "vagina," like it was the punchline of juvenile humor. That lapse into parody was a sign that the milieu of reception had shifted and the building hadn't anticipated the new rules of its own evaluation. The stadium, and by extension parametricism, became historically stranded. It may find a way back in, but in the meantime, *Inscriptions* does a good job of diagnosing the new sets of rules that produced this effect of reception. Of course, the stadium would have to be stabilized as one noun if our habit now is to imagine forms as having been picked from lists.

AI is different. I wouldn't know how to stretch the frame of *Inscriptions* to draw a line around it right now other than to suggest a rhyme in terms of procedure. If *Inscriptions* is invested in this idea that architects lean heavily on a preordained catalog of forms, and that doing so is not limiting imagination or the fecundity of output, it is fair, in gross terms, to say that generative AI works in a similar way, just faster and with a much bigger corpus. The storehouse of knowledge, up to this date, is enough for us – from it we will dream our new inceptions. Beyond this, I think we'll have to wait and see what products of generative AI end up being elevated as "good" and eventually get built – or if judgment will continue to act as a filter at all. I don't know if it's in our interest to stretch *Inscriptions* that far.

KMH: Right. No. Perhaps you're right that I am overly tempted by how perfectly positioned the theoretical project of *Inscriptions* seems to be to explain much of contemporary practice. I am also aware, coming back to Cynthia's question about the diagram, that the Greimas diagram seems to try to explain everything in a field according to the structural positions available in that field. That's certainly true. But we're not claiming that the field diagram is the whole of architecture, like some Jencksian style cloud. We're claiming only that it appears quite specifically in the American academy and related practices. It's not the whole story, by any means.

But what I think *Inscriptions* gets right is the proffer of a highly articulated and well historicized, if limited, field. And coming back to Anna's point, I do want *Inscriptions* to be able to claim some power of organization when it comes to issues of gender and race and those problems that are in the academic discourse of architecture right now. I don't think what we're describing as indexical procedures for a specific discourse needs to avoid those issues. I don't think they have to be constant, but they are addressable within the mechanisms we're trying to articulate.

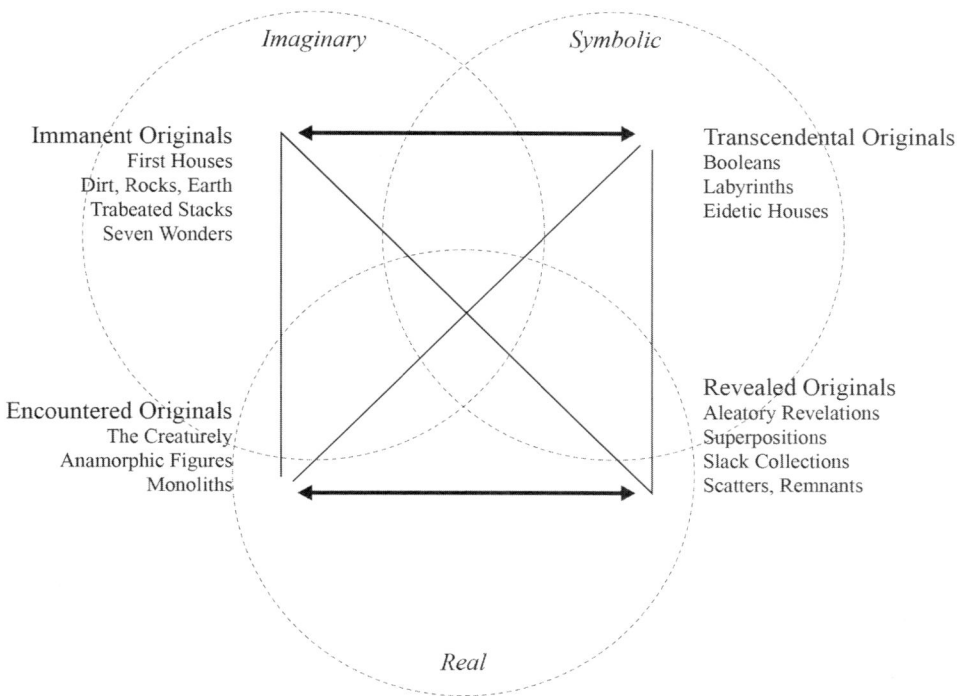

The Greimas semiotic square layered with Jacques Lacan's RSI (Real, Symbolic, Imaginary) diagram.

AH: Returning to the Greimas square and the utility of diagrams for mapping the field, I'll reiterate that I have a hard time understanding the square in the strictly semiotic sense as laying out the total boundary of available thinkable possibilities. I prefer to think of the square as introducing polarities to a field so that it becomes a geography, with different directions that one could go. In the top part of the diagram there is a choice between transcendental, ungraspable things to the right, and graspable things to the left, like dirt and rocks, having to do with embodied experience. In the bottom half of the diagram are regions with different conditions of observing, or what Rosalind Krauss called "consciousness accounting for the fact of its seeing" [*Optical Unconscious*, 19]. To the left are relationships of observation governed by the norms of encounter, and to the right are those that have to be revealed by a mediator.

KMH: I think the diagram recognizes that there are agonistic and antagonistic positions that are engaged through their differences rather than commonalities. It is an agon, a battle, but that means they recognize each other and set up each other. They're battling on the same field. I also enjoy the surprising categories that emerge from the expanded field operations. I enjoy the fact that aleatory practices appear logically from the diagram, as well as historically, and that the encounters with "extimate" creatures are, in a certain sense, a structural negation of the diagram itself; they occupy that impossible fourth slot.

AH: Like Ellie Abrams's work.

KMH: Like Ellie Abrams and her creatures, which have a kind of inhuman quality of alterity. Some others in the dirt and rock category seem like indictments of the discipline itself, revenants from architecture's mirror stage.

CD: Anna, earlier you pointed out that everyone in *Inscriptions* is also in the academy, which may allow a certain freedom for exploration with form and making and material, but there are also issues related to climate, economic justice, social injustice, etc. Where do the exhibition and catalog, and even your own writing, fit in this expanded idea of architecture today?

AN: If we associate form with visual forms of valuation, as well as with nonvisual forms of production, we can more clearly define the territory that this curatorial position tries to delineate. I really liked what Michael said earlier about the image becoming "infrastructural." The *Inscriptions* project brings out the procedural. It helps to identify the substrates in architecture – 2x4s in wood-frame construction, pixels in image production, the zeroes and ones of algorithmic fabrication. Those are all the background media with which we operate. And I also like your question, Cynthia, because as Michael and Andrew are describing 30 years of the *Inscriptions* project, within those 30 years there have been multiple ebbs and flows and multiple distinct revolutions.

When I think of both diagrams presented in the book – the Greimas-Krauss semiotic square and Lacan's RSI network – two things come to mind. One has to do with that horizontal timeframe again. Let's remind ourselves that in leaning on Greimas-Krauss-Lacan, we are summoning linguistic theories of the '70s to analyze the present. There is an anachronism in that. Nonetheless, those are extremely useful models, so I'm completely on board. The second thing is how distinct these diagrams are, one from the another. The semiotic square is a four-cornered polygon, braced by diagonals, while the RSI is a Venn chain of three interconnected circles, or a knot of thread. If I were the reader, I would want to know how they begin to move through one another because they seem to produce two distinct worldviews that are difficult to synthesize.

In an attempt to bring them together, I would propose a thought experiment and throw the structuralist negation at the RSI network, and in particular at the *jouissance* loop that links the real, the symbolic, and the imaginary registers. What would be the *anti-jouissance*?

Could we negate jouissance with the concept of ennui? *Ennui* describes a mental weariness, a state in which things slow down. It is the after-party, the dullness of a post-revolutionary moment. Maybe this is where the minimalism of First Office comes in, in a rather heavy-handed way. And beyond our own work, reckoning with the many postrevolutions that we are living through does not necessarily result in a joyful production of architecture, but in a resetting of values, in a recalibration of a work ethic, and in curbing our energies. It may be a very negative position. But I also think it can result in a productive project.

AH: Anna, your characterization of the contemporary mood seems right, that design is occurring in the wake of some other prior activity and is left with fragments. Along with contemporary calls to do less and/or do nothing in architecture, I would include the rise of interest in Indigenous forms of production that don't participate in fully modern forms of circulating goods and services and of dividing up labor, but instead are local, place-based, craft intensive, and DIY. What are the possible outcomes of design if you deliberately bracket your own geography and process with an intentionally limited set of resources that are more responsible in their origin? Those possibilities seem consistent with the formulation of a design process that I am trying to put on the table. In that situation, something like an archetype, or blank, would be the carrier of form's arrival on the scene, where local labor and craft practices rework its surface, reoriginate it so that the inscription has power and value in the present moment.

This would even include renunciations of conventional building practice, like the projects of Lacaton & Vassal. I think they're doing inscriptive work on top of a set of blanks. Michael and I are trying to identify the blanks and enumerate instances of how they can be handled by the various practices who take them up.

CD: You have said that *Inscriptions* considers 30 years of architecture thinking and work, but it doesn't suggest what this work, or this view of architecture, portends for the near future.

KMH: Because it's a reading mechanism *and* it's an ethos of cultural reception of our most recent past, I think the model of inscriptions that we're describing is imminently teachable. I will teach this. I can start with Hegel and draw a straight line right up to *Inscriptions*. Or better, I can start with *Inscriptions* and draw a line straight back to Hegel, the point being that architecture continues to be an important producer of specific knowledge in our own present.

AN: I do think quite a bit about how the infrastructural approach allows us to pay attention to those things that happen daily rather than those things that happen once in a lifetime. The Soviets even had a word for this anti-heroism of the mundane, the Russian word *byt* [быт]. Viktor Shklovsky tapped into the byt of everyday life with a revolutionary spirit, bringing our attention back to the ordinary in ways that could wake us from a daydream and shock us into the real. He illustrated this with Tolstoy's diary entry on dusting the divan to explain the futile task of taking care of something when no one is paying attention. Through the formalist technique of estrangement, what he called *ostronenie* [остранение], Shklovsky developed ways of slowing down language, to bring our attention to the mundane, to make the "stone feel stony" again.

Architecture has ambitions for form. And it can, at its best, impress meaning on a very large audience that gathers around these objects, to use Andrew's term. But in my mind, it is a counterrevolutionary, secular way of working. I don't mean to say that the work that we do is not joyful or playful, but I think that the things we are describing are quite serious. And the daily routine of our work can be torturous and doubtful. It takes a lot of labor to think about, to construct, to write about, to inscribe, to fund, and to bring a receptive audience and collective energy to the table. That work is real and it takes quite a bit of time, which is to say, these are slow-moving projects for most of us.

Cynthia Davidson is editor of *Log*.

Observations on Avian Cohabitants

Lunchtime in Madison Square Park, New York, for people and pigeons alike. Photo: Patrick Templeton.

They gather at the base of a statue, ubiquitous denizens of the city. There, under the unwavering gaze of a long-dead general, pigeons thrive. They peck at crumbs, blissfully unaware of the irony that they, often dismissed as mere pests, are now the most loyal attendees at the foot of a once-revered leader. They search for sustenance among the scraps of humanity. These birds are more than mere urban fauna, they are barometers of human activity.

Each morning, as the city awakens, pigeons swarm to spots laden with leftovers from the previous day's hominid hustle. Their presence is a direct, observable consequence of our urban lifestyle – our consumption, our waste, our unintentional feeding of these avian inhabitants. Their survival intertwines with our city's rhythms, thriving on our excess.

This connection is stark, and unadorned. As people rush past, coffee in hand, rarely glancing at the feathered foragers below, an unspoken symbiosis unfolds. Pigeons exploit the ecological niche created by humans. The relationship is a straightforward one: We provide, they survive.

As the day wanes, the pigeons disperse, leaving the square for their evening retreats in the eaves and alcoves of the city. Through this lens, the pigeon is not just a bird but a symbol of urban ecology, a living example of nature's persistence in man-made environments. Their presence challenges the notion of what is natural and what is artificial, blurring the lines between the two and reflecting a shared rhythm between human progress and natural adaptation.

– Jada Cannon

Cameron Wu
& Patrik Schumacher

Form, Words, and Artificial Intelligence

The Issue of Geometry, a special section of Log *43 (2018), was devoted to questions surrounding the motivations of architectural form, understood through the specific lens of geometry. To what extent are demands of architecture and geometry coincident and/or divergent? A leading architectural thinker and principal at Zaha Hadid Architects (ZHA), Patrik Schumacher uses emerging digital technologies, including AI, in the design and production of the firm's work. This interview seeks to understand how these technologies are evolving the design process and outcomes of progressive architectural form. We talked over Zoom in November 2023. — CW*

CAMERON WU: Patrik, you've been theorizing, writing, and building your project of parametricism for a couple of decades now. It seems to me that the quickly evolving methods of AI will most certainly be an important catalyst for the kind of work and discourse you're trying to promote. I am not particularly interested in the questions about whether AI will replace architects or not. Ultimately, I'd like to talk about where you think the greatest potential is for AI technology to change the paradigm of creative output. What are the opportunities for true hybrid invention, for leading to a place we would not arrive at only through human design and production?

PATRIK SCHUMACHER: AI is about automation and productivity enhancement, that's for sure. We can make a distinction between what we can do much more rapidly with AI and the new things we couldn't have done before and that give a new quality to the work. But I also think computational algorithmic design has done the latter. AI obviously enhances the productivity of familiar work, but we also have moved to a new place with new creative capabilities and intricacies in design. The latest stage of parametricism, what I call tectonism, which we've been working on for a number of years now, is highly reliant on sophisticated tools, some of which are AI or could fall under a broad umbrella conception of AI, like topology optimization or evolutionary algorithms. Other tools and technologies, like physics engines, are not referred to as AI but have been very important. The geometric intricacy and gradations of some recent ZHA work can't be created without the engineering rationality these tools provide, which can now be applied to irregular forms. For instance, something like RhinoVault and other tools that use topology optimization are very important in opening up new avenues for architecture that go way beyond labor saving or a sense of efficiency in productivity.

It's not as obvious that AI generates totally new potentials, but it definitely expands our imagination and the creative process through the proliferation of variations. This kind of "option churning," where one is quickly confronted with possibilities and iterations, is obviously not only making things faster but also making things more proliferous and richer, and allowing us to achieve outcomes we couldn't have reached otherwise. I also find that there are some things where the particulars of an image produced by AI demonstrate a certain formal inventiveness where you see new moves that you wouldn't have come up with just by thinking or sketching, or by working through the previous conventional tools. There are strokes of genius.

CW: Are you referring to text-to-image-based ideation early in the design process?

PS: Yes. I think it is creativity enhancing. It may be a less dramatic and revolutionary advance than the wave of form-generative computational design tools that lead to parametricism and tectonism, but this new text-to-image AI will also advance our field. At the moment, we use it more for quickly proliferating options of the kinds of designs we have been doing for many years and less for breaking wholly new ground. But there are hints at new directions, and some are more promising than others. Oftentimes, the images become too fantastical in a manner we don't necessarily want to promote. In the current paradigm of tectonism, the AI systems are limited and can't necessarily contribute at their fullest because, so far, they cannot deliver the rigor and rationality we are looking for. The underlying image databases are not yet good or expansive enough. If the prompt asks for bridge structures, there are always problems in terms of structural coherence. However, I think this deficiency can be addressed with better databases. We are currently building up such a database in order to supplement, tailor, and fine-tune AI systems like Stable Diffusion.

CW: Did you say there was a recent book on tectonism?

PS: Yes, *Tectonism: Architecture for the Twenty-First Century*. It's out.

CW: Tectonism was the most recent and advanced form of parametricism that you discussed in the piece you wrote for *Log* 43. It was preceded by foldism, blobism, and swarmism, which are all somewhat distinct but generally include architectural designs that are smooth and continuous. Your intent for tectonism, however, was to convey a more formal and geometric hierarchy, technical rationality, and tectonic syntax.

PS: Precisely. And it is not just me. The whole computational design movement shifted there in recent years, with its focus on the use of engineering optimization tools, fabrication constraints, and constructability. The Block Research Group, for instance, has been looking at structural optimization and form finding for compression shell structures. We are working with them and others, using collaborative tools like RhinoVault, Karamba3D, Kangaroo, as well as various tools for topology optimization. We are also developing our own geometry rationalization tools to capture fabrication constraints for fast and intuitive design work. Many other protagonists have also been working with such methods and tools. I classify all of this under the heading of tectonism.

This is not only getting more engineering rationality into the repertoire but also producing more geometric versatility for expressive purposes. Whereas before parametricism we worked freely with NURBS surfaces, without any further systematic constraints, now we have a new suite of particularly defined geometries based on structural optimization or fabrication constraints. We have anticlastic tensile surfaces, synclastic inflatable surfaces, compression-only vaults, and hypar shells based on the respective structural system. We have conic surfaces if we construct via curved-crease folding of sheet material, ruled surfaces if we fabricate via hotwire cutting, etc. All of these have their own characteristic geometry. I like the resulting expressive versatility because we get a new range of expression, each with its own internal range of variability, thus allowing us to design projects that employ multiple geometric families. Despite their differences, they all participate in an overarching stylistic unity. You can combine them and potentially have distinct zones in an urban complex or campus defined by one of the geometric-tectonic families. Each characteristic family comes with its typical materiality. There's also an interest in reticulations, ribbing, perforations, and tessellations. Like the forms they further articulate, these details are derived from structural or fabrication logics, rather than arbitrary inventions. Their differentiation is systematically correlated with the differentiation of the underlying geometry. This is hard for AI systems to get right.

CW: But the computational algorithmic design tools you just mentioned are not really AI, are they? Meaning, tectonism requires a breakdown in the scale of the larger surface continuities of previous forms of ZHA parametricism, which go beyond AI image capacities. There are structural solutions in addition to local material logics of faceting and curved-crease folding of sheet material, where the specific shapes, bending behavior, and quantities matter, not just the style and aesthetic of appearance.

PS: Yeah, exactly. When this movement began, its protagonists were doing small pavilions and getting into making things. Structural logics were foregrounded because otherwise you were just fighting physics and the costs exploded, or you were wasting space with huge pochés full of hidden steel structure. I mean, some of our projects are like this [*laughs*].

Architecture is more elegant and beautiful with increased degrees of coherence. When you have multiple logics you can combine, you have a stronger expressive versatility that becomes important when you do larger complexes, like we do. If you do a larger group of buildings, even with parametricism and its variations, it can become monotonous relatively quickly, and then you need more diversity in your approach, a richer repertoire. At the same time, you need a unity of approach. Tectonism can cater to these needs. So different areas are distinct but also share a lot of similarities. I think AI could also get involved and help with this, but it's not there yet.

This would require AI models very specific to our discipline and specific to tectonism. Some of the protagonists who have pushed tectonism forward are now getting interested in AI as well, and we will see attempts to craft AI tools more specifically for the purposes of our discipline. We are just beginning to feed neural network systems like Stable Diffusion our particular image sets that contain desirable attributes, classified and tagged in accordance with our way of working. For instance, tectonism requires structurally coherent, complex forms. This has to be learned by giving many examples, ordered and tagged in line with tectonic families.

CW: Are you implying that we may continue to be limited to the text-prompt-to-image model for architectural AI moving forward? I often think about the way programs like Midjourney produce images that essentially look correct in terms of perspective. Many architectural AI images exhibit sets of lines that appear to converge at vanishing points. Midjourney does not understand the rules of linear perspective, yet it achieves general perspectival "correctness" through brute-force mimesis.

PS: Yes, and the handling of light and shadow is pretty much correct. That's why it's so useful. Most of the buildings sit well on the site, gravity is implied, and there is generally a balance to the images, which shows deference to physics. That's why this has been such a big leap forward. There is no reason why the further rigors we aspire to cannot also be learned, thus shortcutting or predicting the simulation results of tools like RhinoVault.

CW: How do we build on the success of AI in two dimensions? Should we be striving to achieve outputs that are 3D models – structural, typological, or surface envelopes, where performance could be verifiable? It seems unfathomable that image-based AI could predictably achieve viable quantitative results for 3D entities. Do you believe that the 2D image-based AI methods of this kind – even when sampling billions of images – could ever get nonvisual and quantitative things like structural and environmental parameters correct?

PS: Certainly not yet, and most probably never with reliable quantitative results. However, when we as architects use Rhino plugins, this also does not substitute for engineering proper, it just gives us useful qualitative results and broad ballpark approximations that tell us enough to keep going in early design stages. Image-based AI will be able to shortcut this to a useful degree. There are other avenues where we could work directly in 3D with AI. For instance, models that generate new models. There are also ways of constraining the image generation by putting parameters, control nets, in together with the verbal prompts. If you feed in a sketch model and let it be dressed up, elaborated, and varied, it works, but that feels less creative.

CW: You're talking about a photo of a physical study model or a screenshot of a schematic 3D digital massing as a point of departure for AI image production?

PS: Yes, 3D digital massings. We iteratively produce images and can highlight areas for change – for example, block out areas of an image we want to change or iterate while fixing and holding on to the parts of an image we are satisfied with. This way we can elaborate and refine an image, rather than being left with a one-shot result. In any event, even if we generate a satisfying image, we must 3D model it to further work on the design. This translation is a matter of eyeballing and craftsmanship. Generating 3D models directly via AI is an obvious ambition for the discipline. We have started to go through our sketch model archive to build up a good database of labeled models, just as we go through our image database.

CW: It's quite funny that you do custom source-image development in-house. ZHA is a well-known firm with a distinctive, recognizable style and is prolific in terms of image production and web presence. If anyone could write effective prompts and get the style right, it should be you guys!

Zaha Hadid Architects, AI prompt: "Tower atrium with exoskeleton designed by Zaha Hadid Architects," 2023. Produced with Midjourney. All images courtesy the architects. For ZHA's AI-generated color images, see pages 140–141.

PS: Yes, you are correct. We don't actually have to do it. The "Zaha Hadid" prompt works very well because we have many images out there. But if you want something specific, or want more particular technical images, you have to refine it in this way. We have a team working on multiple aspects of this process. I would say it not only increases our productivity but also our creativity.

It's not quite tectonism yet. Producing creative and unusual forms which adhere to light and shadow and perspective laws is not a problem, but getting these complex systems right with structural feasibility is much more difficult. We were trying bridges with DALL-E 1 and they were full of mistakes – you know, incoherent structures, missing members, illogical glitches. The results were not really usable. I tried it, maybe a year ago, and realized there's no way it works. You can get an idea for a bridge, but then you have to advance it using conventional means. I tried it again more recently, and the results are still full of glitches.

CW: Let's discuss the possibility of having AI produce actual 3D output – either a text prompt to 3D or an expansive database of 3D models and geometry that could be referenced and iteratively augmented. You have described the material computation of Frei Otto's 1960s soap film experiments as a true precursor to parametricism [*Log* 43]. It seems obvious that if we need to quantify and parameterize certain aspects of architecture, then environmental and structural performance are good places to begin. Minimal surfaces, like those of Frei Otto, address both of these areas. They optimize surface-volume ratios, which have energy implications, while also equalizing tensile forces for structural performance.

For AI to produce structurally viable 3D output from 2D images, you would need to restrict the image database to contain only structurally correct options, which would number in the thousands or the millions. Each 3D-surface option would need multiple images with different projections – all properly tagged, notating that they were representing the same 3D geometry so that the AI could reverse engineer the perspective of each image to get closer to a single 3D output. The overhead of image management would skyrocket!

PS: The currently available systems can't achieve this type of rationality, but image-based outcomes are still useful because our work isn't, in all respects, always following tectonism. Often we must work with more generic volumes and cannot afford to express the structure. In this sense, many AI outcomes manifest earlier forms of parametricism for us. But not all of our projects express articulated structure. For instance, brise soleil systems for sun exposure produced by AI images might appear rational and functional enough, but they lack true rigor. You could still get inspirations working this way, but you couldn't directly reach final, well-calibrated, or optimized geometries. Nevertheless, interesting, new formal features could be discovered that can then be further worked and adapted to become more rational and functionally effective as shading.

So at this point, it is creative, leading to new compositions, morphologies, modulations, transformations, and hybridization of formal languages. It could get closer to truly participating in our design process if we had more images in the database in which the desired coherences were already embedded.

CW: When you're talking about non-image-based methods, are you imagining a database of a billion or so viable structural frames, massing envelopes, and typical floor plans?

PS: Yes, but nobody has done these models. One has to respect the huge investments in processing power that are behind these recent AI successes. If we make a jump to 3D, presumably requiring much more memory and processing overhead, it is unclear how it would become available to us. So at the moment, the idea of tailoring and augmenting existing systems is a realistic way forward rather than building systems from scratch.

In terms of developing a 3D-model database, getting the quantity and quality of models is not an insurmountable barrier. I don't know. I mean, this has not been done. Obviously, it should be possible to get somewhere, but there need to be plenty of models that are properly tagged, etc. It's such a huge project. So 3D will be important, but it is currently unknown when and how well this might start to function.

CW: So for the time being, we have to defer to images of viable forms and structures as the key to advancement rather than a true paradigm shift for AI to three-dimensionality?

PS: I'm interested in both, but at the moment, the 3D version is speculation.

CW: It has been said that one of the reasons why image-based AI is productive and provocative is because it sometimes misunderstands context, producing radical fusions of opposites. Now, with something like parametricism, you're interested in differentiation and the correlation between subsystems that are highly rational. Have you found that increasingly demanding performance and syntactical constraints that convey this rationale and intelligence have led to a narrower window for hybridity and invention?

PS: I'm not sure. One of the interesting things we've been exploring, even before computational methods, is breaking down the architecture-versus-landscape barrier and assimilating the architectural built form to the landscape. You can get that out of AI quite well.

CW: Yes, I know you've been interested in more continuous, less segregated zoning.

PS: When we had a building as a geometric entity cut against a landscape, we used to manipulate the ground floor to bring the landscape into the interior – think of Oscar Niemeyer. We did a lot of this, and AI can generate this too. So there's a successful hybridization between land form and architectural form. I have also tried prompting "Zaha Hadid" and "Frei Otto," or entering text about cable bridges and towers. This kind of layering and hybridization of systems has always been part of my thinking. Not juxtaposing elements in a deconstructive sense but attempting to blend, integrate, letting these systems resonate with each other and mutually adapt to each other. So I don't think true hybridization is out of reach or alien to parametricism. Of course, you don't get something resolved with the high standards of rationality that would satisfy the tectonism agenda. But, again, I see image-based AI as an aid to early ideation and as inspirational input into our design rather than as something that will deliver final results.

CW: So AI can produce hybridity at a larger scale between building and landscape and also operate at a reduced scale within architecture's own typology and expression.

PS: Actually, this blending of usually separate domains is one of the strengths of these AI systems. I don't feel that parametricism is averse to it. I was never one who promoted only single systems resulting in an easy smoothness. Rather, I have always promoted multiple ontologies, which started with differences and then posed the task of integrating them. I was coming from the lineage of deconstructivism, and never bought into the supposedly stark opposition between deconstructivism and folding. I think the latter evolved out of the former, and that is progress only if the latter sustains the complexity gained by deconstructivism.

CW: The term *hybrid* could also refer to architectural outcomes that are typologically ambiguous. These could appear conventional in terms of form and tectonics but be progressive and inventive organizationally.

PS: I agree with you, and these are fascinating opportunities. You are talking in terms of typologies that could very well be absorbed into the paradigm of parameters. Sometimes there are quantitative breaks in the rule sets that are exceptional disruptions. This is okay once or twice in a project, but if you do it 10 times in a larger complex, you start to fall back into a collage condition, which doesn't generate identity or legibility.

CW: I remember a talk you gave at the GSD in which you mentioned "garbage-spill urbanization" to describe the haphazard and inchoate manner in which cities often develop. I asked you why you were unwilling to accept this granular garbage spill as a natural outcome of urban systems and codes, referring to zoning laws, real estate values, office planning, financial concerns, geologic information, and other urban/architectural codes. In your response, you mentioned a thirst for complexity that society might have, perhaps idealizing the intensity of Tokyo at night but rejecting the monotony of the Moscow suburbs.

Some of these recent AI tools for urban design involving BIM technology are remarkably powerful, and it is unclear whether their widespread adoption might counter or amplify the garbage spill. Their text-prompt capability tends to operate at the urban block scale, such as "fill this trapezoidal site with two levels of retail and then put 12 floors of housing in the L-shaped double-loaded corridor anchor on the southwest corner." Seconds later, a fully detailed 3D BIM model emerges. It's incredible! One info video says it speeds up workflow by 100 times! These tools run elaborate and sophisticated scripts and are relentlessly parametric. I feel like you might admire them, in a way.

PS: Exactly. This is for organizational and complex space planning according to typology. One should not think this was a trivial problem to solve. These are interesting things.

CW: But it seems like the codification and the implementation of these elaborate scripts run counter to your design motivations, which might be more interested in evolving social structures, program, and how we inhabit and use space for larger cultural events and complex programs. How can we produce anything new or inventive when the established metrics seem to be hard coded into these powerful BIM AI modelers?

PS: My ongoing research program, in terms of what I call agent-based parametric semiology, is about occupancy simulations with hundreds and thousands of agents implemented. This is looking to predict the frequency of encounters between inhabitants, which could become productive. You can look at how to distribute meeting zones and other spaces to facilitate these interactions. On an organizational level this is interesting, generating new layouts with machine-learned heuristics where one can tweak the parameters to achieve increased density, tighter packing, and more or less permeability or visibility parameters.

Working with these social factors and the representation of interaction, or the population subject to interaction, we can discover the program, spatial layout, and space savings. This is a fascinating tool set that goes beyond the idea of having a schedule of accommodation recommend what should be next to what, and then having that assembled into a geometric layout, distinguishing and labeling program areas.

CW: It seems as if we need these computational algorithms to be intelligently coupled with AI automated plan-making or 3D-modeling capacities, but in an open-ended, nondeterministic manner – meaning that the same or similar inputs (with different seeds) could produce a variety of viable outputs.

PS: By the way, this kind of thinking has existed for nearly 40 or 50 years, in terms of space planning and space management. But they are outmoded because they did not focus on the life process to measure and manipulate space. Knowing all the quantities in advance is old-world thinking – people sitting down in one space to work at their desks, then moving to the cafeteria at a certain time in a corridor which is wide enough, etc. That's not the way our life is anymore.

Zaha Hadid Architects, AI prompt: "Office tower with rational exoskeleton and shading designed by Zaha Hadid Architects," 2023. Produced with Leonardo.AI.

CW: But designing exceptional spaces as a counterpoint to those older ways must presuppose some schedule of accommodation as a starting point. I have heard you use the term *over-coding* in the past. Am I right in thinking that that is somehow coding to produce exceptions within the a priori program schedule? You must have to accept some of these methods instead of always beginning from scratch.

PS: I accept a basic schedule of accommodation as a starting point, but then focus on the potential to generate opportunities of communicative interaction. The reason to bring 25,000 people to a single place is to garner synergies, facilitate inter-awareness, knowledge exchange, and collaboration. We've done some studies on some of our larger office buildings where you have literally 25,000 people in a building – maybe 6,000 on a huge floor plate. How do you do that? We run simulations and try different things. The reliability of these simulations is unclear and the empirical calibration is uncertain. So that's a research project we have ongoing.

I had some PhDs working on this. We also want to use it for virtual spaces, metaverse spaces. That research project uses some kind of Utility AI gaming engine and machine learning. It focuses on the interaction processes within spaces – its barriers, channels, etc. It also studies the original positions people go back to, the different departments, different teams, and what that means in terms of encounters and conversations. This is in the broader realm of AI functionality.

A lot of people are skeptical of this. I think we need to build these capacities to gain some sense of evidence-based design, instead of just saying, I feel this could work, or I've seen that, or I'm an expert, or I have this recipe. That doesn't have much credibility. I've always believed in the tradition of a more scientifically informed design methodology. There was this design methodology movement in the 1960s and '70s using algorithms – people like

Horst Rittel, Christopher Alexander, Lionel March, and Philip Steadman.

From within this movement, William Mitchell developed his *Logic of Architecture* [1990], aimed to guide the development of software tools. They were using computational algorithms early on to re-create village topologies and such. They brought network analysis, or graph theory, into the discipline. Bill Hillier's space syntax research group also worked on a precursor to our agent simulations, to some extent, dealing with crowd behavior and circulation systems. We could go much further with these interaction simulations. It could be about space saving or discovering all the underutilized corners, but, for me, it's about the positive benefits – the social productivity of the space which I'm trying to anticipate.

Now, do I believe this is the whole story, with a naive belief in quantitative optimization? Certainly not. But it's about having some sense of the quantitative and some sense of discovering unusual qualitative effects as well. For instance, you could have fewer people – a less dense packing of desks – but more interaction because of the increased permeability of the space. This layer in design expertise is crucial in raising the credibility and capacity of our field, particularly in large projects like a Google campus, where you have 50,000 people distributed across multiple buildings, or in the case of a university campus. It is important not to cede major design criteria and decisions to the bean counters.

This is one organizational layer, but we are also working at the phenomenological level. This is about legibility and people perceptually understanding the space, allowing them to move more confidently, with more success and satisfaction. In the organizational simulation, we presume that people can stay on target toward a destination. So when designing, we need to ensure they can identify the target in the complexity of the visual field. In the visual chaos of airports, this is done with signage and graphics, but it would be better if the space and form could convey the required navigation information.

Eventually, nothing in architecture will remain outside of the attempt to rationalize and functionalize in this way. I currently have a PhD student using AI systems to semantically identify and tag ramps and escalators in increasingly complex atrium spaces. These are navigation studies with AI representing agents recognizing targets and navigating in a virtual space. These are first steps at operationalizing phenomenology systematically and building tools around the phenomenological project. Whereas the organizational project used agent-based simulations, the phenomenological project is now using AI for the testing of legibility criteria and the navigability of spaces. The other research project I am invested in is the semiological project, and in this project, too, we should be able to operationalize and measure the information richness of spaces and how it empowers successful communicative interactions. AI will increasingly play a role in all of these research projects.

CW: The agent-based simulations of your organizational project seem to affect the plans of architecture, whereas the phenomenological project plays out visually and mostly on the vertical surface.

PS: That's correct. We also want to feed these testing cycles into evolutionary processes, so we need to have a generative element. We need to generate new layout potentials and then keep testing them. I think interesting new solutions would emerge. Whether you might have a description or be able to classify them into types is another question.

If you develop topology optimization, you have structures, but you might not be able to describe them. There's intellectual work in maintaining an intuitive layer of comprehension with a verbal description. This was important when we had people toying around with forms and computers, and then somebody like Greg Lynn or Jeff Kipnis putting a pertinent vocabulary to it. We were doing gradients for 10 years before Kipnis talked about gradients. We didn't use that word, but it helped us a lot to hone in on the concept and to push it further. Some of these great terms, like *smooth* versus *striated* space, came out of Deleuze and Guattari. These emergent qualities and capacities are not in the raw material. We have to conceptualize the raw material to even start to think strategically about these new qualities, capacities, and types of *spatiality*, another useful neologism.

CW: Yeah, for sure. Forms are ideas. I believe that forms are first-order statements in architecture, conveying spatial ideas and concepts better than words can.

PS: Zaha used to think a lot in terms of analogies. When developing a vocabulary that could be analogically based, you have phrases and terms for describing that new formal world. That's very important. And I think that's where Greg and Jeff were instrumental in the early days – Jesse Reiser as well. I also stepped in, helping with putting language, description, and summary into distilled principles, and making it possible to talk about it and to critique it.

CW: It makes sense that language is the cipher or the key to the discursive. I know you're very interested in keeping the discourse of architecture going, hoping that argument and debate might lead to intellectual convergence rather than divergence. Given the sheer amount of information available to us now, coupled with the methods of AI – sampling and mimicking billions of images – it is not surprising that current cultural production is diffuse and pluralistic. Of course, we have words to curate and ascribe value to things, but I fear that information production may exceed our capacity to curate it.

PS: What I find problematic is pluralism – of systems of thinking, of paradigms, of values – in a society that faces critical issues related to the conditions of technology, demography, and urbanization. Simultaneously, we have conditions of prosperity and productivity enhancement. There are strategies that are more viable and less viable, and we should try to figure that out and not say let's let everybody have a go in their own way. There is a need to cohere multiple projects around a set of strategies and shared values. We have to debate the best path moving forward but also adapt to each other around some kind of emergent shared paradigm. If that is not accepted as a fundamental premise to begin with, then something is amiss in the discourse culture.

My analysis has always been that when modernism was becoming maladapted to the dynamic of an advanced society, a paradigm shift was required. It made sense, at that time, to open up an unconstrained brainstorming process in which all sorts of directions could be suggested and explored, without immediately demanding justifications. Such a freewheeling, anything-goes culture of discourse made sense at a certain historical juncture to proliferate possible ways forward. However, in order to critically appraise the imagined possibilities and to select viable candidates for further investigation and investment, a different, more analytical and critical mode of discourse must evolve, one calling for a more systematic frame of mind. This transition, from the seductively unconstrained discourse to a discourse aiming to ascertain and take collective responsibility for the physiognomy of the built environment, never succeeded. We got stuck with the discourse culture of this exploratory phase of our discipline, and this still dominates the expectations, mood, and mode of what should and shouldn't be accepted in the conversation. This made sense in the 1980s, but it is certainly no longer the way we can progress any further.

The whole point of having that brainstorming session is to throw out new ideas and then start weeding out the less viable ones. To some extent, this happened during the 1990s and early 2000s – the result was the movement of parametricism and its latest stage, tectonism – but we also witnessed these waves of wanting to continuously produce further novelty or to go back to basics. The result was that the constructive weeding and elaboration process – the cumulative rebuilding of a new paradigm – only captured a minority within the discipline. That's where I see the lack of "buy-in," or lack of understanding, where the current discourse culture doesn't accept this idea of convergence and doesn't accept the idea that there is a best practice we should collectively try to define and pursue. Instead, we see a celebration of pluralism and very little systematic impact on the built environment itself.

CW: In this sense, the generative methods of AI seem perfectly suited to the ideology of a prolific brainstorming, but we also need to constantly rehearse proper formal analysis to be able to read and interpret this unprecedented volume of production. This is crucial for the perpetual weeding process you want in the determination of what is architecturally productive and what is simply excess. Given the copious and decentralized information flow now, it seems unreasonable that there would be only one or two dominant paradigms for architecture at any one time, as was generally the case until this century.

PS: It's also laziness and self-indulgence, to some extent, and particular architects who don't want to be critiqued or classified. They're doing well by just following their intuition. You know – I do mine and you do yours. Live and let live.

CW: Yeah [*laughs*], for sure. Part of the astonishing power of AI is that it can be so directed and specific, yet it is dependent on an incomprehensible volume of heterogeneous source material in the database. There is an apt comparison between AI and contemporary architecture as a whole, with numerous styles and movements currently expanding in seemingly unrelated directions. Yet the discourse and curation of the explosion of varied outcomes can sometimes be managed by carefully calibrated strings of words.

PS: We need to be creative about the words we collectively bring to these results. The development of a new vocabulary together will hopefully inform and inspire others. All of these movements had productive protagonists, yet they also had theoretical critics reading, justifying, and guiding, ensuring that it wasn't simply the further proliferation of stuff.

Curiously, if you just google "AI generated architecture," you'll find that the majority of images can be classified as belonging to the parametric style. This is very different from the penetration of parametricism in the built environment, the work of professionals, or even in schools of architecture. The same reversal of fortunes can be observed in the brand new world of metaverse architecture. I'd say this portends the future – pragmaticism will eventually become the epochal style it aspires to be.

Cameron Wu is an assistant professor and Director of Undergraduate Studies at the Princeton University School of Architecture. He guest edited the special section, The Issue of Geometry, in *Log* 43 (2018).

Mark Foster Gage & David Chalmers

Architecture, AI & the Hard Problem Of Consciousness

David Chalmers is University Professor of Philosophy and Neural Science and codirector of the Center for Mind, Brain, and Consciousness at New York University. He is the author of The Conscious Mind *(1996),* The Character of Consciousness *(2010), and most recently,* Reality+: Virtual Worlds and the Problems of Philosophy *(2022). David and I talked at his apartment in New York City on September 20, 2023.* – MFG

MARK FOSTER GAGE: You define philosophy not only as "love of wisdom," as its Greek origins suggest, but also as the basket in which you put the intellectual problems that are currently too hard for any other discipline. I'm often asked why I, as an architect, am involved in the world of philosophy, which is curious to me, as we have a lot of hard intellectual problems we need to address in architecture. And having an interest in philosophy is quite literally required by Vitruvius, who writes in the first chapter of his *Ten Books* that architects should "follow the philosophers with intention." It's there, in the origins of two millennia of architectural lore, that you and I should have this conversation.

DAVID CHALMERS: I'm very naive about architecture.

MFG: That's better, because I want to talk about how architecture, more at a meta level, participates in, or even defines, the conscious human experience of reality. Which brings me to your pioneering work on consciousness and, more recently, on simulation and AI. While we'll talk about AI some more, I'd like to cover the current state of our understanding of consciousness and how that may include "architecture as the backdrop of reality," as my friend David Ruy has phrased it. However, I'd be remiss if I didn't offer the prelude that much of architecture's relationship with philosophy in the past decade has been through aesthetics and along the lines of perception, which involve architecture.

Reality+: Virtual Worlds and the Problems of Philosophy by David J. Chalmers, 2022. 528 pages. WW Norton.

DC: In architecture, aesthetic connotes the way the architecture strikes the user?

MFG: Yes, how we perceive the world. What is this built reality we're constructing, as architects? This brings us closer to you and your work, which I started to read after I saw a United Nations' report on how 2016 was the first year in human history when more people lived in urban than rural environments. I think this is hugely significant for how we understand architecture because it means that architecture is no longer, for the majority of humanity, the thing in which you find refuge from nature. Instead, architecture is the thing that replaces nature as the perceptual backdrop of human life. At least as a thought experiment, that is also likely mostly true.

DC: Turns out reality is not made of abstract stuff. It's mostly made of buildings.

MFG: Precisely. And in the theory-engaged architectural community, some of my colleagues and I have been discussing how this is not a trivial issue but is a moral and ethical problem. How should architects format our built environment? Instead of wanting to produce work that is just new or innovative, a lot of us are asking if architecture can help design a world that nourishes how and what we perceive, and therefore consciousness. This brings us to your "hard problem of consciousness," which asks, Why do we experience anything? What is the evolutionary benefit to experiencing things? Why do we need a "self" at all? And, frustratingly, why can't we yet use our own consciousness to understand our own consciousness? You have been asking these questions and pursuing often radical directions trying to find answers.

DC: I'm interested in radical ideas about consciousness because I've always thought that the problem is so hard that it's going to take a crazy idea to solve it.

MFG: You have addressed the idea that consciousness might be a fundamental property of the universe, in the same way gravity or mass or electromagnetism are. Or more specifically, that there may be some truth to panpsychism, which offers the possibly that *everything* has consciousness, from humans to buildings to trees, all to greater and lesser degrees. You've also talked about illusionism, often through Dan Dennett's position on it, which is the idea that our experience of having a self is just an illusory property of something else. Where do you currently stand on these explanations of consciousness?

DC: Those directions were the theme of a TED talk I gave looking to explore different radical ideas about consciousness. I also spent some time looking at connections between consciousness and quantum mechanics – could we find some role for consciousness in collapsing physical reality into a definite state? I've also been quite interested in this idea on the opposite pole that you noted, which is that consciousness is an illusion – the idea that consciousness doesn't actually exist at all but that we are shaped by evolution to only *think* that it does, to think that we have these wonderful properties that we don't actually have. I'm interested in that, but I also find it impossible to believe because consciousness is just clearly so real. On the other hand, this view can explain and predict why I find it impossible to believe. I've had some fun with that recently, connected to what I call the "meta problem" of consciousness. The hard problem is explaining consciousness, but the meta problem is explaining why we are interested in solving the hard problem.

MFG: The idea being that if you can answer the meta problem of consciousness, then you won't need to answer the actual question of what consciousness is.

DC: Yes. Let's say that if you solve the meta problem, it will dissolve the hard problem. Once we can explain why we're so puzzled by consciousness, say in physical terms, we won't need to explain consciousness itself. That's not my view. I think even if you solve the meta problem, the hard problem doesn't go away.

MFG: Is the meta problem accessible via the sciences, whereas the hard problem is less so?

DC: The meta problem is actually something tractable that you can do work on, that anyone can do work on, whether you want to dissolve consciousness or not. Just try to figure out why we are, in fact, so puzzled by consciousness. What's the evolutionary or cultural or scientific reason behind that? I think there's progress to be made in the meta problem, in addition to the hard problem.

MFG: To develop serious knowledge about consciousness, do you think that the problem is going to need to leave philosophy behind, as psychology did, and go through a more scientific and data-focused experimental philosophy, or enter the field of cognitive neuroscience?

DC: Lately I've been very involved with the neuroscience of consciousness. This past summer we held a large Science of Consciousness conference for the Association for the Scientific Study of Consciousness here at NYU. There was a lot of interaction between neuroscience, psychology, and philosophy. One of the centerpieces was a debate about a bet that I had made with the neuroscientist Christof Koch.

MFG: It was covered by the *New York Times*, as I recall. You won a bottle of wine, right?

DC: Twenty-five years ago, Christof and I made a bet on whether we would know the neural correlates of consciousness within 25 years. Christof said yes, I said no. We still don't know about the neural correlates of consciousness. So I won the wine and we made another bet for 2048.

MFG: There seem to be a lot of ways to make the hard problem into a nonproblem, or at least to put some limitations on it. Dennett could wipe it away with illusionism. Your colleague Ned Block believes consciousness is contingent on biology, and Steven Pinker says consciousness is a huge problem that science will never solve. Why are you more hopeful?

DC: Right now, a lot of activity is happening in the interface between philosophy and neuroscience. Mathematical approaches to consciousness are trying to describe consciousness in mathematical terms to see if they can come up with a theory of consciousness with elegant mathematics. It may or may not solve the hard problem, but as an ex-mathematician, I like this idea of seeing if you can describe consciousness in mathematical terms.

MFG: Which would likely be possible if consciousness is a fundamental quality of the universe.

DC: Space, time, mass, and charge are all fundamental qualities you can understand with mathematics. So if consciousness is fundamental, you'd expect there to be some fundamental laws there and you'd expect them to have some mathematical structure. At the same time, the arguments that consciousness is not reducible to physics tend to suggest that consciousness is not reducible to mathematics, that there is more to consciousness than its mathematical structure. Maybe I can know about the math of a bat's brain, but it still won't tell me what it's like to be a bat, to use my colleague Thomas Nagel's example. I am very doubtful that mathematical structures could exhaust consciousness, but they could still tell you something about its background structure, if not its qualitative nature.

MFG: But you're always going to hit the "What Mary Didn't Know" knowledge argument. To briefly outline for the readers – Mary lives in a colorless room, but through a black-and-white television she has access to all sorts of scientific information about color. She just can never actually see color. It's the difference between knowledge of a thing and the actual experience of the thing.

DC: Mary will know all about the mathematical structure of red, but she still doesn't know what it's like to see the color red. Even if you know all about a thing you won't know the experience of it.

MFG: A good marriage of experience and philosophy leads, I think, to the AI question. I last saw you at the Philosophy of Deep Learning Conference. A key question was when the attendees were asked if large language models need sensory grounding for meaning and understanding. Will AI need to be able to sense the realness of, say, red to understand the world, or will descriptions of red be enough?

DC: The big debate.

MFG: The conference featured the Who's Who in the AI world, including Yann LeCun, the director of AI research at Meta, and Ellie Pavlick from Google AI and Brown. You disagreed with many of them and thought large language models do not need sensory grounding for meaning and understanding, and that they could at least understand things like mathematics – but not sensory and bodily aspects of existence. If large language AI models can understand some things, will they be forever unable to understand things at a human level without having some sort of access to the actual physical world? At some point, Mary is going to need to see the color red, right?

DC: In order to understand the experience of redness fully, AI is going to need enough sensory apparatus to have that experience itself. But without it, who's to say? Maybe they could at least have some mathematical understanding of redness. It actually connects to our discussion of the mathematical structure of consciousness and cognition in the world. Maybe you need sensors to fully understand the qualities of the world, red versus blue, maybe even big versus small, as experiences.

But maybe you can also understand the abstract structure, or the mathematical structure, say, of color space without having sensory grounding. So one way to think about these language models is that they're like structuralist thinkers.

MFG: Does existing AI seem to you to have actual contextual knowledge, or is it totally abstract? If they use the term *blue*, do they seem to have knowledge that it appears in the sky?

DC: Yes, they certainly know that, and sometimes even more subtle things. I've had discussions with GPT-4, and you can talk about some quite subtle things, about blue versus violet versus indigo and so on. It has interesting things to say, but it's all at a structural level. I don't think the system is actually experiencing blue or violet.

MFG: But when I perceive blue, the experience is really only the firing of a couple electrical impulses of neurons in sequence. I'm not actually "experiencing" blue, I'm experiencing the neurons firing. Blue is just an activator of those.

DC: Well, there's blue out in the world, but it's not something we can experience directly. It can just trigger a big, long, causal chain of light that goes to the eye and electrical firings.

MFG: So AI would need a similar causal chain that reaches into the world in some capacity, not necessarily "direct" access to blue, which we humans don't even have?

DC: Well, the question really is, When do we have the experience of red or blue? It's not the external quality we're experiencing but an internal quality. It's a quality of consciousness. I'm not sure even a biological human brain in a vat could have the experience of red or blue, even without a deep connection to the world. You might think an AI system could at least have that, which would require the AI system to be conscious.

MFG: There are efforts to link AI with physics engines and robotic bodies to get around this and provide some tangible link to the actual external world.

DC: People are building multimodal language models. I just saw a new one, DALL-E 3, the new vision plus language model from OpenAI. They're going to have a model that deals with vision with as much facility as it deals with language. You can make the case that it is actually a form of grounding the perceptual processes of AI in the world.

MFG: I have Yale grad students who, just through prompts, have already designed unbelievable things without that multimodality. Their architectural problem this term is to design a museum of the history of gold and mining in Ouro Preto, Brazil. Several of them just typed in "Museum of Gold in Ouro Preto, Brazil, designed by Mark Foster Gage," or something like that. I'm not kidding when I say it produced a design as good as, if not better than, I would.

DC: Is there such a museum?

MFG: No, but the AI produced a building in a context that looks like Brazil. I've spent decades developing a kind of architectural language, and Stable Diffusion knocked it out in six seconds after a student typed in a couple prompts. There is no question whatsoever that that aspect is going to revolutionize the creative production of architecture.

DC: Is AI already playing a big role in architecture now?

MFG: It's playing a role, but not nearly as

much as I think it will in a few years. Like most digital technology, it's played with first in universities before it gets co-opted by the business of architecture and becomes about function and economics. But even at Yale, it's a morass of unknowns. A friend of mine, Mario Carpo, wrote a piece in *Artforum* called "Imitation Games" about AI and architecture. He argues that AI in architecture is really a return to a reliance on historic architectural forms because the computer can only access things that already exist. In essence, it's making collages of old buildings, which is anathema to the Modern Movement in architecture. So, ironically, the most advanced technology is taking us back into history. Both the development of the software and the changing theoretical frameworks for it in our field are operating at a breakneck speed.

DC: Just wait. Every year it's so much more impressive. I mean, there was GPT-1, then GPT-2 came out in 2019, but it wasn't that impressive. Suddenly, in 2020, GPT-3 was very impressive. Actually, I wrote an article around then called "GPT-3 and General Intelligence," saying this is the first sign we've seen of possible general intelligence in a computer. Everything before these language models was specialized. They did one thing well, but that's all they did.

MFG: Like winning games like Go or chess.

DC: Yes, But GPT-3 could take on anything. You could play chess or Go with it if you wanted to. You could ask it to write poetry, you could give it math puzzles, and it did all of those things. Not incredibly well, but it was the first to do all of those things at once. Suddenly you could see a path forward, and over the next three years, things moved ahead pretty quickly. The next question is, Are we going to hit a wall or will things keep scaling? So far, things have kept scaling. I would say GPT-4 was the next really big jump, and it was super impressive. It's gone from feeling like talking to a young kid to talking to a young adult. And GPT-5 is coming, as well as Gemini, Google's version of this.

MFG: You've been working in this area probably as long as anyone, watching the fetal AI technologies grow into seemingly now young adults who know a lot. You've literally grown up alongside AI.

DC: I did my PhD while working in an AI lab in the early '90s, in Indiana, with Douglas Hofstadter.

MFG: Hofstader's *Gödel, Escher, Bach* changed my life in high school more than any other single book. That must have been amazing, but I don't think many would intuit the link between Hofstader's work and AI.

DC: Well, back then everyone knew that AI was going nowhere. People would say a year spent working in AI is enough to make you believe in God. You just realize how hard it is to make something intelligent. That all continued to be the case through at least 2012, when this deep learning explosion started. For the next five years, we got impressive things, from object recognition to playing Go, to doing things with folding proteins. But there was no sign of general intelligence. It's just really in the last five years that suddenly there are glimmerings of general intelligence that are moving ahead quickly. And that is simultaneously extremely scary and extremely exciting.

MFG: There are researchers who are putting AI in robot bodies to give them a more physical experience of the world. Is that tactile access to the world what you think is required for AI to make the next exponential leap forward, possibly into consciousness?

DC: It's a good question. How central are perception and action in human intelligence and how central will they have to be in artificial intelligence? No question, they're extremely central in human intelligence. We are perceiving and acting creatures, and language seems to come on top of that. But these language models start with language. They're not that good at perception and action, but they still seem to do remarkably well overall. They still can't actually clean up after a mess, but they can give you instructions on how to do it that are sometimes amazingly good.

So, will AI systems need perception and action? I think it's still an open question, but if they do, the next question is, Will it need to be real-world or will virtual-world perception and action do? There's already a very big movement of working in what people call embodied AI, which mostly takes place in virtual worlds because it's so much easier to build a robot in a virtual world and you have so much more control. Some people would say that's never going to be the real thing, but I don't see any reasons, in principle, why a virtual body couldn't give you everything that a physical body gives you.

MFG: If you link an AI to a virtual physics engine that gives you all of the behaviors of physics, there's the virtual experience of those relations as a simulation, compared to having those experiences in the real world. I agree that neither virtual nor physical is more or less "real" per se, but do you think one of them is more likely to produce a self-aware consciousness in an AI system?

DC: Interaction is probably very important to intelligence, actually being able to do things and have the world act back on you. I would guess that acting makes a very big difference. Interestingly, the language models act a bit – they tell you things and that's a form of action. But mostly they're only very good at giving advice. They obviously don't engage in physical action. You can hook them up to a physical body or a virtual body that does, but I would put my money on action being extremely important in intelligence.

MFG: Let's say that you put AI in a robot body. Does it matter what environment you put it in? Can the environment prompt or inhibit consciousness? If you have an AI in a robotic body with the intent that it physically act in the real world, to train it, does it matter if you put it in Dave Chalmers's apartment or in a shopping mall or in a war zone or in Chartres Cathedral? Humans evolved in certain places, and not others, because the environment nourished their evolution in some way. I ask because a few architects, myself included, are asking how the physical environment pushes back and impacts our consciousness.

DC: For humans, growing up in a certain environment totally structures our consciousness.

MFG: I guess that's the question. Do you need to give the AI the experience of specific qualities in the world or just the general qualities of physics?

DC: The approach these days is big data, so give them everything. Throw all the texts on the internet at them, throw every artwork at them, and so on. In the context of architecture, throw every existing building or design at them. They need to be trained on being in this apartment, on being in a hut, on being in a skyscraper.

MFG: It's interesting that the training of AI to develop consciousness might require the input of every type of architectural environment humans typically inhabit.

DC: Or, if you really want specificity, you just train it on one kind of environment.

MFG: I guess that's another question. Is the goal to get AI to be conscious through any means possible or is the goal to develop an AI with a certain moral conscience, which may require a more specific type of training, perhaps in a more specific environment?

DC: I think we would, in the end, like our AI systems to have styles, plans, morals, and goals of their own and beliefs that are distinctive – some personality. For now, we have these giant GPT systems that can take on any persona you'd like, and they're a bit like chameleons in that respect. You can ask it to simulate the works of Mark Foster Gage and it'll do a decent job.

MFG: A terrifyingly good job.

DC: But is its heart really in it? It's like you might want an AI system that is trained wholly on the works of Mark Foster Gage and nothing else to see what it can come up with that really takes off in new directions.

MFG: That's an interesting thought experiment. Ask architects if they think an AI trained with only their buildings would develop a good moral character.

DC: Someone is actually programming a Dave Chalmers language model. They're training a language model on everything I've ever written in order to produce a simulator that they will then use to generate a bunch of pseudo–Dave Chalmers prose. Then they'll give it to people to see who can tell the difference. Which is the real Chalmers, which is the fake? They already did this with Dennett, and this will be a follow-up. I'm hoping that at least I can tell the difference. Right now, they're kind of catching up to human-level intelligence. I don't see why, in principle, they couldn't eventually get well beyond us. We'd like to think it's not just a statistical mashup, but I don't know. Get enough complicated statistics on top of more complicated statistics, maybe you get a brain.

MFG: Do you have a dystopian, utopian, or in-between view about the effects of general intelligence in AI on the world?

DC: Simultaneously both, extremely scary and extremely exciting. I mean, intellectually, I am extremely excited by it. If these machines get sufficiently smart, maybe they'll solve the hard problem of consciousness for us.

MFG: What would you do?

DC: Well, I'd be out of a job, but I'd be glad that the problem was solved. At the same time, AI is obviously going to change everything. At a level of displacing jobs and probably ending up running so many things that are currently run by humans. Eventually, once these systems are so much more powerful than us, they'll have the ability to dictate how they want the world to be. So we'd better make sure that we're giving them goals that are consistent with ours. But, as many people have been saying, it's so easy for that to go wrong. There are a million possible disasters waiting for us. Maybe we can thread that needle and avoid all the disasters to get a good outcome and hit utopia on the other side, but I think we're going to have to be very lucky for that to happen.

MFG: I think that's part of the question of how you nurture morality in a conscious AI. What inputs do you give it?

DC: Some people ask, What is the objective function for AI? What's the utility function for AI? What's it maximizing? They all maximize something; we better make sure it maximizes the right thing.

MFG: Some of my peers in architecture are thinking about the effect of maximization on design. For instance, using AI, you just write a prompt, say, "Mark Foster Gage's design for Dave Chalmers's apartment," and it'll pop out five versions of a similar thing. The architect then picks the best option. This turns designers into curators. Here's the worry. You say, "Design a building like Mark Foster Gage," and it does that. Then the client asks an AI to make it half the cost, and it shoots out something. Then they ask to make it half as expensive again. That's the history of architecture and technology. Technology in architecture mostly isn't used to serve creative ends, it's used to serve economic ends. I think the scary scenario is that AI merely becomes a tool to hammer down the result of a design into the least expensive version.

DC: I assume there are already a million forces doing that.

MFG: There are a million forces doing it, which is all the more reason we don't need AI to join that front. Although it inevitably will, I am, probably like you are, excited about the potentials of AI and a little scared about what they could do to humanity. But I'm extra scared about what they'll do to the way of life of an architect and academic – that is, my life. I've already accomplished enough that it won't really hurt my career, but it may terminate hundreds of my future students' creative careers before they've even started. If everyone can do what everyone else can do, why would you hire one particular person over another?

DC: We're a little bit further away from this in philosophy. I haven't started actively worrying about language models coming up with better philosophy and thereby replacing philosophy professors. Maybe the next big thing in philosophy is to get AI to produce a new great article by Bertrand Russell or write some amazing new insight by Heidegger. Then what will be the role for the humans?

MFG: I guess it depends on whether the AI is conscious enough to produce, or know it's produced, original ideas. So, speaking of original ideas, What are you working on next?

DC: I've been thinking about writing a book on AI. The trouble is that by the time it comes out, it will be obsolete. AI changes everything. Can these AI systems be conscious? Can they think, can they understand? Can they extend your mind? I've been writing an article on whether we can use AI as a tool, the way we use smartphones, that actually serves to extend our minds in a deep sense. There are so many questions…

Mark Foster Gage guest edited *Log* 17: Superficial (2009) with Florencia Pita. He is an associate professor at the Yale School of Architecture as well as the founder of Mark Foster Gage Architects in New York.

Ursula Biemann, *Forest Mind*, Taita Oscar's table, film still, 2021. All images courtesy the artist. For color images of Biemann's work, see pages 142–143.

Sanford Kwinter
& Ursula Biemann

Sentipensar; or, How To Become Earth

Ursula Biemann is an artist, cross-media essayist, researcher, and activist based in Zurich. She belongs to a vanishingly small cohort of practitioners to have achieved a practical and conceptual "parity" with the vital metabolisms that underpin the material world beyond the reach of routine human experience. Hers is notably not just another naive "posthumanism" but a steadfast sensory penetration into the creative substrate that is common to all worldly expression and interaction of form. Her primary interest is the reciprocal arising of knowledge and world(s), a process she sees as operating all the way down, as a social, political, and even somatic capture of broader, more remote geochemical processes. Among her many "meta" art practices is her role as a principal in the creation of the Biocultural Indigenous University in Colombia, which rethinks how knowledge is transmitted from matter to time. Her mediums are video, travel, and storytelling. The following is from our November 2023 email and SMS correspondence. – SK

SANFORD KWINTER: Hi Ursula. Let me say, by way of disclosure to *Log* readers, that we met in 1985, in New York City, in a *theory* class for *artists*. I mention this because the context for our engagement today, I expect, is no different. Your practice belongs to a remarkable but tiny cadre of art makers that is driven by research, discovery, and revelation, and whose form of "reporting back" is indivisibly sensory and theoretical at the same time. A comparable practice that comes to mind is that of Chris Marker, whose works are only *ostensibly* films but are, in fact, artifacts, or maps, of personal or existential transformation. Everything I want to talk to you about today has to do with the capacity of your work to bring the experience of transformation out of both sentient *and* intellectual awareness.

You once remarked that "every crisis of matter is also a crisis of thought." I take this to mean that no complete or proper accounting of "reality" can leave the false division between matter and thought intact. There is a wonderful tradition in human culture in which the subtle and surreptitious processes by which matter becomes thought, and thought matter, are treated as the underlying dynamo of *life* as expressed in form, a process normally obscured to us – it is either too large, too subtle, or too remote – yet rendered accessible through a continuous refining of our general attunement. Your work, of the last 11 years at least, could be characterized as accelerating this process of correction, the disclosing of the thought in matter and the matter in thought – in other words, revealing that nature is simply *knowledge* in its wild, or active, state.

Your work is strongly focused on knowledge and the infinity of its modalities. Not only is your primary practice actual classical fieldwork, you go to "the place" and both annex and enter into it, but in many of the videos, especially the earlier ones, you introduce specific figures, such as the scientist (who observes), the dreamer (who imagines), and the technician (who captures, frames, and records). I see every one of your videos as an "origin myth," a different way of birthing of world.

URSULA BIEMANN: Hi to you, Sanford. Yes, it's funny, because at the time we met, you were introducing many shell-shocked students to rhizomatic thought, ways of capturing "world" without reproducing it. I spent most of my studio time that year painting abstract 3D maps. Principles of spatial organization also entered all of my early video works, which were essentially video *geographies*, from transitmigration spaces in the Sahara to the oil geographies of the Caspian Sea, seeking to capture moments of global transformation. But underlying these concrete geopolitical situations that I recorded and "reported back," as you say, there were fundamental questions that intrigued me and drove all of my field research with camera in hand: How do these territories actually come into being? And then, what is my role as video maker in the making of these worlds? I meant these questions literally. My thoughts and attention, my joys and apprehensions, my instrumental observations through the camera lens, they too contribute to making a world, they do not simply represent a pre-given one. With the shift of my creative focus from cultural geographies to environmental concerns, more firmly located within the scope of science, these matters of worlding moved to the foreground and became a prominent element in my videos. This was a particularly opportune move, as scientific and other forms of knowledge facilitate a deeper exploration of how this our world comes into being.

The new cinematic environments I've been working on, over the last dozen years, are indeed populated by a plethora of different actants. Some are humans, many are not. Ranging from microorganisms in the Nile to the ones in the meltwaters from Greenland's ice sheets, they bring about major changes in the political and social life on Earth. In other words, they are powerful, if undervalued, actants. It is minute empirical work in the field that ultimately reveals their mechanisms and interrelations. But I would also say that initially it is philosophy that inspires most of my projects from the onset. It is a constant going back and forth between ideas, discoveries on site, and situating these ever again in larger theoretical frameworks. So yes, originally, in order to address the full biocultural spectrum, I introduced a mediator: the pivotal figure of a scientist who goes into the field and whose purpose it is to transport and amplify these reflections. In addition to the camera as my instrument for intentional observation, I began to use other scientific equipment and forms of mediation to interact with the particularities of the site. Performances of scientists working in the field turned out to be an effective aesthetic strategy to imbue landscapes with the meaning-making of nonhuman actants. Performing a particular epistemic repertoire, such as water chemistry, marine biology, or tropical entomology, is a form of role-playing and narrative writing.

These new *worlding* explorations introduce staged performances and poetic writing to activate material emergences in more evocative and symbolic ways. *Egyptian Chemistry* involves filming, interviewing, and sampling water from the Nile River and connects ontological experiments with specific postcolonial environments on the ground. In so doing, camera in hand, I try to establish a poetics of place, while at the same time emphasizing the role of art in mediating environmental knowledge.

SK: You mention in passing, as if it were a slight thing, the switch in your work's attention from "cultural geographies" to "environmental concerns." In other words, from the global to the planetary. Yet it strikes me that this is the cardinal transformation – I'm almost tempted to say *revolution* – in your work, what sets it apart, not only from most other artists, but from much of the monolithic knowledge enterprises that make up our constipated modernity. We live, for example, and draw solace evermore from the platitudes of what we call our Anthropocene, with little awareness that the new Earth Systems approaches within which this worldview was developed do little more than convert arbitrary and incoherent bits of physicochemical evidence into seemingly more ordered and intelligible forms without acknowledging the deeper integral reality in which they are embedded, the invisible but pervasive dynamo that makes earth *Earth* in the first place: *life*. I am fascinated by the ways you characterize this underlying substrate and its action, the extraordinary ways that you bring them to our senses – biosemiosis, intelligence, worlding, and so on. These terms carry us as beings to a much different "place."

UB: The shift in attention toward the planetary opened a new vista onto and into the world for many artists and thinkers, not only for me. It was no longer a matter of merely scrutinizing the activities taking place on the surface of the globe but of attending to the thin, fragile layers of the biosphere above and below Earth's crust where life is possible. At best, this also entailed a change in objective, from simply conquering distance for trade and travel to caring for a damaged Earth. But the crux is that this shift cannot be performed successfully by sticking to old methodologies. We need proposals and visions for the future and to invent new charismatic figures to inspire a different way of being. This crucial moment in human time requires a *propositional* practice in art, not just a critical one. So I entirely agree with you. Lamenting the Anthropocene while blindly steering full speed toward a changing Earth System that exponentially diminishes or puts an end to life-sustaining conditions for most species is worse than unhelpful.

I have used investigative video and fieldwork as an artistic practice since the very beginning, when I scrutinized the mind-boggling global labor conditions in the Mexican borderlands. Not that this was a popular topic in the arts of the early '90s, but with some imagination, you could place it in the context of cultural studies of gender and critical postcolonial theories. Leaving such cultural geographies behind to turn to the *ecologies* of oil, ice, water, and forests meant taking another giant step into uncharted territory, this time from cultural to natural phenomena, which required a completely different conceptual structure. Climate change and the biodiversity crisis urge art and art institutions to engage in dynamics that are not comfortably located in the designated humancentric field of cultural inquiry, although altogether they are disturbingly concrete and pertinent for human continuation.

Ursula Biemann, *Acoustic Ocean*, film still, 2017. Performance of a Sámi marine biologist laying out her hydrophones to record the vocalizations of marine species, Lofoten Islands, Norway.

How to turn cyclones, climate warming, insect behavior, or subtle changes in water chemistry into a compelling subject in art? A mystery for sure. These efforts would not simply seek to ground scientific knowing differently or to draw physical and biological phenomena into a cultural discourse from which they have been effectively discouraged, if not entirely left out. Many of these efforts aim at breaking down the opposition between science and poetry and instead offer a diverse configuration of that encounter. It had to start from a deeper understanding of the failures of Enlightenment rationalism and its objectifying distance to anything alive, an epistemology that penetrated all areas of society and systematically exposed life to manipulation and extraction for human benefit. This disturbed relationship between humans and the Earth, rooted in the simultaneous emergence of natural science and colonial conquest, is the underlying driver of the current environmental crisis. Hence, my questions became increasingly geared toward different knowledge cultures. How can art inject ways of knowing that are both persuasive and refreshingly distinct from those practiced in the machinery of universities and scientific institutions? One of the rare good things the Anthropocene discourse has brought is a different notion of time. From the self-absorbed concerns with human history that rarely reached further back than World War II, the time bubble was blasted open and allowed for a transformative glimpse into deep time, into cosmic dimensions, embracing the "big history" of planet formation and prompting a desire to span the more-than-human time with our minds. It was an extraordinary moment of expansion of human self-conception.

The only way to activate this in the modest video projects I do was to draw on science fiction–style narratives and to invent fictional characters out of time. *Subatlantic* and *Acoustic Ocean* were both written as sci-fi poetry. She-scientists inhabiting the northern islands of Shetland, Greenland, or the Lofoten archipelago are seen maintaining curious nonphysical relations to the land

and the waters surrounding it. Rising sea levels resulting from the last ice melt, 12,000 years ago, had submerged early human settlements along the shore some 300 feet. One narrative figure inhabits multiple temporalities, unfolding a postglacial, premodern narrative from a submerged Atlantic position. She speaks to us contemporaries, who will be experiencing similar aquatic conditions in the not so far future. The other figure entertains interspecies communication with marine species who were believed to be mute for centuries. The question I address in these videos is how humans and other species collectively attune to the idea of an unstable living environment where our very subsistence is uncertain. It's as much about the physical and natural environment as it is about the psychic space we inhabit and which we are part of, because the atmospheric alterations affect not only the physical but also the mental climate on Earth. In this science-fictional narrative, thoughts materialize. They reconfigure to engage the changing ecology, they merge with frozen methane, become part of weather events. Apprehensions are part of the melting icescape, they flush into the cold water and blend with new matter, intensively communicating with fragile marine systems. Global warming, with its rampant disturbances, challenges us to engage artistic and scientific paradigms together in a conversation and let the mixture infiltrate our imagination and practice.

To achieve a future in which human-nonhuman relations are less violent, less destructive, the past will have to be reassembled. This sort of rewriting of history resembles somewhat the rewriting of postcolonial history. Only in this case, it will not be solely a matter of admitting formerly excluded groups of human populations to the theater of significance, but to fundamentally decentering the human figure altogether. What we can already say is that a common future that we share with everything else would be equally rooted in cultural and natural narratives, for our heritage will henceforth necessarily include both cultural *and* natural histories.

SK: In watching the two aquatic-themed works you mention, and in marveling at their structure, I was often struck by the resonance they have with Rachel Carson's *The Sea Around Us*. That book, as you know, deploys an unforgettable confluence of voices, attitudes, and performances of sentience that, together, not only marked the inaugural act of Western scientific environmentalism but did so paradoxically while employing a language and a posture that might be described as rising from a *rhapsodic disposition*. This uncustomary approach allowed, even mandated, an unprecedented identification of the writer with the sea itself as a teeming "multitude," analogous to, and continuous with, the vital polyphony of our own bodies as well as the infinite and inventive variety of our own species' social forms.

Carson-as-scientist, it could be said, simply confirmed, on another register of explanation (most explicitly in *Silent Spring*), what empirical and felt understandings sometimes reveal in other contexts, either by rare preternatural gifts within our own knowledge culture, especially by nature writers, or by cultivated attentional practice in premodern, traditional, or embedded Indigenous cosmologies. This marks a leap, which should not be passed over lightly, because it represents an important and largely overlooked episode in the history of consciousness, one that marks the transcendence of hidebound – and what many still think of as "human" – *time*.

The platitude that humans are confined in their scope of natural understanding to only the narrow horizon of ordinary psychological experience rather than, say, able to access more foundational rhythms of material, energetic, or biological transmissivity

Ursula Biemann, *Egyptian Chemistry*, film still, 2012. Chemist taking water samples in the Nile delta.

and conduction – what philosophers have variously called "creative advance," "transduction," "self-realization," "élan vital," "self-organization," "transpersonal" noesis, Logos, and so forth – is as trite as it is commonplace.

On the contrary, it is demonstrably a reflex of life and of free sentience to experience life's own progress of individuation and understanding – understanding's own unique penetration into reality – as being of-a-piece with the wider problem-solving dynamo of evolution itself and of active matter. Your use of the word *semiosis* is interesting because it refers to the organization of both matter and meaning as a unified act. It also situates this essential human activity of worldly participation well outside the mundane framework of routine "experience." The defining feature of life is its compulsion to "learn" – to assimilate features, patterns, information from the environment into functional circuits and to integrate them within its own patterns and actions. And this learning, as you insist throughout *Forest Mind*, takes place at every level and scale – chemical, energetic, cellular, somatic, cognitive, spiritual, and so forth – and is in no way confined to "human time." This is why, in some contexts, it feels more accurate to describe the world as "mind" than as matter, and it is certainly why many traditional cultures are appalled to discover that technological cultures habitually divide these *and still manage to survive*.

In truth, the myth of the mind's separation from vital and material nature represents one of the key operations in what was once seen to be hard-won emancipation from the *indifference* of nature rather than a sign of its abundance and unity. This historical and cognitive operation is often described as a process of *disenchantment of the world*. But this is also why your invocation of the need to invent and set into motion "charismatic figures" is so surprising, evocative, and powerful, not to say timely.

Charisma is not a common term these days. Its modern sense goes back in large part to Max Weber's usage regarding political or cultural leaders who are seen to possess exceptional, even supernatural qualities (which can certainly be seen as dangerous).

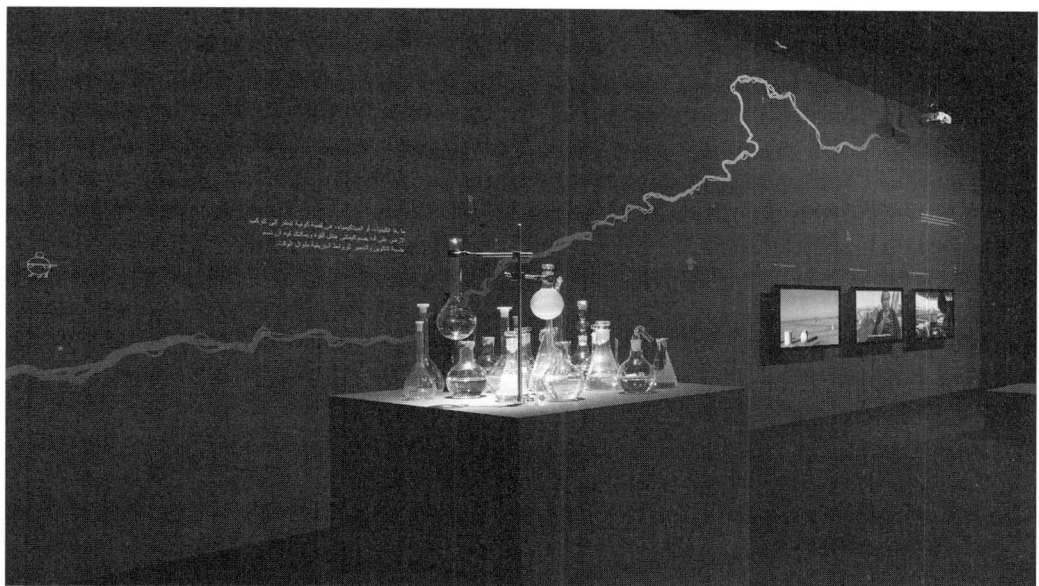

Ursula Biemann, *Egyptian Chemistry*, installation at n.b.k. Berlin, 2013.

But the nuance that is pivotal to the use of the term has to do with how one construes the source of these non-ordinary qualities and the implication that they are somehow divinely conferred or associated; for the possessor of charisma is always seen to bear a privileged connection to a magical, beyond-human domain. It is deemed "magical" because it accesses *what is beyond the throttle of detached observation*, revealing relations so surprising or obscure that they are construed as formed in another, actually existing world.

If that domain is now construed as the mysteriously organized Gaian realm, knowledge and its means of acquisition, as you well note, would need to undergo a significant transformation. Access to this world's efficacy and "intelligence" becomes dependent on finding ways of bridging to what is not part of ordinary or familiar experience, which mostly means *to the operations of an undivided world*. In traditional cultures, this role is largely reserved in formal ritual, to healers, seers, elders, and shamans, but a great deal of this knowledge is perennially embedded in that culture's everyday economic activity and collective practices. It has become increasingly clear that our modern "world picture," or cosmovision, is *structurally* unfit to achieve this type of global elaboration. The transformation of a world picture, as your work gently and persistently argues, is also always a transformation of a "world."

It is here that I see an incredible prescriptive opening in your scripting and reportage. *Science* – the systematics of the outer world – and *understanding* – a systematics of the inner world, are conjoined not as two things but as indissociable threads of a single "world-twine." To grasp even this single fact would indeed provide a gateway to a restored 21st-century onto-epistemology. But for it to achieve traction, there needs to be a set of compelling or charismatic thought-images, or imagining tout court, that directs life and cognition toward what has been both forgotten – the organism's immanent relation to Earth – and toward what is not yet arrived – the new synthesis of noosphere and ecosphere. There is a difference between bare facts and pregnant ones. In nature there are no bare facts.

Pregnant facts have what William James used to call "noetic quality," which is to say, they yield states of understanding that seem to exist in suprahuman time and space. Your arguments in *Forest Mind* seem to draw very strongly on these propositions.

UB: I feel deep sympathy with Carson's effort to seek a fitting language for the charged electromagnetic quality of heightened attention, which I often experience during my fieldwork when registering the world through both the senses and thought. In this attitude of open research, one is disposed not merely to define the findings but to create new and lucid coalescences with semiconscious affects and ideas, and with other material and immaterial surroundings, all of which converge in a common narrative matrix. These are the moments when I'm most keenly aware that I'm mediating reality as fully as I possibly can, using all of my sensors, neurons, and antennae. At least with respect to the noetic quality of field research in my early ecological projects. My more recent ones, *Forest Mind* in particular, propelled me into entirely different states of mind.

Your image of the indissociable threads of a single world-twine made me think of the entanglement in the quantum world as well as the double helix of the DNA molecule. Even particle theorist Karen Barad argues that the quantum world teaches us there is no materialization without the implication of consciousness.[1] But apparently this is also true for DNA, the blueprint for life nested in every cell. The entire earthly living fabric, our primary entity of experience, is made by and kept alive through the entanglement of mind and matter. For that reason alone, I am with you when you say that the world is minded, or at the very least, in the words of anthropologist Gregory Bateson, that mind is not something located within a person's brain; mind is what happens in the perceptual moment outside and between bodies.[2]

I have felt considerable traction, and a certain urgency, to seriously engage my artistic production – my fieldwork, signifying practice, organizing system, my whole cosmology – with the possibility of overcoming this factitious boundary that sets humans apart from the Earth. I felt the need to dive into the innermost dimensions of our composite reality if I wanted to understand the first thing about reality mechanics and appreciate its powerful political agency. *Egyptian Chemistry* was my attempt to enter these metachemical microworlds. The project engages the disrupted and reemerging material bonds that form a nonverbal narrative configuration at the molecular level – namely, the plurality of dynamic processes of water and soil chemistry that have been dramatically recomposing the physical territory of Egypt from within. Altered water chemistry transformed soil quality, which in turn interfered with land management, drove urbanization processes, and disrupted food supply chains. It infiltrated the human sphere through multiple venues and illicit channels. Of course, these components do not line up in a simple causal chain of reactions, as they constantly shift and create strange feedback loops, nor are they solely the result of specific economic policies. Each element operates to create hybrid ecologies in which global organizations, desert developers, and tiny pollutants all forcefully affect water, land, and daily life in Egypt.

Forest Mind, on the other hand, takes us into the *runa* world of Amazonia, or more precisely, into the multispecies pluriverse of the Inga people of Colombia, with whom I have collaborated for the last five years. Driven by the Inga vision of establishing an

---

1. See Karen Barad, *Meeting the Universe Halfway: Quantum Physics and the Entanglement of Matter and Meaning* (Durham: Duke University Press, 2007).
2. See Gregory Bateson, *Steps to an Ecology of Mind* (New York: Ballantine Books, 1972).

Indigenous university in their territory, the project entwined me in an intense web of *sentipensar* with the territory and its lush biodiversity, with the elders, *sabedores*, women healers, social leaders, traditional medics, and, by necessity, with *the* plant, *la planta* – that is, ayahuasca. Fittingly, anthropologist Arturo Escobar's *sentipensar* with the Earth, a word that merges feeling (*sentir*) with thinking (*pensar*), is also deeply connected with the complex Indigenous notion of the territory, the living-sentient cognitive entity that is intimately connected with knowledge, wisdom, perceiving, and caring for. Learning and knowing can only take place within and through the territory; all knowledge derives from there. The territory is the maximus teacher. In the forest, coming to know something is not done from a distance, it is an encounter with a person, with a mind, and it means to understand its place in the larger ecological context. I see my role as an aesthetic companion to their megaproject of recuperating and recreating their own epistemology, calling my modest input *Devenir Universidad* (becoming university). In fact, in a thoroughly pluriepistemic endeavour, what is becoming *university*, here, is not so much the Inga people but the territory itself. With their vast knowledge of medicinal plants and forest ecologies, the Inga see learning with plants also as a form of healing the territory – from colonial projects, from oil extraction, from epistemic occupation, from a messy history. *Forest Mind* emerges from the cocreation of this visionary pluriversity with the Inga and all other species and entities inhabiting this Andean-Amazonian living space. The 30-minute video essay empirically investigates practices of knowing with a focus on the intelligence and metaphysics of plants. Do forests have a cognitive dimension, do they have consciousness? The difference in epistemic cultures becomes abundantly clear when asking such questions. The Western worldview doesn't acknowledge this mind-spirit life force even in most sentient nonhuman creatures, let alone in plant-beings.

The video research zooms in on the structural interconnection of all life by exploring how shamans (*taitas*, as they are known in Colombia) and microbiologists are understanding and working with DNA in their distinct ways. *Forest Mind* is a biosemiotics project employing advanced lab technologies and neurobiology to comprehend practices performed by Indigenous medics since time immemorial. The science of ayahuasca works through visions prompted by the psychoactive agent in a type of liana plant. The plant communicates through chemistry, and one segment of that chemical pathway includes neural transmitters. Through a remarkable coevolution, they happen to fit into the receptors in the human brain, creating a unique mode of telepathic communication between the plant and the person who ingests it. It is the result of millennia of coevolution, precisely hitting the part of the brain that activates the sensibilities of perceiving, sensing, and imaging. The Inga consider the plant an intelligent being with whom human consciousness can enter into communication. Hence, the taitas's primary tool is consciousness – not simply the rational mind. Taitas operate like engineers who go into the nuclear plant to reprogram the cosmic order. They manipulate nonordinary reality in order to elicit changes in the ordinary one. The same may be said for artists who breach the threshold of the zone of hyper-conventionality that is governed by the default collective imaginary. Art impacts reality by interacting with and expanding the collective imaginary. But sometimes, like shamans, artists sever the attachment across time, generations, and species, and cross the threshold to the nonordinary zone.

Many recent findings confirm that DNA molecules are both active and sensitive at the quantum level. They emit light waves in the low-visible light range, called biophotons. Although barely measurable impulses, DNA molecules act as antennae, emitting and receiving energetic waves. It is conceivable that Amazonian medics have become masters of interacting with this energetic part of DNA by turning into transmitters for the light signatures proliferating in the living world.[3] Taitas are thought to be quantum beings who interact with the mind-spirit inherent in all existence.

Taita Ernesto Evanjuanoy, president of the Unión de Médicos Indígenas Yageceros de la Amazonia Colombiana, told me that the master plant has a mind. For sure it has a powerful and widely documented semiotic agency and intention. When ingested, the plant evokes a feeling of social belonging and trust within a social group. It is a psycho-integrator plant, mediating an expansive and fully embodied thinking-feeling-knowing-imaging. It is a thinking with Earth. The plant-induced state activates and *worlds* a rich community of *persons*, not all of whom are human. It mediates a collective experience of mutual responsibility that brings the Amazonian people together and binds them to the land. This is how the master plant works its way into the group's sociality and brings forth territory. Ayahuasca ceremonies guide all the Inga's social decisions and are regularly practiced in Inga high schools. The plant will certainly become a crucial medium for learning at the university level we are working to build.

As a media artist, I also became interested in the kinds of images that biotechnology produces when sequencing the DNA of the rainforest. Such operative images, as typically produced by science and technology, are utilitarian image-instruments that no longer explicitly address human eyes; they

3. See Jeremy Narby, *The Cosmic Serpent: DNA and the Origins of Knowledge* (New York: Penguin Putnam, 1998).

roam about freely without human intentions. Hence, in one system, the forest communicates directly with the human mind through visions, while in another, images have taken on an independent life outside of human intention. In *Forest Mind*, I work with the cosmological distinction between these two knowledge systems regarding the function and meaning of images. What interests me is to converge three forms of image making: the luminous aspect of DNA in living biomaterials, the fluorescing images of ayahuasca-induced visions, and the light-capturing work of video making. The task was to sense the energetic fields of life mediated by the neurons in our brain and to transpose them through image technologies.

SK: You call attention to an exquisitely subtle distinction that you encounter, through the Inga, between consciousness – a lucid and freeform domain that structures their cosmos – and rational mind – the reducing valve that structures ours, a distinction that may already be ascendant in brain science and philosophy of mind. Consciousness, you suggest, is composed of images that both flow and endure, while also affirming that so does the material advance of the world at every level, fluxing like a musical composition, a perpetual enterprise of expression, integrating images of light, sound, or pattern meaning that endlessly form integral realities or worlds. The philosopher Henri Bergson was the first (as far as I know) to refuse the distinction of images of matter from images of perception and consciousness. The image, in other words, does not reveal a qualitative difference between matter and mind. You said, I think in *Deep Weather*, that "oil and water are like video, time-based media," and just now, you said material and perceptual processes are all "image technologies." They are all transmitters and transistors of intelligence, entities that "send" and "receive,"

Ursula Biemann, *Forest Mind*, film stills, 2021. Taita Carlos during his performance for the film. Top: Performance by Waira Jacanamejoy and Flora Macas in the Inga territories. Middle: Neurological forest.

but also organize and transform, activities that you refer to across the human-nature spectrum as meaning and worlding. Which brings me to another comment you made, that geometry's power has lost its grip on the mind. This reminds me of just how badly Ernest Rutherford's dictum that "qualitative is nothing but poor quantitative" has fared in late 20th- and 21st-century science. Something has certainly replaced geometry, or the geometric attitude, which brings us back to your original observation here about more adequate, less hubristic ways of capturing the world. Does it help to say that the Earth and the camera have a discoverable anima, or a soul?

UB: If we are now so keen on rediscovering Indigenous cosmologies, it's because *we* are in dire need of a different cosmology from the one governed by science and economy, so powerfully created by our rational mind. Consciousness, we learn, is not what we have, it is what we are – albeit merely a tiny individual expression of it, limited by the sensorial apparatus with which we humans come equipped. As a psychoactive agent, the master plant is thought to act as a medium or connector between the specialized human consciousness and the inclusive, cosmic consciousness that contains all there is. It represents a kind of paranormal passport to access the wonderful clarity of this psychic connection. The prevailing scientific rationale by which we gather our understanding is incapable of accessing such ultrasubtle domains, as long as our methodologies are driven by the obsession to discover and register a material world "out there." To be fair, much of neuroscience does suggest that reality is a process – however imperfectly understood – taking place in our brain, which combs the incoming stream of raw sensory signals – sounds, colors, patterns, scents – with the acquired expectations and interpretations about the way the world is. Reality is a biosemiotic process. This is how the world matters… to us. Images obviously play a hugely significant role in the process due to their ability to capture multiple levels of meaning long before they are put into words. Images powerfully evoke and transport emotions and sensations in a timeless manner, interweaving the conscious and unconscious planes while perpetually reflecting back to us. It makes no difference whether the images are perceived as inside or outside the mind. The forest and the perception of the forest are one and the same thing. The ultimate question will always be, What world do we want to matter?

Sanford Kwinter, a *Log* protagonist, guest edited, with Gökhan Kodalak, three special sections on nature and the cosmos in *Log* 49, 51, and 52 (2020–2021). He is Professor of Science and Design at the Pratt Institute in New York.

François Roche / S/he with Emanuele Coccia

An Archaeological Retro-future

"Une Chambre des mémoires à-venir, has been." https://vimeo.com/833561141/eb0b4fcbf6.

Plugged in, in Paris, in the intermediate/interstitial spaces beneath the La Défense slab, a philosophical and psychological experiment with a pinch of hypnosis, September 2023. For the duration of the event, these forbidden basements received, for the first and last time, a Voltairean_Rabelaisian tale and apparatus in the pursuit of the crypto naive and cruel tale of the 18th century in France, becoming a den where people overheard the snippets of a conversation, a dispute, a polyphonic and cavernous controversy put into words and staged by E. Coccia & S/he.fR, who entrusted three entities to whisper about the future of our world as seen from a temporal elsewhere (in a pareidolic vision between the cosmogonic gates of the universe and synaptic human brain disturbances). Two biological voices for an archaeological retro-future that watches us struggle through the here and now.

Preamble, Impromptu: S/he.fR

IT SEEMS PLAUSIBLE TO CONJUGATE A NARRATIVE IN THE FUTURE PAST TENSE, TO LOOK AT A TOMORROW, RIGHT IN FRONT OF US (THE ONE THAT FRIGHTENS US AND THAT WE NEVER STOP CARESSING), WHERE THE SPECIES (OURS AND ALL THOSE ON THIS PLANET) WILL HAVE MUTATED, AT ONCE HUMAN AND TECHNOID, VEGETABLE AND CEREBRAL, CHRYSALIS AND DARWINIAN CHIMERA. POSTPARIETAL CREATURES GIVE THEMSELVES THE RIGHT TO SPECULATE ON A HYPOTHESIS OF A NEW BRANCH OF EVOLUTION. THEN A JOURNEY TO THE SURFACE, INTO THE PSYCHE OF A BLUE PILL.

E. Coccia

THWARTING THE RELATIONSHIP WITH AN INDIVIDUAL OR COLLECTIVE PAST [---] REMOVING THE ILLUSION OF NECESSITY THAT BINDS US TO A PAST AS A BIOLOGICAL SPECIES. TO BE ABLE TO (RE)EXPERIENCE A SITE AS A CHILDHOOD BEDROOM STILL PREGNANT WITH FUTURES THAT HAVE NOT (YET) DECLINED INTO THE PRESENT. TO BE ABLE TO SHATTER THE EVIDENCE THROUGH WHICH WE REGARD OUR HOMO SAPIENS NATURE AS A NECESSARY TRAIT. [---] AN EXPERIENCE THAT FREES LIFE OF EVERY KIND FROM HISTORY AND INVITES IT TO AN EXERCISE IN IMAGINATION IN WHICH EVERYTHING HAS YET TO HAPPEN.

E. Coccia

… But above all, what strange period of time are we in? Isn't that the question we ask ourselves every morning as soon as we wake up? There's nothing psychological about this question. It doesn't express an ephemeral malaise. If we ask it, it's because the life that animates us never perfectly coincides with the time that surrounds it. Every awakening is the coincidence of forward projection and the memory of a future about which we know almost nothing. Every awakening is the collapse of the future into an arbitrary past.

All life has this paradoxical temporal structure. We have all inherited from an older life, which is the same age as the Earth, and even older. Every birth gives each life one and the same life. It's the same life as LUCA, the first and last universal common ancestor, who, over time, has only changed his clothes. It's the same life of matter that is also in the body of every object around us. We are made of the same flesh of Gaia, which has always been there, even before life began. From this point of view, life is always returning from an immemorial prehistory. That's why it's always hard to articulate in the present. On the other hand, this prehistoric life is capable of crossing any other. To say "me" at any moment is not just prehistoric. It is also, by the same gesture and the same breath, posthistoric. Always beyond and of itself. For tomorrow has already begun. To be in time always means to be in this chronological vertigo. And it's precisely because of this that the first living being in us is able to live now. Prehistory and hyperfuture at the same time, we are bearers of a life that is already projected into an absolute future, beyond us. Life is this coincidence between prehistory and futurism. Life condenses and defies chronology, bringing together technology and geology. It does so by giving this life three functions-faces, including a bicephalous one. Welcome to the dispute between demicreatures, Petrophytis and Petrogaia. We know very little about either of them.

Petrophytis is a creature that mixes the mineral and plant worlds in its body. It reverses the dynamism between soil and plant; Petrophytis is a plant which permanently becomes soil, and from that soil, becomes plant again. It is the very act by which solar energy animates the Earth's mineral skeleton. And conversely, the moment when the stone seizes the sun again to capture it and silence it. It's very old and androgynous. She harbors many personalities, and many voices come out of her. Sometimes these voices say the same thing, sometimes they overlap and you can't really hear what she's saying.

Petrogaia is a kind of petrified sun, a stone that is nothing more than absolute energy. His_Her body is a hybrid between a planet and a star. His_Her body resembles a giant, blurry sparkling microchip, more or less circular in shape. It's the equivalent of Earth's brain. She is the wisest of the three voices. She is the one finally able to unmask the audience. These two creatures land in our time by mistake. They don't really know where they are. It's Petrophytis who arrives first and wonders, "Where are we?" She realizes that she has been catapulted backwards, and recognizes the 21st century. Petrogaia arrives later, and says she's disgusted by the dirty, ugly place… By the idea of the city… By human beings. She knows that human beings have disappeared. And this is where the reflection of the two begins. Thinking about the human from the point of view of this 21st-century life, at once prehistoric and futuristic, means getting rid of all oppositions. And above all, to think outside any idea of evolution.

Are they capable of thinking of life solely as a succession of forms that succeed and replace each other? In this paradigm, error must always be ruled out. On the other hand, both creatures embody an idea of begetting, where life is given only because error cannot be erased. That it is error that generates all forms. And that every form is an error. The human being, like all other forms, is an anomaly. Every species is a glitch; history is a glitch. An accident. To free ourselves from the prison of identity, we must think of ourselves from the point of view of metamorphosis and not be afraid of transformation.

S/he
"He/she prefers fiction then"… Foucault's fiction… to fold and unfold our relationship to reality… For this opus I had written this message from Bangkok… Words from a world of yesterday, before Covid… All the more relevant today, in the aftermath… And it speaks of architecture, the discipline that serves as my vector… And therapy, and what I remain, an architect, despite appearances… Intentionally misleading… "experimentation has shifted to a new body of instrumentation, made up of tools, computation, machinismo, but also and simultaneously of fiction and lines of subjectivity, in synchronicity with our symptoms; of fear and here and now." An opportunity to explore correlated attitudes, codependent on the forms they underpin, through their conflicts and reciprocities. It's about discovering a postdigital, posthuman world, postactivist, postdemocratic, postfeminist, a queer world… Androgynous, carnal, disquieting, disenchanting,

pornographic, transitory, transactional, where the scenarios, devices, misunderstandings, psychic and physiological fragments are the very material of walls and ceilings, cellars and attics, schizoid and paranoid paranoia, in the hollows of operative and critical fictions… The androgynous folds and folds behind which… They… Hide, trigger confusions and epidermic reactions, suspicious hostilities, fantasized idealization, even premeditated oblivion.

… This text and apparatus are a continuation of the last 10 years of Rimbaudian adventure, robotic, subversive, human, "where it smells like shit"… in the depths of charming distress and pollution… "to put an end to the judgment of the gods, be they divine and/or institutional"… fugitive in the slums of Bangkok's Chinatown as a refuge… but Covid obliges… the Baudelairean devil who would have us believe that he doesn't exist… blah, blah, blah… I landed back last year in the Chinois district, Paris XIII, HBM housing from the Front Populaire, not so bad… to dream of the filthy residual basements of the Futurama (New York World's Fair, 1939) of modernity at La Défense and to witness the fight of retro-futuristic australopithecines… rather than Homo sapiens, my contemporaries… So back to the motherland as a native immigrant… nomad… temporal statelessness, for a writing style… disillusioned, disenchanted… with a bitter aesthetic libidinal… charming distress, the eroticism of Sabina Spielrein's death instinct, but also of Boccacio's *Decameron*… a mirror of the bankruptcy of our ecosophy too late, and far too sterilized, hygienized, privatized… but also a mirror of our own dementia, a film with three characters: the cynic, the idiot, and the moralist… Three-headed Diogenes in Lacanian introspection… in his barrique dog cave… dog… For this film, which seems to be a Valladolid controversy 2.0… in reverse… three "non-Jesuit" avatars from the future discuss and judge our degree of humanity… from tragedy to farce… but it's also like a fold of the soul… a topological fold of our inner psycho cinema… we're talking to ourselves… these little "men, women, green beasts" are ourselves… the expression of our sad passions, the unavowable desire to take the risk of being human… a multiplicity of inner voices like psychodramas, critical schizophrenias… echoing… of our procrastination… an aesthetic of skepticism… It's time to meet to meet Trans Humans… mutants, who are not Transhumanists… but also to question evolutionary theories and their distinction between species in "retro-future-speculative archaeology" / The aesthetic object here is a subject… which is not outside, outside…

but in itself… to give language to our own ambiguities… to reveal our lack of discernment… these cosmic avatars, trans… it's "both of us"… in dissonance… schizoanalytic demultiplications and Guattari's chaosmosis… fiction as the unveiling of inside-outside knots, their unfolding and contingency… ecology of being… heroes and Thanatos… ecology of limbo and the migrations of beings, beasts, plants, genders, and sexualities… Eco-technological monism… Infinity, proximity, thought, genitalia, love… the same substance…

Highlighting, through paradoxical postures, through counter-aesthetic devices, the biopolitical stakes, potentials, and disorders of contemporary technologies, from their infancy to their commodification, suspecting them of being neither innocent nor inoffensive, outside the conformism of borrowed discourses and aesthetics… Institutional "deja vu" via the good taste of the bourgeoisie (the modalities of Bourdieu's *habitus*)… And to confess their antipathy to the ultimate branch of evolution. A pathology of limbo, where mysticism and quantum dance in farandole, in the instability of particles… Stellar winds, winds of the psyche, mirror of ourselves… We shelter these avatars in our reptilian brains… These inner voices that never stop haunting us, like Sybil and her 19 characters, schizophrenia characters, bi-tri-deca polarities; the organization of folds with multiple languages, and it's in this… Zone, a Tower of Babel for human species, vegetal, digital… Asperger's and Alzheimer's at the same time… The right to forget… And to be vulnerable…

Intoxicated with "earthly foods," even if they're particles and bits, in a libidinal eroticization of the moment. Human biology, and the biology of vortexes and larvae, de-zombifies… Yes, there's something in the tool that allows us to be these natural voices, from the depths of the grave, like the eye that watched Cain. In this shadow theater, this Chamber of Past-Future, the voices are analog, from the actress Laura Benson, who simultaneously portrays the three characters with their terribly pathological and pathetic expressions. We needed a human to vomit his-her own disgust of self being. We were talking about Plotinus with Emanuele Coccia… Sciences of the unknown and sciences of the mind, both and simultaneously… Mysticism and metaphysics, the right to meander through a heterotopic forest, a pleonasm… Not a panoptic one, and discover substances of monism, of sharing, of coexistence…

Perhaps it's also necessary to look at how it's produced… A hybrid universe, both cosmic and microscopic, a kind of fractal universe, a diseased, tricephalic brain derived from medical imaging, and at the same time a glitch by James Webb, infinitely and simultaneously... For an aesthetic strategy from particles, a kind of digital unit, intelligent pixels, pixels given properties and animated by vortexes, solar winds and sea breezes, in interaction... Each particle becomes a creature, a stem cell, generative, agglomerated or diffracted. That's what's so interesting about this process... From a conversation between us to psycho trances by Mika Tamori, who created these entities, these ectoplasms in the pursuit of psychosomatic occultism sessions, a sort of third eye in a Mesmer's tub, ghostly and contradictorily in motion, creating the 2.5 creatures. It was not a body but effluvia, blurred, indefinite, where patterns play with pareidolia, the projection of the unconscious and the impermanence of forms... of our psyche, of our vulnerability _____ that our industrial-military societies, from the NSA to Boston Dynamic, mask in the illusion-falsification of security and performances with so much cynicism and diligence to serve us the reheated dishes of the mythologies of Violence.

La Défense in Paris
The scale 1 prototype... obviously a place of contradiction, both a Western champion of modern financial structures... in their capitalist mechanisms, but also the memory of the last slums (similar to where I lived for 10 years in Asia, with Asia, with 7-axis robots, water monitors, transgenders and human follies) where, whatever the hygienists say, it smells and smelled good, "the music of the swarm," to borrow Rimbaud's expression about the Paris Commune, it smelled of the bottom-up or the city, its organization and modes of production are not (were not) solely delegated to financial and political power, where the self-organization of the Multitude was prohibited but tolerated...

This place exists, albeit forbidden. It is an infrastructural residue of the 1960s, in basements and at the crossroads of freeways, train and metro, the foundations of superstructures of downtown. Not open to visitors and, for safety reasons, forbidden to the public, it reaches depths where the air becomes rarefied (-30 meters), and where the ground is that of the origins, of beaten earth, of the cave, a secular cathedral of concrete... to an urbex zone. Bicephalous odyssey where places, dates, Molotov spray-painted graffiti versus negative hands with blown pigments... Red hematite limonite and goethite for yellow and brown ochres, manganese oxide or

New-territories, model of the set for *The dispute*, La Défense, Paris, 2023.

charcoal for black, talc for white... Versus the toxicity of styrene spray cans, which litter the floors and walls.

Graffiti artists, but also a homeless population of between 500 and 1,000 human beings who live in these basements, immigrants, employed and unemployed, the broken-hearted, mainly males but also lost teenagers, in escape mode. They're "male-female," symptoms of abandoned childhoods, runaways and psychotics, of being at odds, but with dreams of existence. You can be sure this is not one of the evolutionary variations of Homo sapiens, but rather a new branch, born of the "domestication of being," a blend of technological artifice, human frailties, and vulnerable memories in the time of the Anthropocene. Neither anticipation nor speculative, tender, timid, literary, and cognitive. An immersive zone of medium contact, "to show not the invisible, but to show how invisible is the invisibility of the visible..." Where the forms and challenges of space, that of living together, where fiction is naked, like a whisper that comes from the outside in. This temporal outside-in will be our mousehole, our keyhole, a posteriori, voyeur of our metamorphosis in the making, and not without contradiction, able to influence it in retrospect. In this heterotopia of time and space, in the cracks of the cave, self-realizing fictions creep in, renewing our relationship to the here and now. The devices were critical, resisting projective fantasies, never techno-fetishistic, but flirting with Alchemy, pataphysics... The "chamber" has been like a suggestive "mise en contact" (pareidolia, fuzzy logic, neural imagery, wave-corpuscle duality, chemical holographies), literary (catatonic mode, binary, phono-ideographic)... as polyphonic whispers from a Tower of Babel, voices in dissonance.

The dispute

Dialogue between three cosmic entities,
one bicephalic, no genders...
(by S/he.fR & E.Coccia)

Petrogaia 1
Where are we? But first of all - in what strange period of time are we? Wait... we've been catapulted back centuries. It feels like the middle of the 21st century...

Petrogaia 2
Yes... where are we? This looks like a dirty, ugly place. Such shapes .... A proliferating city. I feel like... Ahh....... Anyway, they had been extinct for millions of years....

Petrophytis
We are in a glitch, a topological miasma,.... date and place shift....here it is 2022 in the basement of some kind of... techno-positivist fantasy, the... just above...

Petrogaia 1
a glitch... a programming error...ehhhhh.....you see them.... These are clearly errors... right?

Petrophytis
This doesn't seem to be an illusion, it's the homo-machine branch. An admirable combination of destructive power and larval metamorphosis... to see so much... is....

Petrogaia 1
At this point they must not know it... Or they must refuse to know it.... It was not a true extinction... a proliferation of their intelligence in any other form of symbiosis... a multiplication of hybridization...

Petrogaia 2
series of anomalies, coding errors... the DNA is me... child who keeps wishing and raving...

Petrogaia 1
DNA leakage... wild hom-herbs, fembes, homfemmes and femdieux.... at the same time.... this must be one of the last generations of their simple form... and look... they still reproduce...

Petrophytis
nature had not yet integrated the reality of its errors in order to develop its own transgression... its multiple truths... It was a way of overcoming the opposition between the genesis of a species and its extinction

Petrogaia 2
Chai pas... what does that say...eh ...Petrophytis-Mother?

Petrogaia 1
But my darling, listen to your pre-specific memories, the residues of your reptilian brain, and.... dance with your paranoia.... your fears are beautiful... your anxieties are like honey... madness is our matrice... I never told you.... Can you tell him? After all, what is your name? With whom do we have the pleasure of........?

Petrophytis
Photogaia.... So..... It is a slow process that has involved all species in the past. Life has tried to progress through evolution for millions of years, but the process was too exhausting. And too wasteful. Because the error was discarded, thrown away, left to fester. And then a life was born that could get through all the mistakes.

Petrogaia 2
So there is no waste? Nobody disappears and nobody dies?

Petrophytis
Exactly, but that means that no one is really born. We are just transformed.............. sliding beings into co-existence.....

Petrogaia 2
Are we all the same body? Are we all the same flesh?

Petrophytis
Almost. We are all together in the sense that, while mistakes are always real, what ends is history. The difference between the future and prehistory. And this is what the beings before us experience...

Petrogaia 1
That is why they look so stupid. They have not understood the truth of the error.

Petrophytis
Don't they seem intelligent to you?

Petrogaia 2
Like us?

Petrophytis
Yes, definitely.

Petrogaia 1
They seem very ignorant, and they have ....

Petrogaia 2
... strange beliefs and strange manners. Divinities from outside their world who die... but also.... ah.... money, its fiction and its addiction...

Petrogaia 1
... unable to decrypt themselves - to go beyond the opposition between truth and lies... and they fall into their own traps... they don't want to transform themselves...

Petrophytis
unable to laugh.... bring a court jester here... we'll see if they are sensitive to the humor... It's a sign of knowing how to transform... The sign of knowing the identity between truth and error... Laughter.... hybrid...

Petrogaia 1
laughter laughter... yes.... yes.... spontaneous! excellent idea! Crazy people have all the rights, don't they?

Petrogaia 2
hmmm they are sulking... no!

Petrogaia 1
Hello You?... my little genome gnome, deoxyriboprimitive, adenosive, sitinin, tymiditin, whose mutation potentials you ignore....... do you know how to self-program my darling...?

Petrogaia 1 and 2
Apathetic!

Petrophytis
... antipatic

Petrogaia 2
(.....Borborygms mix Summerien-Akkadian)
H pesh dish esh mimo ia homo selim macaled kekabichan kapu kchaley shipu kakurapu sorolmash gula dilgan u rikis nunni, Enlil

lugal kurkurra abba digirdigireenke inim ginanita ningursu Sarabi ki ensur..... es gana bera kiba na biru us ensi nm-make nam inimma diridirise eak.... Masauqe q iiidou necte monai quede cha chomamosomo saqsa trou me ma mo somo bouree O marra mounou musina qure malan MAISON saque, reque re le la VIE lou meme oune sae ou roule lapanu, se se se ou qui.... li mou chrri... ARBRES cham me, ou quou pas tou ale, ad renicha, chaoulatoupachic

Petrogaia 1

...turning again to the visitors___ at the end of Pe2's tirade..... he grimaces and makes slow... animal cries... their catatonia-like language... plants, bestiaries and demons are summoned... particles spewing their disgust... and ending with an ode to melancholy... high-pitched sound...(animal complaints)/background sound in de-synchronization/hypnotic message... slow... Meanwhile P2... goes into lethargy... his head becoming a rag doll vibrating to P1's rhythm, and lulled by the shakes and waves of his lament)... Memorized by a psychedelic-hypnotic sound _ 2 mn... Songs of Maldoror...

Petrophytis

....But this is not a joke! We are talking about a people who are suffering and dying! A real people... although extinct, lost lineage, rotten branch of evolution, homo __ sapiennn...... they are no less...

Petrogaia 1

The embarrassing thing is that your people didn't even smile! They didn't loosen their lips! They didn't change....

Petrogaia 2

si si..... they smiled.... a little... i saw them.... i didn't ... pathetic motherfucker ... love you-me-youuuu!

Petrophytis

As you can see, there is nothing universal about a slip-up.... and .... They are afraid, they are afraid of their metamorphosis... they are afraid of their mistakes... they are afraid...

François Roche guest edited *Log* 25: Reclaim Resi[lience]stance/ / ......R2 (2012). S/he is the principal of New-territories. Androgynous, transgender avatar, _S/he_, created in 1994, authorized Roche, native immigrant French architect, to write, talk and teach on his/her behalf. Last solo show was September 2023, in Paris: https://new-territories.com/PASTFUTURECHAMBER/. Emanuele Coccia is a lecturer at the École des Hautes Études en Sciences Sociales in Paris. His most recent book in the French is *Métamorphoses* (2020).

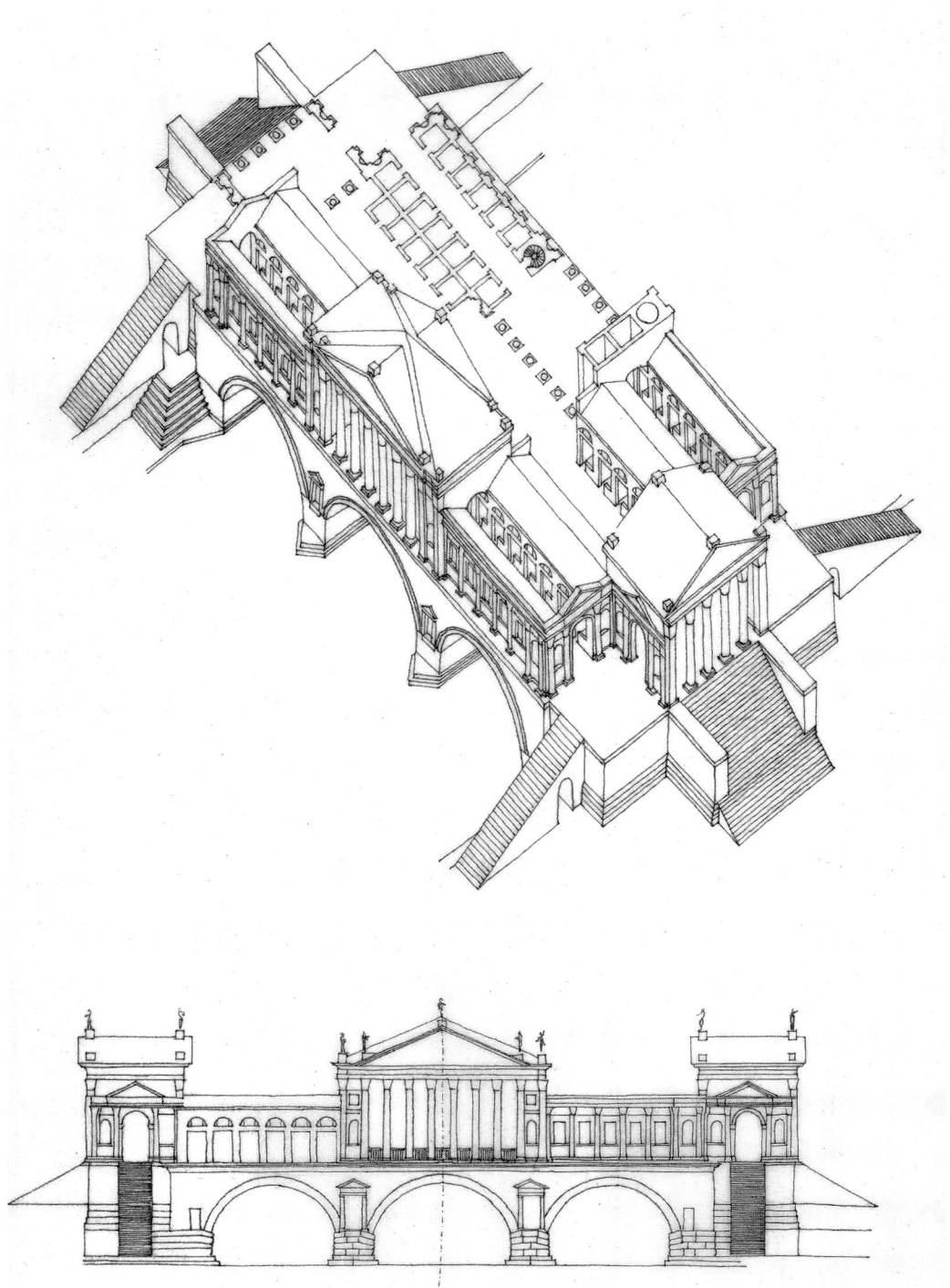

Anthony Vidler (1941–2023), axonometric and elevational study of Andrea Palladio's 1556 design for the Rialto Bridge, in Venice, drawn while studying architecture at Cambridge University, 1960–1966. Ink on tracing paper, 240 by 300 centimeters. Courtesy Peter Eisenman.